GW00585053

STUDIES IN IMPERIALISM

General Editor: Andrew S. Thompson

Founding Editor: John M. MacKenzie

When the 'Studies in Imperialism' series was founded
by Professor John M. MacKenzie more than twenty-five
years ago, emphasis was laid upon the conviction that
'imperialism as a cultural phenomenon had as significant
an effect on the dominant as on the subordinate societies'.
With well over a hundred titles now published, this remains
the prime concern of the series. Cross-disciplinary work
has indeed appeared covering the full spectrum of cultural
phenomena, as well as examining aspects of gender and sex,
frontiers and law, science and the environment, language
and literature, migration and patriotic societies, and much
else. Moreover, the series has always wished to present
comparative work on European and American imperialism,
and particularly welcomes the submission of books in these
areas. The fascination with imperialism, in all its aspects,
shows no sign of abating, and this series will continue to
lead the way in encouraging the widest possible range of
studies in the field. 'Studies in Imperialism' is fully organic
in its development, always seeking to be at the cutting edge,
responding to the latest interests of scholars and the needs
of this ever-expanding area of scholarship.

Beastly encounters of the Raj

Manchester University Press

SELECTED TITLES AVAILABLE IN THE SERIES

MUSEUMS AND EMPIRE
Natural history, human cultures and colonial identities
John M. MacKenzie

BORDERS AND CONFLICT IN SOUTH ASIA
The Radcliffe boundary commission and the partition of Punjab
Lucy P. Chester

THE COLONISATION OF TIME
Ritual, routine and resistance in the British Empire
Giordano Nanni

GENTEEL WOMEN
Empire and domestic material culture, 1840–1910
Dianne Lawrence

IRELAND, INDIA AND EMPIRE
Indo-Irish radical connections, 1919–64
Kate O'Malley

Beastly encounters of the Raj

LIVELIHOODS, LIVESTOCK, AND VETERINARY HEALTH IN NORTH INDIA, 1790–1920

Saurabh Mishra

MANCHESTER UNIVERSITY PRESS

Copyright © Saurabh Mishra 2015

The right of Saurabh Mishra to be identified as the author of this work has been asserted by him in accordance with the Copyright, Designs and Patents Act 1988.

Published by MANCHESTER UNIVERSITY PRESS
ALTRINCHAM STREET, MANCHESTER M1 7JA, UK
www.manchesteruniversitypress.co.uk

British Library Cataloguing-in-Publication Data
A catalogue record for this book is available from the British Library

Library of Congress Cataloging-in-Publication Data applied for

ISBN 978 0 7190 8972 5 *hardback*

First published 2015

The publisher has no responsibility for the persistence or accuracy of URLs for any external or third-party internet websites referred to in this book, and does not guarantee that any content on such websites is, or will remain, accurate or appropriate.

Typeset in Trump Medieval by
Koinonia, Manchester
Printed in Great Britain by
TJ International Ltd, Padstow

To Menka and Vivan

CONTENTS

Illustrations – viii
Acknowledgements – ix

Introduction   1

Part I – Veterinary health and the colonial state

1 Horse breeding and the ideologies of the early colonial state   11
2 Beasts, murrains, and veterinary health   36
3 Ticks, germs, and bacteriological research   59

Part II – Caste, class, and cattle

4 Cattle, famines, and the colonial state   77
5 Food adulteration, public health, and middle-class anxieties   102
6 Cattle poisoning and the Chamar identity   123

Conclusion   145

Bibliography – 149
Index – 167

ILLUSTRATIONS

Figures

1 Cartoon regarding the cattle plague in Britain. The Patient says: 'Oh, if they'd only leave off quarrelling, and just try "United Action", it might be the saving of me!' (source: *Punch, or the London Charivari*, 17 February 1866) *page* 42

2 The Muktesar Laboratory (source: J. D. E. Holmes, *A Description of the Imperial Bacteriological Laboratory, Muktesar: Its Works and Products* (Calcutta: Superintendent Government Printing, 1913)) 67

3 Sketch depicting the famine in Bellary district (source: *The Graphic*, 6 October 1877) 78

4 A satirical sketch depicting the 'real sources' of milk supply in cities (source: Roshan Lal Anand, *The Milk Supply of Lahore, 1930* (Lahore: Civil and Military Gazette Press, 1933)) 109

5 A 'typical Chamar leather worker' (source: Geo W. Briggs, *The Chamars* (Calcutta: Association Press, 1920)) 125

Table

1 Mortality among plough cattle, Delhi (1899–1900) (source: *The Punjab Famine of 1899–1900, Vol. I: Government Resolutions and Statistical Tables* (Lahore: Punjab Government Press, 1901)) 79

ACKNOWLEDGEMENTS

I started research on this theme in 2009 and, over the last five years, have received a huge amount of help and support from several friends. I owe my greatest debt to Mark Harrison, who not only encouraged me to work on this theme, but also shared some primary sources in order to get me started on the project. His constant support over the years has made all the difference to my work. My deepest thanks also to Biswamoy Pati and Indrani Sen, who have been so generous with their love, support, and advice over the years. I am also grateful to Waltraud Ernst who has shown a very keen interest in this project and gone carefully through the first draft of all the chapters. This book looks and reads much better because of her inputs. Thanks also to Pratik Chakrabarti and Nandini Bhattacharya for their friendship, support, and generosity.

I would be failing in my duties if I did not thank the staff members at a number of libraries and archives who made it pleasurable to carry out research. Thanks to the staff of the British Library, the Wellcome Library, India Institute Library (Oxford), the National Archives of India, and the Nehru Memorial Museum and Library. Thanks also to the photocopying staff at the National Archives of India, who coped with my huge pile of requests without much complaint.

A massive thanks to the Wellcome Trust, which funded my project and made this monograph possible. I am also grateful to the *Journal of Social History*, the *Indian Economic and Social History Review*, *Bulletin of the History of Medicine*, and *Modern Asian Studies* for allowing me to print revised versions of articles that were published by them. Thanks also to Emma Brennan at the Manchester University Press, who has been extremely patient and helpful throughout the process of finalising this manuscript.

Finally, my parents and siblings have always been my greatest source of strength over the years, and my son Vivan has been a welcome distraction during the last couple of years. My biggest debt, though, is to Menka – my editor, bouncing board, and stern critic. This book is as much hers as mine.

INTRODUCTION

'If I have a buffalo and a murungei tree', says a Tamil proverb, 'I can make people happy at the coming feast'.[1] These, and numerous other proverbs of a similar kind, emerge out of the peasants' obvious dependence on tamed animals. Indeed, such is the level of dependence that it is difficult, if not impossible, to picture the Indian rural landscape without livestock. To anyone with the faintest familiarity with the agrarian context, their massive significance would be quite self-evident: they were a form of property, a means of transport, an agricultural tool, a source of food, manure, and fuel. Equally importantly, livestock was not seen as mere chattel – it was often linked to its owner through strong emotional ties.

The importance of cattle was not the same in every region, though, and could vary significantly, depending on livelihood patterns, soil types, climate, and various other variables. However, no matter what these conditions, there was always a degree of dependence on cattle. In areas with dry soil, for example, several ploughings were required to prepare the fields for cultivation, whereas in wet regions that carried out intensive cultivation and multiple cropping, 'cattle power' was quite obviously a necessity.[2] Similarly, while settlements at high altitudes were based almost entirely on cattle rearing, they were no less important in the plains where both the agricultural and dairy output depended on it.[3] Further, nomadic and peripatetic groups such as the *banjaras* could not imagine an existence without cattle, as it allowed them to retain their mobility, while pastoralist groups were, of course, defined by their ownership of cattle.[4] It is hardly surprising, then, that within such a scenario, even the poorest peasant family sought desperately to own cattle. In fact, the need to own or purchase cows or bullocks was such that it was often seen as one of the chief reasons for peasants' indebtedness.[5] Also, in those cases where it was difficult to borrow, peasants often resorted to what was known as the *harsajh* or *tijara* system of sharing cattle. In the former, peasants pooled their resources to buy cattle, whereas the latter referred to an arrangement whereby they worked someone else's fields and were allowed the use of their cattle in return.[6] Having struggled to lay full or partial claim to livestock, peasants were quite understandably very proprietorial about them, and showed great reluctance to sell them, even during periods of great financial distress. This strong attachment to cattle can be seen clearly during certain episodes such as the Rangpur *dhing* (insurgency) of 1783 in Bengal, which was partly caused by the local landlord's decision to capture cattle and sell it off at a reduced price in order to recover revenue deficits.[7]

Besides being an essential cultivation tool, the presence of livestock also determined the degree of access to the market. This was a matter of crucial importance, as reduced access to the market often created a space where the merchant-moneylender could proliferate.[8] Equally importantly, though, cows or bullocks tied outside a peasant's hut could signify prosperity and wealth like little else could, and this was a strong inducement behind the decision to buy cattle even at the cost of lifelong indebtedness. This comes across clearly in Premchand's *Godan* (or 'the gift of a cow') where the protagonist Hori Mehto simply could not resist the temptation of owning a cow, even though he was quite aware that this desire could not be supported by his meagre means.[9] For Hori, noted Premchand, the cow was 'not just a thing of worship but also a show-piece, a living symbol of prosperity. He wanted people to point to his house and say: *there, that's Hori Mehto's house.*'[10] These literary sources also point towards an extremely strong bond between the peasant and his cows or buffaloes, and it is therefore not difficult to imagine the extreme distress that the former must have suffered during periods of large-scale cattle mortality such as epizootics and famines, which are some of the themes that this study is going to focus on.

Keeping all this in mind, it is surprising to note that, though there is an extensive body of historical work on agrarian processes and structures, the intrinsic importance of cattle in the life of Indian peasants has received comparatively scant attention from historians.[11] Cursory references contained in certain works do bring livestock's centrality to the fore. Jairus Banaji, for example, makes the significant observation that cattle were so integral to the peasant economy in nineteenth-century India that any household without it 'was a household on the verge of extinction'.[12] However, very little effort has been devoted towards exploring this link between cattle and the agrarian landscape any further.

What lies behind this curious omission of a subject that not only has the potential to provide an insight into rural life, but also into the nature of the colonial state in India? The answer might lie partly in the recent trends in historical writing which, at least in South Asia, seem to have steered firmly clear of the 'old Marxist preoccupation' with the peasantry and agrarian relations. With the onset of 'colonial discourse analysis' and literary criticism, historians have tended to engage with new kinds of themes altogether, and studies focusing on the agrarian context have, consequently, tended to become less frequent. This study seeks to bring the agrarian question back into focus. Simultaneously, it also raises several valid arguments regarding the nature of the colonial state and its policies.

The question of cattle has been ignored not just by scholars working on agrarian conditions, but also by historians of medicine in India. The latter have completely sidestepped the question of veterinary health in South Asia in spite of the huge cattle mortalities that were caused by epizootics and cattle diseases. Such lack of interest is especially surprising keeping in mind the fact that veterinary medicine was part of the overall apparatus of public health in India – a subject that has been at the centre of many historical works in the recent past.[13] Admittedly, a debate was taking place during the late nineteenth century, both in Britain and in India, over the question of whether veterinary medicine was really a part of the larger public health administration. However, by the 1880s, growing concerns over linkages between animal and human disease, and over the ill-effects of ingesting infected meat, had allowed veterinarians to make inroads into public health administration.[14] In India, too, zoonoses such as bovine tuberculosis and anthrax raised major concerns, even though they did not lead to any remarkable increase in the authority of the veterinarian.

Due to this strong link between veterinary health and the larger public health policies, a thorough examination of the subject would yield several fresh insights about the nature of colonial medicine. One of the most striking features of veterinary administration, for example, was its preoccupation with the health of horses and military animals until the end of the nineteenth century (see Chapters 1 and 2). This forces us to reconsider the existing scholarly consensus regarding the increasing separation between the medical and the military establishments, which is supposed to have taken place from the 1860s onwards.[15] It also becomes quite apparent, upon examining veterinary records, that colonial officials were much less imbued with the 'white man's burden' when it came to preserving indigenous cattle stock. Perhaps this was due to the fact that notions of charity and public welfare could be set aside with much greater ease in this case than they could be in the case of human health. As a result of this relative lack of the benevolent spirit, the question of finances and funds attained greater prominence, and increasingly became the final arbiter for colonial policies. Chapter 3 shows that the question of finances could influence areas such as laboratory research, as is evident in the operations of the Imperial Bacteriological Laboratory at Muktesar. This preoccupation with finances also comes across clearly in Chapter 4, which deals with famines and cattle mortality, and highlights the meagreness and ineffectiveness of relief measures. This chapter also brings to light indigenous responses that were adopted in order to compensate for the inadequacy or inappropriateness of colonial policies. In doing so it underlines the fact that many of the peasant responses were not 'irrational', as many colonial officials perceived them to be, but had been arrived at after much weighing of all possible alternatives.

While discussing these issues, the book does not lapse into a straightforward and monochromatic narrative of colonial neglect and excesses, and the peasants' silent capitulation under this *zulm* (injustice). In fact, this work consciously tries to move away from the bleak picture presented by scholars like Laxman Satya, who single-mindedly record the relentless and ruthless destruction of the nation's cattle wealth by the colonial masters.[16] This is not to negate the fact that the colonial decision to 'fence the forests' caused a significant diminution in the stock of fodder available to peasants,[17] and that this situation was worsened further by repeated outbreaks of famines and epizootics that severely depleted the livestock population. These facts have been clearly documented in this monograph too, but an attempt has been made to move beyond these questions in order to discuss other equally interesting themes connected with livestock in India. For instance, the question of livestock in India was connected very closely with the issue of middle-class consumption practices, as milk continued to be the food item *par excellence* even in urban India at the start of the twentieth century. This theme is examined in Chapter 5. Another theme that is discussed is the question of caste identities, especially that of the Chamars (popularly known as leatherworkers), which is studied in Chapter 6. This chapter explores, in detail, the process whereby stereotypes regarding caste groups were formed, and how they came to be crystallised over time. In examining these diverse themes, we hope to have opened up new pastures for research. This shift away from traditional narratives (especially in the context of cattle) was initially made by David Gilmartin in his remarkable study of cattle theft, to which this work is greatly indebted. Gilmartin's work showed clearly how something as seemingly innocuous as theft of cattle could reveal, upon further examination, extremely interesting stories regarding community ties, tensions, and the changing idea of property rights.[18]

Overall, this monograph attempts to write a social history of livestock. This social history of livestock also insinuates itself into the narrative when we look at specifically veterinary developments. Far too often there has been a tendency, especially among scholars looking at veterinary history in non-Indian contexts, to have a sort of blinkered vision that shuts out every social reality connected with cattle and livestock.[19] This book consciously avoids this trap, though this does not mean that medical questions have been neglected in this study. In fact, this book began its life as a predominantly medical history project, and some of its chapters still deal with subjects such as bacteriology and the veterinary administration. Most of the other chapters also have a running medical history theme, as they deal with issues such as toxicology, medical jurisprudence, and the nature of early veterinary institutions. However, as research progressed, it became clear that medical issues could not be divorced or completely separated from other themes. For example, while studying early veterinary history, it is quite simply impossible to block out the question of horse-breeding, as it was the major preoccupation of early veterinarians. Similarly, in studying the rate of cattle mortality in the subcontinent, one could not avoid the subject of famines and focus only on epizootics.

Another central concern of this book is to study the nature, priorities, and guiding principles of the colonial state. In doing this, we have tried to examine colonial responses to a wide variety of stimuli – to famines, to the concerns over veterinary/public health, to the military needs of the early colonial state, and to the question of caste identities – all of which have been framed or linked together by our core thematic engagement with the question of livestock in India. Though there are a number of subjects that are being addressed together, this can be of great use in studying the nature of the colonial state. Studies of the colonial state in India have really come of age in the last few decades, and there are various contradictory or complementary perspectives. There are those who argue for a limited, fractured, or non-interventionist state, while on the other hand there are arguments in favour of a highly reformist or interventionist state that received validation from the logics of civilising mission, progress, development (scientific or otherwise), etc. This is of course simplifying a huge diversity of research, but one needs to highlight the fact that conclusions about the nature of the colonial state emerge out of certain thematic or regional foci that have been adopted by scholars. For example, any study of plague during the 1890s will inevitably conclude that the colonial state was a highly interventionist one, whereas a micro study of a small district, or *taluka* will no doubt find areas that were untouched by colonial presence.[20] The wider thematic and regional scope of this monograph might allow us to avoid these pitfalls by making it possible to look at the state from various angles and delineate its contours.

Finally, the book also adopts a long-term perspective, choosing to study a rather long chronological period. This allows us to not merely look at various facets of colonial policies and indigenous life, but also makes it possible to examine the changes that took place within these over time. The narrative starts in the 1790s – the decade that saw the

[5]

recruitment of early veterinarians within the military administration in India. The decade of the 1920s have been chosen as the end point, as the colonial veterinary administration and bacteriological research had started coming into their own by this period. We will start, in the first chapter, by looking at some of the early veterinary developments and horse-breeding policies.

Notes

1 Rev. Herman Jensen, *A Classified Collection of Tamil Proverbs* (London: Trubner, 1897), p. 350. The murungei tree is considered to be extremely versatile and useful. In the north Indian context, besides these proverbs, there are also several examples of special offerings being made to certain deities in order to preserve cattle. William Crooke gives us the example of the Santals, who apparently made offerings to a deity called Brijnath, whose special function was to protect cattle from beasts of prey. *The Popular Folklore and Religion and Folklore of North India* (first published in 1896, reprinted by Kessinger Publishing, Montana, 2004), p. 182.

2 David Washbrook, 'The Commercialization of Agriculture in Colonial India: Production, Subsistence and Reproduction in the "Dry South", c.1870–1930', *Modern Asian Studies*, 28(1) (Feb. 1994), 129–64.

3 Dhirendra Datt Dangwal, 'State, Forests and Graziers in the Hills of Uttar Pradesh: Impact of Colonial Forestry on Peasants, Gujars and Bhotiyas', *Indian Economic Social History Review*, 34 (1997), 405–35.

4 According to certain sources, 200 tribes (or nearly 6 per cent of the country's population) are engaged even today in some form of pastoralism. This number would have been much higher during the colonial period. V. P. Sharma, J. Morton, and I. Kohler-Rollefson, *Pastoralism in India: A Scoping Study* (Delhi: DFID, 2003), p. 4.

5 David Hall-Matthews, *Peasants, Famines and the State in Colonial Western India* (Basingstoke: Palgrave, 2005), p. 35.

6 Shahid Amin, 'Small Peasant Commodity Production and Rural Indebtedness: The Culture of Sugarcane in Eastern U.P., c.1880–1920', in Ranajit Guha (ed.), *Subaltern Studies I* (Delhi: Oxford University Press, repr. 2010), p. 54.

7 The Rangpur *dhing* has been seen as 'the first formidable peasant uprising against the rule of the East India Company'. Jon E. Wilson, 'A Thousand Countries to Go To: Peasants and Rulers in Late Eighteenth-Century Bengal', *Past and Present*, 189 (Nov. 2005), 81.

8 Neeladri Bhattacharya, 'Lenders and Debtors: The Punjab Countryside, 1880–1940', in Sugata Bose (ed.), *Credits, Markets and the Agrarian Economy of Colonial India* (Delhi: Oxford University Press, 2004), pp. 197–247.

9 Munshi Premchand (1880–1936) is widely regarded as one of the greatest Hindi novelists. He wrote fourteen novels, nearly 300 short stories, and also a couple of plays during his relatively short creative life as an author. His *Godan* was first published in 1936 and is arguably one of his most famous and accomplished novels. The story of this novel revolves around a poor peasant and his desire to own a cow. For an English translation of the novel, see Jai Ratan and P. Lal (tr.) *Godan: A Novel of Peasant India* (Mumbai: Jaico Publishing House, 2002).

10 Ratan and Lal, *Godan*, p. 36.

11 Marxist historians have, understandably, been responsible for much of the pioneering work on agrarian structures. However, they seem to have ignored Marx's own belief in the transformative potential of mobile forms of property in India. In a letter to Vera Zasulich, Marx noted that mobile property would lead gradually to differentiation of wealth, thereby making it possible for conflict of interests to arise. In second draft of a letter to Vera Zasulich, dated 8 March 1881, quoted in Suniti Kumar Ghosh, 'Marx on India', *Monthly Review*, 35(8) (Jan. 1984), 41–2.

12 Jairus Banaji, 'Capitalist Domination and the Small Peasantry: The Deccan Districts in the Late Nineteenth Century', in Gyan Prakash (ed.), *The World of the Rural Labourer in Colonial India* (Delhi: Oxford University Press, 1992), p. 124. David Hall-Matthews also draws attention to livestock in his *Peasants, Famines and the State in Colonial Western India* (Palgrave: Basingstoke, 2005). Others like Neeladri Bhattacharya have drawn links between livestock and access to markets, in 'Lenders and Debtors: The Punjab Countryside, 1880–1940', in Sugata Bose (ed.), *Credits, Markets and the Agrarian Economy of Colonial India* (Delhi: Oxford University Press, 2004), pp. 197–247. Significant among works that deal directly with cattle in nineteenth-century India are David Gilmartin, 'Cattle, Crime and Colonialism: Property as Negotiation in North India', *Indian Economic and Social History Review*, 40(1) (2003), 33–56; Laxman Satya, *Ecology, Colonialism and Cattle: Central India in the Nineteenth Century* (Delhi: Oxford University Press, 2004). Satya's book, however, focuses entirely on colonial measures that led to a degradation in Central India's cattle wealth and ecology, and does not explore other aspects of the livestock economy of the region.

13 The most notable among the existing full-length works on the subject are Mark Harrison, *Public Health in British India: Anglo-Indian Preventive Medicine, 1859–1914* (Cambridge: Cambridge University Press, 1994); David Arnold, *Colonizing the Body: State Medicine and Epidemic Disease in Nineteenth-Century India* (Berkeley, CA: University of California Press, 1989); Mridula Ramanna, 'Western Medicine and Public Health in Colonial Bombay 1845–1895 (Hyderabad: Orient Blackswan, 2002); Poonam Bala, *Imperialism and Medicine in Bengal* (New Delhi: Sage, 1991); Roger Jeffrey, *The Politics of Health India* (Berkeley, CA: University of California Press, 1988); Anil Kumar, *Medicine and the Raj: British Medical Policy in India, 1835–1911* (New Delhi: Sage, 1998).

14 Anne Hardy, 'Pioneers in the Victorian Provinces: Veterinarians, Public Health and the Urban Animal Economy', *Urban History*, 29(3) (2003), 372–87. See also Keir Waddington, *The Bovine Scourge: Meat, Tuberculosis and Public Health, 1850–1914* (Woodbridge: Boydell Press, 2006).

15 See for instance David Arnold, 'Crisis and Contradictions in India's Public Health', in Dorothy Porter (ed.), *The History of Public Health and the Modern State* (Amsterdam, Rodopi, 1994), p. 341.

16 David Gilmartin also makes the same point in his review of Satya's book: http://eh.net/book_reviews/ecology-colonialism-and-cattle-central-india-nineteenth-centuryReview (accessed 5 December 2011).

17 Several scholars have made this argument. See for example Mahesh Rangarajan, *Fencing the Forest: Conservation and Ecological Change in India's Central Provinces, 1860–1914* (Delhi: Oxford University Press, 1999); Ramchandra Guha, *The Unquiet Woods: Ecological Change and Peasant Resistance in the Himalayas* (Delhi: Oxford University Press, 1989); Akhileshwar Pathak, *Laws, Strategies, Ideologies: Legislating Forests in Colonial India* (Delhi: Oxford University Press, 2002).

18 'Cattle, Crime, and Colonialism: Property as Negotiation in North India', *Indian Economic and Social History Review*, 40(1) (Jan.–Mar. 2003), 33–56.

19 See for example Clive A. Spinage's ambitious *Cattle Plague: A History* (New York: Kluwer, 2003). Though very useful, the book has a tendency to get mired in scientific/technical details, while ignoring larger social realities.

20 See for example Anand A. Yang, *Limited Raj: Agrarian Relations in Colonial India, Saran District, 1793–1920* (Berkeley, CA: University of California Press, 1989).

PART I

Veterinary health and the colonial state

CHAPTER ONE

Horse breeding and the ideologies of the early colonial state

In 1984, the Directorate General of Veterinary and Remount Services commissioned a work that would 'place on record the glories [of the corps] spread over two centuries'.[1] Faithful to this clear brief, Lieutenant Colonel J. S. Bhalla outlined the evolution of the corps, starting with its 'inception' in 1794, touching upon its magnificence during the two World Wars, and ending with a paean to its contemporary splendour.[2] Like all sagas of past glory, this narrative elided over episodes of relative failure, mentioning them only as brief halts in an inexorable journey towards modernisation and efficiency. However, these episodes were so frequent and prolonged that it is quite possible to invert the prism and retell the story in a somewhat pessimistic tone, which is partly what this chapter is going to attempt.

More importantly, this chapter will situate the practice of horse breeding within the institutional matrix of colonialism, highlighting its affinities with the economic impulses that animated the Raj during these initial years, when the question of land revenue settlement, property rights, trade, and markets were being extensively discussed. It is sadly forgotten nowadays, under the influence of the new linguistic turn in South Asian historiography, that colonial discourse did not consist solely of the tropes of cultural difference, displacement, 'Otherness' and assimilation; it also consisted of several economic themes that have received relatively inadequate attention in recent years. This neglect or omission is not entirely involuntary and has been seen by critics and economic historians as the outcome of a 'holy fear of economic reductionism', or a 'profound disinterest in economics'.[3] This chapter will challenge this partial occlusion of the economic, and argue that it was indeed the touchstone with which policies around several subjects like horse breeding were examined and implemented by the colonial state. It will also show that the semantics used for discussions around land settlement – undoubtedly the most important

[11]

economic measure during early colonial rule – insinuated itself into debates on other subjects, shaping and forming them in various ways. There were parallels between land revenue measures and colonial breeding policies, indicating that there was a common framework within which such subjects were being approached. Finally, the tentativeness of colonial policies during this early phase has been captured through the indecisiveness on questions which were integral to horse breeding, for instance on the question of autonomy or integration within the 'native' economy. Integration could have the potential benefit of reducing expenses, but autonomy would mean less dependence on unreliable 'native' agents and producers, and the relative merits of both these approaches were discussed for a long time. It was partly the fear of the unknown Indian terrain during this early phase of colonialism that pushed the state towards a policy of greater autonomy, which ultimately went against the economic logic that was so central to its policies.

Before discussing these larger questions relating to colonial policies, it might be useful to briefly sketch the immediate pre-colonial background. This will serve the purpose of elucidating both the continuities and breaks within the horse-breeding network under the East India Company's suzerainty.[4] Perhaps the stable hierarchy of horse-breeding regions represents the most striking continuity, so that Punjab, Rajasthan, Kutch, and Kathiawar continued to dominate the horse-breeding scene even under colonial rule. Though many of these regions provided conditions that were far removed from the lush, humid, and flat landscape of the plains, they were apparently ideal for breeding horses for military purposes.[5] This is also reflected in the great popularity of horses imported from the somewhat inhospitable terrains of Central Asia, Iran, and the Arabian peninsula. Maritime trade in horses from these regions has been traced as far back as c.AD 1000,[6] though imports peaked only in the early eighteenth century at the figure of nearly 5,000 horses annually.[7] This annual influx of quality horses was essential to satisfy the immediate military demand from regional potentates but, equally importantly, this fresh stock was needed to reinvigorate flagging equine strains. The rather intangible and extremely fluid 'character' of horses was, after all, notoriously difficult to maintain.[8] However, though imports from external sources were essential for these reasons, the manner in which they occurred reflects a full and complete integration within internal economies and agricultural cycles in South Asia. This was true as far as overland trade in Central Asian horses was concerned, which were brought in by Afghan merchants travelling with caravans of *Powindah* trading nomads. These merchants either travelled towards northern India via the Khyber Pass or went southwards towards Bikaner, Jaipur, and the Deccan region via the Bolan and other passes.[9] Paying several cesses and dues en route, they travelled extensively within British territories and attended important fairs such as those held in Haridwar or Pushkar, which acted as nodal points for the purchase of horses.

Company officials also recognised the importance of these pre-existing fairs and local networks, but were unable to use them optimally to procure desired horses. In fact, the Company's presence or growth appeared to be detrimental to the regional trade in horses: for instance, as it made greater inroads into the North Western frontier, the horse trade in these hitherto thriving regions diminished. Similarly, as the Company consolidated its reign in the latter half of the eighteenth century, the overall demand for horses came down from the peaks it had scaled in the earlier part of the century. Officials were also unable to fully exploit 'native' markets due to the insufficient funds at their disposal – dealers received much higher prices for quality breeds from regional rulers and were reluctant to negotiate prices with the British.[10] These reasons partly drove the Company towards instituting autonomous breeding experiments, which will be discussed in detail in the following pages. It must be mentioned at the outset, though, that such experiments did not make full use of the existing wisdom on horse-breeding, which is why studs were established in the humid plains of eastern India rather than in the traditional horse-breeding districts. Another decisive break from pre-colonial patterns occurred when the British began to import breeding stock from the homeland in large numbers – a policy that was both financially disastrous and biologically unsuccessful.[11] This chapter will highlight these aspects while discussing their links with larger colonial ideologies and tenets.

Markets as the measure of success

The question of horse breeding during our period was intimately linked to the military needs of the Company; the relentless march of the British army was, after all, handicapped to a certain extent only by the superiority of 'native' cavalries. In his sketch of horse breeding in India, Jas Gommans notes that 'at the end of the eighteenth century, the Company's officials and the army officers became increasingly aware that, in the long run, they could not hold or expand their newly acquired territories without a substantial enlargement of their cavalry establishment'.[12] This was partly true, as the British found themselves at a slight disadvantage against excessively equinely inclined adversaries like Mysore,[13] which was apparent in Lord Cornwallis's abortive advance on Seringapatam in 1791. In the months following this setback there was an increasing consensus that the insubstantial British cavalry, which was totally dependent on allied states for replenishment during wars, needed to become self-reliant.[14] Two hurdles had earlier stood in the way of achieving this: one was the expense involved in recruiting a massive cavalry, a problem that was partly resolved after a realisation of its immense usefulness; the other problem was the far more persistent one of quality, an area where the administration was much less willing to compromise. Horses had to be of a 'good character', had to be 'well formed, proportioned and limbed', and had to be at least fourteen-and-a-half hands tall.[15] Government studs, using only the best stallions from India and abroad, were established in Poosa, Ganjam, and Hissar to address this question of quality. However, they performed abysmally and were written off as bad investments, though they were funded for long afterwards in the hope that they would, at some point, revive and perform the miraculous feats that were expected of them. The urgency and redoubled energy with which horses were sought did not fail to bear fruit though: for instance, the Bengal cavalry, which had no more than 500 horses in 1793, grew sevenfold to have nearly 3,500 horses only six years later.[16] Despite this, Company officials were guarded and often outrightly critical in their assessments of the progress made: it was felt that these returns did not match the level of expectations and financial investments. The supposed grimness of the situation forced a distressed Captain Wyatt, superintendent of the stud in Kathiawar, to even rue the decline of an alleged tribe of marauders called the Kattra, who had been 'distinguished for ages past by the superior breed of their horses'; that this sentiment was expressed in 1814 when the anti-thugee campaign had already begun, further highlights his desperateness.[17]

The only really effective way of ensuring a perpetual supply of exceptional horses in these circumstances was to establish a network of 'native' breeders producing quality horses for colonial consumption. In other words, the Company wished to be at the centre of horse breeders' activities, thereby displacing 'native' potentates from this enviable position. However, it failed spectacularly in achieving this due to the small matter of insufficient demand – where 'native' rulers bought a lion's share of the 600,000 horses traded in the mid-eighteenth century,[18] British purchases never exceeded a few thousand even during those years when this became a priority area. In view of this rather limited British demand, far from being the unenterprising, orthodox, or 'traditional' beings that colonial records alleged they were, 'native' dealers appear to have been very sanguine creatures who were alive to the idea of profit-making. It is also worth remembering that, though Mysore and the Marathas might have fallen, the incessant demand from regional satraps kept the market afloat – even the ruling chief of Bharatpur, for instance, had a cavalry regiment consisting of 1,647 horses,[19] while more substantial rulers like the Amir of Afghanistan had 19,500 or more horses in their employ.[20] This leads us to a formulation that might appear somewhat odd at first sight: that while there was a vibrant 'native' market in horses, the new market in 'quality produce' that the colonial masters wished to conjure into existence never really took root, despite several incentives and gifts. The 'native' market, it appears, was not only spatially separated from its white equivalent – it also followed different economic laws. As late as 1872, more than seven decades after the first efforts in this direction were inaugurated, the government was still hoping that 'with proper assistance and encouragement, the breeding of horses for the market would probably again revive as a profitable enterprise'.[21] It appears that the British notion of quality – imported wholesale from the metropolis and applied unreflexively in the colony – prohibited an unfettered interplay between the forces of demand and supply, thereby stunting the growth of the nascent market.

This failure to institute a Company-centric market was seen as the foremost symptom of the general malaise afflicting horse-breeding operations in India. The strength of this notion of the market as the cure for all ills is not very surprising, considering that this was the age of ascendancy of utilitarian free-market doctrines and physiocratic principles.[22] Also related to this was the introduction of land settlements, which were expected to inject the notions of private property and market into a supposedly inert and supine Indian countryside.[23] It was hoped that these would, in turn, pave the way for the evolution of a society based on status/custom to one based on contract, from closed village communities to larger integrated economies, and from the Asiatic mode of production to the capitalist one.[24] Even during later periods, buoyed by their centrality within the theory of laissez-faire, the concepts of free market and free enterprise continued to be perceived as a talisman for growth and development. In fact, as late as the 1860s, by when the heyday of utilitarian and physiocratic theories was over, senior colonial administrators like Baird Smith still saw markets and freely transferable property rights in land as not merely the most effective means of attracting capital into agriculture, but also as the best form of famine insurance.[25]

Consequently, just as in the case of agricultural tracts, measures were taken to create the much-desired market in horses, and assistance and encouragement began to be offered to potential breeders. Both the cultivation of land and the cultivation of horse-breeds, it was hoped, would reach optimal levels as Zamindars, or 'improving landlords' became gradually imbued with the idea of profits and markets. An official noted in the context of horse breeding that 'I know of no expedient so effectual as that of offering a premium for the greatest quantity [of horses] delivered by the landlords.'[26] Interestingly, this analogy between farming and breeding does not end here; in fact, the two overlapped closely enough to even share a similar nomenclature: both the permanent settlement of land revenue and the new scheme for encouraging horse breeding were known as the Zamindari system. This was quite appropriate too, as both schemes rested on the bedrock of substantial landlords who were considered sedentary and trust-worthy. It could be argued, in fact, that the Zamindari system of horse breeding reflected colonial faith in the ideas of progressive landlords and markets to a much greater extent: after all, colonial officials relied on landlords despite the fact that the latter had very little prior experi-ence of breeding horses for commercial purposes. What was attempted, therefore, was a complete overhaul of the existing system and the creation of an entirely new kind of breeder. The idea of a permanent, stable, market-driven system which was free of any interference from middlemen or dealers drove the Company towards this ambitious scheme, and in this sense both the Zamindari scheme for breeding and land settlement had common ideological origins.

The Zamindari scheme for horse breeding was first formulated in the 1790s by Major Fraser, the pioneer of studs in Bengal, to cope with the spurt in demand from the newly formed cavalry corps.[27] Launched on a small scale in 1798, the scheme initially relied on the expertise of 'native' horse breeders (called *Naulbunds*). Stallions with a suppos-edly excellent character and pedigree were distributed gratis among *Naulbunds*, on the sole condition that the Company would have the right to be the first buyer of any subsequent progeny. They were each assigned a certain village or a certain number of mares and were also paid for the upkeep of stallions. A *daroga* was also appointed to super-intend their work and maintain records. However, since *Naulbunds* were men of small means, their own promissory statements had little value – the weight of added testimony from fellow-breeders or 'respect-able' villagers was required to lend credence to them.[28] Despite a strong emphasis on using local expertise, this initial experiment failed to show any appreciable outcome and was quickly forgotten within a climate of growing expectations from studs. However, the scheme had the twin merits of being relatively inexpensive and supervision free, and consequently made a reappearance in 1816, by which time the failure of the stud experiment had become self-evident to everyone. It was clear that, two decades after the inception of the first institution at Pusa, studs had failed to show any signs of becoming financially stable – in the year 1814/15, for instance, the net expenditure on studs amounted to rupees 406,427, whereas the value of the stock at these studs rose only by rupees 262,966.[29] William Moorcroft, who had the great misfortune of replacing the illustrious Major Frazer in 1808, had to consequently face acerbic attacks from all directions, not least from colleagues and seniors whom he had successfully antagonised. There was little else to do in such a situation but repackage the Major's popular Zamindari scheme and, with but a slight nod of acknowledgement in his direction, present it as primarily his own brainchild.[30] This he did rather successfully, making the one major alteration of including Zamindars within the ambit, thus making the scheme more worthy of its name.

The scheme, in fact, became so dependent on Zamindars during Moorcroft's time that not a single *Naulbund*'s name can be found in lists of beneficiaries that are replete with *Deshmukhs*, *Deshpandeys*, *Kulkarnis*, and *Patils*.[31] It appears that the Company, riding high on the success of its military campaigns and the quieter but more insidious revenue campaigns, had decided that the formerly rebellious local potentates and landlords had finally been vanquished and tamed. In his nuanced and detailed sketch of the Western Indian countryside, Ravinder Kumar notes that this sense of confidence was perhaps justified, as:

> The office of the *Mamlatdar* [had been] completely transformed...The *Mamlatdar* was formerly an officer who exercised considerable initiative. He now became a supine instrument of the collector's will, and his actions were controlled by a narrow and precise set of regulations. The *Deshmukh*...suffered a similar eclipse, the collectors were inclined to look upon him as a parasite and they were reluctant to utilise his services in negotiating the land-tax with the *Patils* and the *Kunbis.*[32]

Whatever be the reasons behind this greater colonial willingness to trust the Zamindars, what is noticeable is that the latter continued to harbour misgivings about colonial motives and were inclined to question the Company's benevolent intentions.[33] Such doubts were partly justified for, though beneficiaries were repeatedly assured that they could 'do as they wished' with their windfall, the official eye was firmly fixed on their activities. In fact, though it ran completely contrary to all notions of free market, the Company's right to be the first buyer quickly dovetailed into the right to levy fines: a 'book of fines and rewards' was maintained and stud superintendents doubled as ad hoc magistrates.[34] The undertakings and testimonials produced on the *Naulbunds'* behalf were also strictly enforced and, in lean years when breeders moved in search of greener pastures, their guarantors were rounded up and reminded of their obligations. This quasi-feudal, retributive system did not coalesce with the avowed objective of creating a free market in quality produce which was so desired by officials.[35] Such inherently antagonistic tendencies ensured that colonial efforts to establish a market did not bear fruit until the end of our period of study.

Far from the 'native' market: horse breeding in colonial studs

The 'native' market was, then, too fickle and unresponsive to be relied upon, though it was the easiest and cheapest route to achieving plenitude. Also, markets could not be simply wished into existence, and though local breeders were encouraged with an eye to the long-term consequences, it was also essential to think of a quick remedy in the short term. In the 1790s, when the urgent need for a strong cavalry was fully appreciated, there appeared but one way of achieving the target quickly – by circumventing the 'unreliable and profiteering' Indian horse dealer and creating a parallel breeding network.

The 'native' horse dealer attracted great scorn and ridicule from British purchasers, his dishonesty acquiring an almost proverbial status. A rogue and a swindler, he was thought to possess several cunning tricks to cheat potential buyers. In fact, buyers were warned to be particularly suspicious of excessively healthy animals, as they could be suffering from what was popularly known as the 'dealer's condition' – implying that they could have been temporarily polished and fattened, thereby conveying an erroneous impression of health.[36] Horses, complained officials, were invariably of an indifferent quality, and on the rare occasion when they were tolerably good, the price quoted was exorbitant. Dealers were also susceptible to acts of sabotage by rival European and 'native' powers who 'being jealous of [British] interests...diverted expected supplies into different channels' at most critical periods.[37] The situation became even more difficult when an individual dealer became powerful enough to form a large conglomerate that monopolised the regional horse trade.[38] Not surprisingly, this stranglehold of middlemen was believed to be stifling British interests, especially in a situation where the option of disciplining or reprimanding wayward dealers was not to be contemplated for fear of antagonising them and reducing future supplies. This fear of antagonising dealers existed also in the context of itinerant trade in other commodities. Writing about the colonial treatment of *banjara* traders, Ayesha Siddiqui notes that:

There had been instances, it was said, where large bodies of *banjaras* passing near army camps, and refusing to offer the grain they carried, had been allowed to move on to the enemy, the dread of alarming them, and thus banishing them for ever, being sufficient to protect them from interruption.[39]

This fear and distrust of the middleman was not limited to the horse trade – it became the central notion around which the colonial stance on many subjects was formulated. The Ryotwari land settlement was, after all, first and foremost an attempt to eliminate middlemen and deal directly with the cultivators;[40] similarly, within the textile trade too monetary advances were made directly to weavers, short-circuiting the powerful middle interests.[41] However, though quickly ridiculed, middlemen were a huge blessing for the British, especially when they had no direct links with producers. This link with producers was especially fragile during the initial years, when the white man was yet to physically stamp his presence on the Indian countryside. The rumour of the white man had, of course, travelled to the remotest regions, but when he appeared in person at a 'native' gathering – as he did, for example, at a cattle fair in Dinapore – he inadvertently caused great alarm and fear.[42]

Until such a time arrived when direct and reliable links were established, it was essential to rely on the services of the rogue middleman. An incident that occurred in wartime Deccan in 1802 captures both the extreme usefulness and the British mistrust of agents. An entire regiment was, in this case, left stranded without any draught animals to carry provisions, when one Venkatarungapilly came to the rescue and almost magically mobilised 30,000 bullocks within a day or two.[43] However, true to their form, officials alleged he had artificially engineered this shortage or disarray in the first place, with the sole purpose of ingratiating himself with the highest authorities by promptly meeting the demand for animals when panic set in.[44] When the agent later demanded payment, a debate ensued about his character's (dis)honesty and his alleged and actual services. Venkatarungapilly eventually ended up being viewed by officials as a suspicious character. Within this climate of suspicion, it is easy to lose sight of the pivotal role played by agents like him within this climate of suspicion, but they helped steady the Company's ship during its turbulent and foundational years.[45] Also, although these agents were perceived as profiteering swines, they had the great virtue of forestalling huge potential expenses on creating a parallel breeding establishment.

However, the distrust of the 'native' dealer and the disappointment in the 'native' market had become so strong that the Company was virtually forced into making this financial blunder. Portents of disaster were evident from the start. Pusa, of which great exploits were expected, produced a paltry dozen or two horses rather than the hundreds that would have been justified by the scale of investment. Also, good stallions of a breeding age seemed impossible to find, and the 'ignorant natives', who were otherwise supposed to be quite innocent of any notion of property, suddenly appeared to become excessively proprietorial about their mares.[46] There was also a crisis of authority within the stud administration, and even animal fodder became difficult to obtain.[47] During the initial years it was easier to represent these as minor irritants, but when they failed to disappear well into the next century, stud administrators struggled to find a reasonable and convincing explanation.[48] Pusa faced the auditor's axe less than a decade after its celebrated inauguration, and barely managed to survive; its equivalent at Ganjam in the Madras presidency was less fortunate and was summarily abolished without much prior warning.[49] The committee that presided over its liquidation noted, after burrowing into the stud finances and weighing expenses against the value of stock, that 'the expense of the stud has not hitherto been balanced by any proportionate benefit derived from the institution'.[50] In such times of extreme fiscal economy, unprofitability equalled failure and studs struggled unsuccessfully to win the battle with the account books.[51] A decade after the abolition of Ganjam, a memorandum circulated by the Bengal government noted rather conclusively that 'the breeding establishment in Bengal has been found, after a trial of twenty years, to be utterly inadequate to the object of introducing into the Bengal province an improved breed of horse'.[52] That Pusa continued to exist despite this damning verdict can be attributed more to chance than circumstance – a similar verdict led to a complete abolition of studs in the Bombay and Madras presidencies.[53]

However, though the stud administrator was heavily censured, his alleged ineptitude – financial or otherwise – was not the sole trigger behind escalating costs. If these were indeed times when thrift in public life was considered a great virtue, these were also times when office holders were infamous for their susceptibility to corruption, and this added substantially to the cost of running the studs and similar institutions.[54] The race to earn the rather oddly termed 'competencies' and a peaceful retirement in the old Blighty contributed in no small measure to what Nicholas Dirks calls the 'scandal of empire', and it led senior officers to trifle with public finances and policies.[55] It is no surprise, then, that the heavily endowed stud plan was closely pursued by the shadow of fraudulence and nepotism since its approval. When Major Frazer initially demanded 300 quality mares for the experiment at Poosa, the contract was immediately awarded – without so much as a token debate – to the brother of Sir John Murray, member of the recently constituted Board for the Superintendence of Horse Breeding Operations. A report later noted that, out of all the mares bought as a result, 'one half...prove[d] barren and the rest bad mares or otherwise objectionable'.[56] The report made much of this initial lapse, though it talked of Sir Murray's indiscretion in euphemistic terms, calling it his 'impatience of losing time'.[57] Apart from such instances of blatant corruption, the studs' autonomy and efficiency was compromised by interference from senior military officers working part-time and gratuitously on the Board of Superintendence, leading to multiple layers of authority and a confusion regarding the lines of supervision.[58]

However, the chief cause for the failure of the stud experiment was, in a way, embedded within the seeds of its birth. Pusa was envisaged as a tranquil island for exceptional horses situated far from the influence of 'native' markets, its climate was likened to that of Britain, and its horses were expected to match English ones in ability and character.[59] The Anglo-Indian breeder was, it appears, gripped by nostalgia of the motherland: it is quite another story, of course, that within Britain itself the exotic Arabian breed, relatively easily available within the Indian subcontinent, was more highly prized than the home-grown ones.[60] This nostalgia, forming the basis of stud policies, perverted their normal operations and introduced certain financially ruinous practices into them, chief among which was the importation of English stallions and mares for breeding purposes. In fact, an elaborate and complex establishment took shape in the metropole to support the Indian studs: this included acquiring a 130-acre farm in Essex, the appointment of a permanent veterinary surgeon and his various assistants at the farm, the formation of a board that oversaw the purchase of horses, and regular maintenance of all records relating to shipment and purchase of horses.[61] These were very expensive measures, which could have been easily avoided had the 'native' market been perceived with a little more sympathy.[62]

However, though it was the underlying rationale for the whole experiment, the utopia of studs as unspoiled European stations in a sea of 'native' markets was quite impossible to implement. Pusa's climate might have approximated Britain's in the wistful Britons' eyes, but the bold experiment initiated there had any chance of success only if a substantial 'native' presence was tolerated within this tranquil island. *Naulbunds* had to be, after all, recruited in their dozens to care for horses despite the allegedly suspect nature of their breeding practices, while 'native' bookkeepers and *babus*, despite carrying a reputation for being sly and guileful, were appointed to ensure that routine duties were performed faultlessly. An incident that flared up at the Hapur stud in 1833 reveals, in an indirect way, the power and authority of the *babu*. A major feud broke out in this year between European officers at the station, and a commission was instituted to inquire into the incident. Instances of insubordination were taken very seriously during these times, and an immediate order was issued to check the veracity of the numerous complaints made by the veterinary surgeon Hodgson and his colleagues against the stud superintendent Captain McKenzie.[63] The future of the establishment hung in the balance and 'native' employees were forced to choose allegiances in this open conflict, which most of them did by bolstering the McKenzie camp. As the enquiries took a decided turn against Hodgson, he was gripped with paranoia and, in his frenzied state, imagined that all *babus* at the stud, and especially one Ramruttun Sain, were conspiring against him. Ramruttun, he alleged, had torn up vital evidence, threatened his subordinates with dire consequences if they dared to reveal the truth, and was perverting the course of inquiry in every conceivable way.[64] Both the commission and the Military Board dismissed his pleas and complaints as the ravings of a lunatic – which, incidentally, worked in his favour as he was spared a court martial due to his supposed insanity[65] – but his tirades reveal to an extent the financial clout and elevated position of the *babu*, and this was substantiated by testimony from other officers too.[66]

However, the history of colonialism has conclusively proved that employing 'natives' does not necessarily translate into integration with the 'native' society or economy. Pusa, geographically distant from any major settlement, was both literally and metaphorically detached from the countryside – so detached, in fact, that basic necessities like animal fodder became difficult to obtain. 'Natives', for instance, appeared excessively uncooperative and were so unwilling to part with their bales of straw that physical or legislative force had to be sometimes used to 'convince' them.[67] It is possible that a different outcome could have been obtained had the countryside and local cultivators been carefully assimilated within the stud plans. This could have had other potential benefits too, for greater integration would have meant greater utilisation of the local ecology and natural resources which would have, apart from several other advantages, made great financial sense. Studs were, however, so hermetically sealed that even common-place information – like the location of local grazing fields or foraging areas – was out of reach. Interaction with the locals was so minimal that when two *charwahas* (cow herders) 'strayed' into the Pusa stud in 1800, they almost succeeded in causing a minor sensation.[68] They were plied with gifts and Major Frazer vexed them with queries about local rearing practices, making a careful note of their responses and acting promptly upon them soon afterwards.[69] On his return trip from the areas mentioned by the *charwahas*, Frazer seemed completely convinced of the benefits of greater integration, recommending:

> The adoption of that measure [by which] the *gualas* [cow herders] will become our ryots [peasants and tenant farmers] and neighbours. By assisting each other and introducing population we shall obtain the object desired without any increase of expense and these lands may probably be brought to yield great assistance of the stud.[70]

However, this laudable objective of 'introducing population' was never fully realised, and isolationism and import remained the two dominant pillars of official stud policy. The same logic of separation from 'natives' and 'native produce', which first pushed the Company into creating a parallel infrastructure, now effectively choked its fledgling stud enterprise. Already facing extreme pressure to conform to the high standards of financial viability, the stud was further crippled by this disengagement from the local setting. Several measures were employed to stem this rot, one of which was the appointment of veterinary surgeons to studs. However, in such a scenario even the veterinarian's role came under attack and was significantly reformulated and redefined, as we shall see in the next section.

Between the treasury and the military: the veterinarian in a colony

A quick survey of the initial years of veterinary medicine in India will allow us to illustrate many of the points we have made in the last two sections. The question of economic utility was, after all, of the greatest importance when recruiting veterinarians: it was only in 1796, when a sizeable cavalry had been acquired and losses through disease became a very real possibility that a regulation was passed proposing the appointment of a veterinary surgeon to cavalry regiments.[71] Another question that was central to the practice of veterinary medicine during these initial years was the use of 'native' resources and expertise; these were not fully trusted but were available readily at negligible cost when compared to the expenses involved in importing medicines from Britain. This led to a dilemma for the colonial state that we have highlighted earlier. The veterinarian also faced the question of economic utility very closely while performing his duties as a horse breeder, and faced heavy censure from authorities for showing inadequate results.[72] Finally, a study of early veterinary developments reaffirms the strong military connection of the subject of horse breeding that we have shown throughout this chapter. Perhaps the efficiency of the veterinarians and horse breeders was, to an extent, compromised due to this strong link with the military.[73]

Colonial officials had little doubt about the superiority of British veterinary expertise, despite the raging debate over the relative advantages of integration and autonomy. The relative merits of 'native' practitioners and British ones were not even perfunctorily discussed, as veterinarians barely trained in the rudiments of the art were imported from the metropole.[74] Medicine for regiments was also purchased in and despatched from Britain through the offices of the ever-helpful Mr Coleman, though *bazar* medicine was resorted to quite frequently in practice.[75] It was soon realised, however, that the demand for veterinarians far outstripped the supply, primarily due to the great reluctance shown by British practitioners in undertaking a stint in India, partly due to the poor pay conditions for veterinarians in India.[76] This recruitment gap could be potentially addressed only by training farriers locally, an experiment that was started on a small scale at Arcot in 1811 when 'half-caste boys' were instructed for short periods and later attached to regiments.[77] The experiment, however, was not a roaring success: the rather short training succeeding only in equipping beneficiaries with a 'superficial knowledge of diseases'.[78] A similar initiative was launched in 1822 at Ballygunge in Calcutta under the superintendence of Veterinary Surgeon Hodgson who had, until then, not acquired the unflattering reputation that we know him for.[79] Working on the theory that a hint of 'whiteness' was immensely preferable to unrelieved negritude, 'half-caste boys' were once again recruited, though even they were found wanting in several attributes. At the end of the training, Hodgson reported that only two out of his eight wards, Mr Hughes and Mr Molineux, were tolerably well informed.[80] These failed experiments, combined with the elevated position of British practitioners, reflect both the growing demand for veterinarians during these times of rapid growth in cavalry as well as a strong distrust of 'native' aptitude and ability to cure animal disease. This, when juxtaposed with the negative perception of 'native' breeders that we have highlighted earlier, underscores the extremely suspicious official stance against indigenous practices when it came to prized British horses. An official noted rather emphatically in this connection that:

> It must be obvious to any one who has paid the smallest attention to the subject that Europeans ... who have obtained a very moderate share of veterinary knowledge must be far more useful in a cavalry corps than the first 'native' solotree [*sic*] in the country whose medical acquirement, if they can be so called, are far below the most ignorant European cow leach in Europe.[81]

Though such statements reflect the dismissive colonial attitude towards indigenous expertise, we must reiterate that in terms of practical measures there was some degree of grudging dependence, reflected in the use of dealers, *Naulbunds* and Zamindars in horse-breeding experiments which we have highlighted earlier. Within veterinary medicine too, 'native' expertise and *bazar* medicine were constantly used and applied. Mistrust coexisted with partial dependence and even a measure of respect when it also came to other aspects of indigenous knowledge, for instance in case of astronomy or human medicine.[82] Such grudging admissions notwithstanding, colonial suspicion, mistrust, and disparagement of indigenous knowledge systems prohibited a greater integration with them.

Where indigenous resources and expertise could not be trusted, autonomous arrangements were necessary, as in case of studs. Arcot and Ballygunge were also steps in this direction. Contrary to the logic of the stud enterprise, however, the question of quality did not determine the nature of veterinary training in the colony, where maximum returns with minimum investment appears to have been the Company's motto. When Hodgson berated the government for its inadequate devotion to the advancement of science, the reply was clear and categorical: all that was expected of him was to train his wards in 'practical matters', not in the 'scientific knowledge of the [veterinary] art'.[83] As the proportion of livestock in the Company's regiments rose, so did the losses suffered through epizootics and other disease,[84] but there existed a strong belief that basic precautions, like proper shoeing of horses and knowledge of certain stock remedies, would significantly reduce losses. This, of course, had the added advantage of justifying the rather elementary but cost-effective training provided at Arcot and Ballygunge, while also setting the tone for contemporary and future Anglo-Indian veterinary practice. Consequently, when William Moorcroft – who later replaced Major Frazer at the Poosa stud – wrote his first and only monograph targeted at veterinarians in India, he chose deliberately to ignore the abstract anatomical and physiological experiments being carried out at the famed French institutes, writing more prosaically about the 'contents of a portable horse medicine chest adapted for India'.[85]

Preventing excessive mortality was, however, only a part of the veterinarian's duty – there was a significant expansion in his remit and responsibilities in the colonies, transforming him severally into a conservationist, an agrarian reformer, a researcher, and even a revenue collector.[86] In the Indian context, he acquired the dual responsibility of being a healer as well as a breeder, not only buying and rearing suitable horses for regiments but also overseeing stud operations. It was in this role that he directly faced the bookkeeper's wrath, especially as the stud experiment failed to show any financial gains. Severely reprimanded for the stud's meagre performance, the veterinary surgeon and the superintendent colluded and devised underhand methods of improving returns. Quantity, not quality, became the new watchword, as the fundamental rationale for studs was challenged in a race to increase the number of stud horses passing into the cavalry. Small wonder, then, that the number of such horses rose manifold from a mere dozen or two in the 1790s to as many as 496 in 1823, though any potential gain in the stud's reputation due to this was offset by the visibly poor quality of the produce.[87] Talking of the methods used to achieve higher targets, an official noted that:

> The object of the superintendent and his veterinary surgeon [is] to get as many of their colts passed as possible. They [are] brought up in quick succession [before the Remount Committee] and subjected to a very cursory scrutiny. I have known colts rejected in the first two three sittings of the committee presented on a future day when the members were less keen on their work and passed.[88]

The economic argument, applied rigorously and carried to its extreme, perverted the very basis of the rather utopian stud experiment. Another crisis was generated due to the fundamentally military nature of the enterprise, which led to a deep-seated clash of interests after the appointment of veterinary surgeons to studs. Hodgson, for example, faced military opposition throughout his career, starting with the Ballygunge experiment and leading eventually to his dismissal from Hissar. An equally prolonged battle took place between Moorcroft and the Board of Superintendence appointed by the Military Board, with accusations flying thick and fast in both directions. Though Moorcroft's life was perhaps a great example of peaceful coexistence with the military,[89] he repeatedly made the point that his difference with the military breeders emerged out of an underlying conflict of perspectives.[90] His grand tours to North India and Central Asia, which so riled his military superiors,[91] might have been partly occasioned by a desire to flee from the dictates of this superiors, though the ostensible motive was to study and obtain cattle of better breed in the region. Such dissidence, coupled with the fact that the late 1820s saw an enthusiastic return to the old policy of recruiting British practitioners, led to a partial strengthening of the veterinarian's autonomy,[92] a development that would have been quite inconceivable during the earliest phase when there had been a complete co-option by the military.[93] However, caught as he still was between military fiats and the treasury's ledgers, it would take him many more decades to achieve any substantial measure of independence.[94]

Conclusion

Veterinary developments both substantiate and resonate a number of trends discussed in earlier sections, including distrust of 'native' practices, military origins of horse breeding and its lasting influence, financial underpinnings of the entire enterprise, and dependence on metropolitan expertise. These trends have been highlighted against the background of several noteworthy processes occurring during this formative phase of colonial rule. The question of horse breeding and a strong cavalry was, after all, of supreme importance during these times of great military campaigns and annexations, and it was closely linked to larger debates about property rights, land settlements, and financial administration. Major Frazer, though only an insignificant military underling, was in this regard a close ally of great and almost mythical personages like Cornwallis, Philip Francis, and Thomas More. All of them worked within a climate that was shaped by the larger utilitarian and physiocratic doctrines and tempered by a healthy financial austerity.

Though the colonial horse-breeding policy had its originary impulse in the concern with quality and in the distrust of 'native' networks, policies and correspondences on the subject were couched in an economic language right from the start – private property, the creation of a market, and the financial worthiness of studs were all discussed extensively in connection with breeding practices. Also, the argument of financial worth was the final basis on which the usefulness of any new policy was judged: the Zamindari system appeared alluring due to the promise it held of cutting down stud expenses, a quality-conscious 'native' horse market was promoted as the most cost-efficient method for acquiring horses, studs fell out of favour due to their inefficiency and unsatisfactory financial returns, and even the fate of the emerging veterinary establishment was decided on the basis of a carefully drawn balance sheet. This financial emphasis was, in fact, carried to such an extreme that it undercut its own basic purpose, leading to half-baked measures and half-way abandoned plans that made a significant demand on the treasury. Though this is purely historical conjecture, perhaps the studs would have succeeded had their operations not been reined in and perverted by this economic logic.

Finally, this chapter has mapped the trajectory of a policy that did not have much impact and never took off. The colonial cavalry never matched, purely in terms of quantity, the ones owned by 'native' states like Mysore or the Marathas during these early years of colonial rule. Yet, a study of these failed measures not only reveals the larger ideological parameters within which the colonial government functioned, but also sheds light upon several areas that have been, till now, approached differently by historians. For instance, though Company *Sahibs* during this early phase of colonialism have been seen as having relatively greater interactions with the 'natives', this chapter highlights a fundamental distrust of 'natives' when it came to actual measures. The white man might have dressed up as a *nawab* and appreciated *Urdu* couplets, but this did not guarantee an approval of all 'native' agents. This distrust might have been partly responsible for an insufficient colonial penetration into the remotest territories which led to the failure of many of the measures outlined above, though the process of gaining collaborators had already started with the implementation of land settlements and similar measures.

Notes

1 Lt Col. J. S. Bhalla, *History of the Remount and Veterinary Corps* (New Delhi, Additional Directorate General Remount and Veterinary, 1988), p. xv.

2 A board for superintending over horse-breeding activities was formed in 1794. If a date of inception for remount operations has to be chosen, perhaps this is as appropriate a date as any.

3 The first phrase was employed by Sumit Sarkar in 'Popular Culture, Community and Power: Three Studies of Modern Indian Social History', *Studies in History*, 8(2) (Aug. 1992), 309. The second was used by Tirthankar Roy in an article entitled 'Questioning the Basics', *Economic and Political Weekly*, 37(23) (8–14 Jun. 2002), 2223–8; see also Sumit Sarkar's 'The Decline of the Subaltern in *Subaltern Studies*', in *Writing Social History* (Delhi: Oxford University Press, 1997), pp. 82–108; Prasannan Parthasarthi, 'The State of Indian History', *Journal of Social History*, 37(1) (2003), 47–54; Dane Kennedy 'Imperial History and Post-colonial Theory', *Journal of Imperial and Commonwealth History*, 24(3) (1996), 345–63. Benita Parry, one of the leading critics of post-colonial studies, looks at this linguistic turn as a strategy that 'reduces the dynamics of historical processes to the rules of language and ... permits the circumvention and relegation of the economic impulses to colonial conquest'. In 'The Postcolonial: Conceptual Category or Chimera?', *Yearbook of English Studies*, 27 (1997), 12; see also Parry's *Postcolonial Studies: A Materialist Critique* (London: Routledge, 2004).

4 This paragraph and the next one are largely based on the comprehensive survey of horse-breeding complexes in eighteen-century India by Jas Gommans, whose monograph is the only existing full-length survey of this subject in the modern South Asian context. See *The Rise of the Indo-Afghan Empire, c.1710–1780* (Leiden: Brill, 1997); see by the same author 'The Horse Trade in Eighteenth Century South Asia', *Journal of the Economic and Social History of the Orient*, 37(3) (1994), 228–50.

5 Comparing horses reared in the plains with the hill-bred ones, Moorcroft noted in his journal that 'there is much difference between the manner in which a horse bred in the plains and one bred in the mountains proceeds ... The former climbs with eager steps endeavouring to overcome the difficulty of the road but does not give himself sufficient time to appreciate and prepare for the irregularities ... The latter sets out slowly and circumspectly, places his feet with deliberate caution and gains his object by a succession of starts proportioned to the obstacle which present themselves. The former, if he make a false step can scarcely recover ... The latter seldom makes a false step through the command he retains over his limbs.' British Library, Asia, Pacific and Africa Collections (hereafter APAC), MSS EUR D. 236, pp. 20–1.

6 Ranabir Chakravarti, 'Early Medieval Bengal and the Trade in Horses: A Note', *Journal of the Economic and Social History of the Orient*, 42(2) (1999), 195.

7 Horses from these regions were also in great demand during the Mughal period. Talking about this period, K. N. Chaudhuri notes that 'the extent to which breeding of fine and specialised horses had become the preserve of nomadic pastoralists in Central Asia, Iran, and the Arabian peninsula can be seen from the fact that the two leading trading nations of Asia, India and China, preferred to import their war horses rather than breed them at home ... as compared to a Badakshan pony or the Arab blood-stock, the indigenous Indian horse remained a second-best choice'. *Asia before Europe: Economy and Civilisation of the Indian Ocean from the Rise of Islam to 1750* (Cambridge: Cambridge University Press, 1990), p. 278.

8 Some empirical justification for this belief is provided by the huge historical variations in the nature of horses. For example the Destrier, a warhorse used in medieval Europe, was much taller, slower, and stronger than modern horses. R. J. Barendse, 'The Feudal Mutation: Military and Economic Transformations of the Ethnosphere in the Tenth to Thirteenth Centuries', *Journal of World History*, 14(4) (Dec. 2003), 513.

9 Gommans, 'Horse Trade in Eighteenth Century South Asia', 230.

10 J. P. Piggott, writing one of the earliest treatises on horse breeding in India, noted about the highly desirable Toorkoman breed that 'From the high estimation and great request in which this horse is held by the natives, a Toorkoman is rarely procured by Europeans, who, in general decline them at price equal to what a merchant can readily obtain from the opulent native.' *Treatise on the Horses in India* (Calcutta: Government of India Press, 1794), p. x.

11 The report on the reorganisation of the Indian army, published in the wake of the Revolt of 1857, noted that 'the introduction of the tall, weak-constitutioned modern English horse into Europe has ruined them as it has done the studs in India ... the introduction of the English horse has been fatal to our studs'. *Papers Connected with the Re-organisation of the Army in India, supplementary to the Report of the Army Commission* (London: Eyre & Spottiswoode, 1859), p. 85.

12 Gommans, *Rise of the Indo-Afghan Empire*, p. 85.

13 Despite this obvious deficiency, the heavy 'native' reliance on horses sometimes worked in favour of the British. Major Durham, for instance, noted that: 'the "native" cavalry in India ... move around in great bodies; but are easily avoided or seldom take effect against our troops who are formed in lines of great extent and no great depth'. Quoted in Romesh C. Butalia, *The Evolution of the Artillery in India: From the Battle of Plassey to the Revolt of 1857* (Delhi: Allied Publishers, 1999), pp. 54–5.

14 The company nearly completely relied on 'native' allied states for supplying them with a cavalry, which did not prove to be a very good idea in 1791. Raymond Callahan, *The East India Company and Army Reform, 1783–1798* (Cambridge, MA: Harvard University Press, 1972), pp. 4–6.

15 This last criterion was very strictly imposed, and was relaxed after several discussions only in 1816 when it was realised that 'by too rigorous an adherence to restrictive regulations ... relating to the height of cavalry remount horses many valuable undersized animals have been lost'. APAC, F/4/543/13257, p. 882.

16 Gommans, *Rise of the Indo-Afghan Empire*, p. 85.

17 The Captain noted that 'their predatory habits, their success and safety in their freebooting expeditions depending so much on the goodness of their horses, was the chief inducement to them probably to pay such attention to the breed ... they were chiefly formidable to their neighbours from their boldness and dexterity and the fleetness of their horses'. Letter dated 14 March 1814, APAC, F/4/486/11667.

18 Gommans, *Rise of the Indo-Afghan Empire*, p. 89.

19 Sir Roper Lethbridge, *The Golden Book of India: A Genealogical and Biographical Dictionary of the Ruling Princes, Chiefs, Nobles, and other Personages, Titled or Decorated of the Indian Empire* (Delhi: Aakar Books, 2005; originally published in 1893), p. 10.

20 Lethbridge, *Golden Book of India*, p. 73.

21 *Moral and Material Progress of India, 1871–2* (Calcutta: Government of India Press, 1872), p. 36.

22 Elizabeth Fox-Genovese notes that 'the authoritarian system of [physiocratic] politics was derived directly from a determination to protect – if not to institute – the market'. *Origins of Physiocracy: Economic Revolution and Social Order in Eighteenth Century France* (New York: Cornell University Press, 1976), p. 46.

23 Ranajit Guha notes that, according to Company officials influenced by these doctrines, 'given permanent proprietary rights and a buyers' market in land, there was no reason why Bengal should not be blessed with the capital and initiative of its own indigenous entrepreneurs'. *Rule of Property for Bengal: An Essay on the Idea of Permanent Settlement* (Delhi: Orient Longman, 1982), pp. 48–9. A lot has been written about the influence of utilitarian and physiocratic doctrines in fashioning land settlement policies in South Asia, and it is generally agreed that these European philosophies did, to some extent, fashion agricultural policies in India. A very good summary of the debate on the relative importance of local Indian conditions and European philosophies can be found in Neeladri Bhattacharya, 'Colonial State and Agrarian Society', in Burton Stein (ed.), *The Making of Agrarian Policy in British India, 1770–1900* (Delhi: Oxford University Press, 1992), pp. 114–39.

24 See Amiya Kumar Bagchi, 'Land Tax, Property Rights and Peasant Insecurity in Colonial India', *Journal of Peasant Studies*, 20(1) (1992), 1–49; Sandra Den Otter, 'Rewriting the Utilitarian Market: Colonial Law and Custom in mid Nineteenth-Century British India', *European Legacy*, 6(2) (2001), 177–88; Eric Stokes, *English Utilitarians and India* (Delhi: Oxford University Press, 1989).

25 Eric Stokes, *The Peasant and the Raj: Studies in Agrarian and Peasant Rebellion in Colonial India* (Cambridge: Cambridge University Press, 1978), p. 10.

26 APAC, F/4/127/2369, p. 37.

27 APAC, L/MIL/431, p. 214.

28 This testimony read something as follows: 'From my own goodwill and opinion of the said ... I agree to become security for the faithful performance of all the duties required of him as specified in his Mutchilka agreement and further, should the said ... leave his residence in the said village of ... taking the said stallion with him, I bind myself to produce the said ... and horse, or to become liable to such punishment as would be apportioned to the said ... should he be produced and found guilty.' APAC, F/4/93/1891, p. 74.

29 APAC, F/4/543/13257, p. 733

30 This did not go unnoticed and one official noted rather plainly and bluntly that: 'of the discovery [of the zemindary system], as of all others, Major Frazer should not be defrauded'. APAC, L/MIL/ 5/431, p. 213.

31 APAC, F/4/1524/60209.

32 Ravinder Kumar, *Western India in the Nineteenth Century: A Study in the Social History of Maharashtra* (Toronto: University of Toronto Press, 1968), p. 58.

33 Captain Jameson from Allygaum noted that: 'Few in the distant districts were at first suspicious of the motives which induced government to give them fillies but on seeing their neighbours in quiet possession of them they have come forward to request that they may also furnished, and when the next supply arrives from the Bengal stud I shall lose no time in distributing them.' APAC, F/4/1524/60209, p. 5.

34 APAC, F/4/1518/59945, p. 17.

35 Ranajit Guha has noted in the context of land settlements that the policy of capitalist enterprise, in the absence of a sovereign market within the colony, could only become 'an apologia of quasi-feudalism'. Perhaps this observation is equally applicable in the context of horse-breeding practices. Quoted in Bhattacharya, 'Colonial State and Agrarian Society', p. 115.

36 Dated 5 October 1864, APAC, L/MIL/7/902, not paginated (hereafter n. p.).

37 APAC, Board's Collections, file no. F/4/127/2369, p. 135.

38 Captain Wyatt, Superintendent of Stud at Kathiawar, for instance complained about one Sunderjee in a report written in 1814, noting that: 'In the circumstance of the breeders of horses in this country having had such little communication

with Europeans is to be discovered one cause to which it is owing that Sunderjee, and other "native" merchants, have been allowed to monopolize the produce of the country.' Letter dated 23 December 1814, APAC, F/4/486/11667, n. p.

39 'Introduction', in Asiya Siddiqui (ed.), *Trade and Finance in Colonial India, 1750–1860* (Delhi: Oxford University Press, 1995), p. 42.

40 Dharma Kumar, *Land and Caste in South India: Agricultural Labour in Madras Presidency in the Nineteenth Century* (Cambridge: Cambridge University Press, 1965); R. E. Frykenberg, *Guntur District, 1788–1848: A History of Local Influences and Central Authority in South Asia* (Oxford: Clarendon Press, 1965); Nilamani Mukjherjee and R. E. Frykenberg, 'The Ryotwari System and Social Organisation in the Madras Presidency', in R. E. Frykenberg (ed.), *Land Control and Social Structure in Indian History* (Wisconsin: University of Wisconsin Press, 1969); Guha, *A Rule of Property for Bengal.*

41 Prasannan Parthasarthi, *The Transition to a Colonial Economy: Weavers, Merchants and Kings in South India, 1720–1800* (Cambridge: Cambridge University Press, 2001).

42 An official noted in 1800 that 'some arrangement might however be useful to prevent any species of influence, in an open and free market where foreigners assemble from all quarters of Hindoostan, hundreds of whom have never seen a European and are of course easily alarmed. I am sorry to state from good authority that occurrences of a similar nature have totally ruined the nuk-na-murd mela (fair).' APAC, F/4/93/1891, pp. 98–9. Gayatri Chakravorty Spivak also talks about the impact of the figure of the white man on horseback stalking the virgin Indian countryside in 'The Rani of Sirmur: An Essay in Reading the Archives', *History and Theory*, 24 (1985), 247–70.

43 APAC, MSS EUR F 128/121, p. 28.

44 APAC, MSS EUR 128/121, pp. 28–30.

45 The role of the 'native' collaborator or comprador during the high noon of the British empire has been sufficiently documented. However, not much work has been done on his activities during the initial years of wars and annexations.

46 A memorandum on studs noted in 1816 that: 'it is universally known that the "natives" of India are extremely unwilling to part with productive mares and any attempt therefore to procure three hundred productive mares in a few months could not be expected to succeed'. APAC, L/MIL/5/431, p. 212.

47 APAC, F/4/127/2369, pp. 34–47.

48 Already in the firing line in 1802, a stud administrator offered the following explanation: 'the first charges are heavy, but the value of the produce soon equals, finally overbalances, the amount. The stud is now in the second of these stages. The heavy disbursements have taken place, the stock in had in equal to them, and if we continue to give an efficient support to the establishment the value of the produce in a few years will exceed by an increasing ration, the aggregate amount of expenditure. The stud is at present in that state, which demands our care, in order that the ends proposed from its institution may be ultimately attained.' APAC, F/4/127/2369, p. 209.

49 In 1804, merely four years before the final abolition of the stud, a committee formed to report on the stud noted that: 'we have deemed the condition of the stud to be such as to answer the expectation entertained regarding the progress and success of the undertaking'. APAC, F/4/166/2833, p. 4.

50 They were therefore 'decidedly of opinion that it is advisable to discontinue entirely the establishment of stud at Ganjam'. In letter dated 30 March 1808, APAC, L/MIL/5/461, n. p.

51 Writing about the frugal lifestyle of Indian governor-generals, Victor Jacquemont noted that: '[One] may easily imagine that there are people who talk loudly of the dissolution of the empire and the world's end, when they behold the temporary ruler of Asia riding on horseback, plainly dressed, and without escort, or on his way into the country with his umbrella under his arm.' Cited in E. M. Collingham, *Imperial Bodies: The Physical Experience of the Raj, 1800–1947* (Cambridge: Cambridge University Press, 2001), p. 54.

52 APAC, L/MIL/5/431, p. 210.
53 In letter from the Stud Committee, dated 30 March 1808, APAC, L/MIL/5/461, n.p.
54 For details on corruption within the forestry department, see Akhileshwar Pathak, *Laws, Strategies, Ideologies: Legislating Forests in Colonial India* (Delhi: Oxford University Press, 2002).
55 Raymond Callahan notes that: 'The company [did] not having any scheme for retiring an officer because of age, ill health, or even gross incompetence ... The only hope of retiring to England, if one had not acquired a "comptetency" [sic] was to apply for a pension from Lord Clive's fund. This trust fund's ... resources were limited and its pensions correspondingly small.' In *East India Company and Army Reform*, p. 22. See also Nicholas B. Dirks, *The Scandal of Empire: India and the Creation of Imperial Britain* (Cambridge, MA: Harvard University Press, 2006).
56 APAC, L/MIL/5/431, p. 212.
57 APAC, L/MIL/5/431, p. 212.
58 Referring to the board's inefficiency, Moorcroft noted that: 'It may ... surely be said generally without offence that men are not apt to attach quite a due degree of importance or responsibility to the performance of duties which are undertaken gratuitously and merely in superaddition to their regular, and more important avocations.' APAC, F/4/543/13257, p. 996.
59 Frazer noted that 'Pusa comes nearer to the climate of England than Arabia and differs but little from that of Parma, where the cows give almost as much milk as in England.' APAC, F/4/93/1891, p. 314.
60 Peter Edwards, *Horses of Tudor and Stuart England* (Cambridge: Cambridge University Press, 1988). The demand for Arab horses continued undiminished in South Asia throughout the period of our study and in fact exceeded supply by a considerable margin, but the new emphasis on British horses at colonial studs reflects the somewhat higher status of home-grown stallions in official reckoning. If Arab horses had replaced English stallions at colonial studs, it would have considerably reduced expenses as Arab stallions were more easily procurable than English ones which had to be imported at considerable cost from the metropolis.
61 This land was acquired in 1801. After the lease ran out on this farm, a similar property was acquired at Kingsbury Green in Edgeware. Letter dated 23 May 1821, APAC, L/MIL/5/460, n. p.; see also letter dated 28 July 1802, APAC, L/MIL/5/461, n. p.
62 Writing in 1794 J. P. Piggott, a Lieutenant in the Cavalry, rated some Indian breeds like the 'Irakee', 'Iranee', 'Candahar', 'Cozakee', and 'Mojinnis' breeds very highly. *Treatise on the Horses in India*, pp. 1–10.
63 The other officers were Captain Barbarie and Captain Carnegy, and the complaints related mostly to the question of personal use of stud resources.
64 In a letter to the Secretary of the Military Board, he urged that 'as soon as possible, for the baboos here may suspect what I am after, you will be pleased to send to the office of captain Hawkings Deputy Commissary General for Kalee Baboo and also for Neelmoney his father, both formerly Sircars at the Hauper stud and have them examined on oath.' APAC, F/4/1518/59945, p. 80.
65 The commission noted that 'in consideration of the length of his service of his large and helpless family and of some circumstances of irritation ... acting upon a weak and irritable mind, it ventures to submit whether he may not in some way be made an object of mercy'. APAC, F/4/1517/59944, p. 12.
66 The *babu* apparently not only had access to stud finances but was also privy to the personal finances of English officers at the stud. APAC, F/4/1518/59945, pp. 13–15.
67 The Collector of Berhampore suggested, with respect to the Poosa stud, that: 'I conceive, the authority of the government may make a provision for the delivery of a reasonable share of the straw of each village and introduce a clause to this effect, in the public grants, under which the proprietor holds its right of possession; few villages will be induced voluntarily to dispose of this article, even if an extraordinary compensation were offered; but, I do not apprehend they will consider it any distress or hardship should a provision be made, in the manner I suggest.' APAC, F/4/127/2369, p. 35.

68 The administrator, however, 'soon realised that their principal motive for visiting me was to complain of various vexations to which they are (or suppose themselves to be) subjected, and that their aim was to solicit the protection of your board'. APAC, F/4/93/1891, p. 292.

69 The *charwahas* were also 'presented ... with turbands [*sic*] and some trifling presents to conciliate their good opinion, for they are almost as wild as their cattle which are brought up in the woods of Surriance [*sic*]'. The visit also represented an opportunity for 'reciprocal benefit', and Major Frazer tried to convince them to use Nagore bulls for breeding, but they seemed suspicious of British motives in lending them the bulls. APAC, F/4/93/1891, p. 293.

70 Letter addressed to the Board of Superintendence for Horse Breeding, APAC, F/4/93/1891, p. 301.

71 APAC, L/MIL/5/395, p. 75.

72 Veterinary medicine, more than any other branch of modern science, was insepa- rably intertwined with the question of financial viability. Before the farmer even called in the farrier, he asked himself if the benefits derived from the animal justi- fied the cost of treatment. Of course cost was seriously contemplated in case of human treatment too but humans were perhaps not as easily dispensable as animals. See Michael Worboys, 'Germ Theories of Disease and British Veterinary medicine, 1860–1890', *Medical History*, 35(3) (1991), 312.

73 Contrary to this, the veterinarian's primary battle in the mother country was fought against his more glamorous colleague practising human medicine, who assumed authority in several areas that should have been the veterinarian's domain. See Lise Wilkinson, *Animals and Disease: An Introduction to the History of Comparative Medicine* (Cambridge: Cambridge University Press, 1992).

74 These practitioners were required to have the following attainments: 'they must have attended Mr Coleman's lectures and practice at the college three months at least, whatever might have been their previous qualifications, before they can claim an examination and they must also have attended lectures on human anatomy, physiology and surgery, material medica, chemistry, and the practice of physics, either before or since they have been at the college.' APAC, L/MIL/5/395, p. 80.

75 APAC, L/MIL/5/395, pp. 75–80.

76 An official noted that: 'regiments have frequently been for long periods without veterinary surgeons, there being no inducement to go out to India, but on the contrary from the probability of remaining on foreign service for many years and being obliged to return home for recovery of health with broken constitution ... to retire and linger out a miserable life upon half pay, besides being paid by the Honourable Company in India, the increase of King's pay does not go on.' APAC, L/ MIL/5/388, p. 83.

77 These 'boys' were to be 'instructed in the duties of a farrier such as shoeing, admin- istering medicines, performing operations, the knowledge of diseases of horses, with the usual remedies. When old enough [and] considered by the superintendent qualified to act as farriers, they [were] posted to the different regiments.' APAC, L/ MIL/5/388, pp. 87–9.

78 The only clear benefit it had was that it facilitated the shoeing of regiments, an operation for which cavalry regiments earlier had to rely on the expertise of *Naulbunds.* APAC, L/MIL/5/388, pp. 87–9.

79 APAC, L/MIL/5/395, pp. 61–111.

80 Hodgson noted that 'it is with regret I state that the country born young men I have under my charge have not been of such description that I could undertake to teach again as this class labours under disabilities that prevent further advance- ment'. Letter dated 18 May 1822, APAC, L/MIL/5/395, p. 80. Hodgson also argued that his wards should not be employed at full pay and *batta* as they were not fully competent. This proposal was, however, rejected by the Medical Board. APAC, F/4/738/20145, pp. 1–2.

81 Captain R. H. Sneyd, Commanding Officer, Governor General's Body Guard, APAC, L/MIL/5/395, p. 80. Major Frazer also noted in 1794 that 'I am convinced that the

natives of India have no rational system of treating the diseases of horses being totally unacquainted with anatomy and circulation of blood.' Quoted in Bhalla, *History of Remount and Veterinary Corps*, p. 6.

82 C. A. Bayly, *Empire and Information: Intelligence Gathering and Social Communication in India, 1780–1870* (Cambridge: Cambridge University Press, 1996), pp. 247–83.

83 From the Medical Board to Hodgson, APAC, L/MIL/5/395, p. 93.

84 Severe cattle diseases broke out in the Bengal presidency in 1817, 1824, and 1836. Dr D. C. Palmer, *Report on the Calcutta Epizootic or Cattle Disease of 1864 in Calcutta and Its Neighbourhood* (Calcutta: Government of India Press, 1865), p. 2.

85 *Directions for using the Contents of the Portable Horse Medicine Chest, Adapted for India and Prepared by W. Moorcroft* (London, 1795).

86 William Beinart, *The Rise of Conservation in South Africa: Settlers, Livestock, and the Environment 1770–1950* (New York: Oxford University Press, 2003); Diana K. Davis, 'Brutes, Beasts and Empire: Veterinary Medicine and Environmental Policy in French North Africa and British India', *Journal of Historical Geography*, 34(2) (2008), 242–67; Karen Brown, 'Tropical Medicine and Animal Diseases: Ondersepoort and the Development of Veterinary Science in South Africa, 1908–1950', *Journal of South African Studies*, 31(3) (2005), 513–29; Daniel Gilfoyle, 'Veterinary Immunology as Colonial Science: Method and Quantification in the Investigation of Horse Sickness in South Africa, c.1905–1945', *Journal of the History of Medicine and Allied Sciences*, 61(1) (2005), 26–65.

87 The Secretary to the Military department noted, in a letter dated 15 September 1851, that 'there appears to be not the slightest doubt that the stud bred horses are now not only bad but far worse comparatively than they were thirty years ago'. APAC, L/MIL/5/389, p. 24.

88 Letter from J. Currie dated 9 September 1851, APAC, L/MIL/7/9626, n.p.

89 Moorcroft travelled extensively to the northern parts of the subcontinent and as far as Central Asia while working as a stud superintendent. Though these trips were ostensibly made to study and procure breeds of horses, he has been seen by historians as a military spy and one of the first actors in 'the great game' on the northern fringes of the Indian colony. In *Dictionary of National Biography* (Oxford: Oxford University Press, 2004).

90 He noted, for example, that 'the whole point of the present turns upon the comparative competency of judgement of the two parties as applied to the subject of horse breeding in Indian both generally and in detail. It may be supposed either that I am inadequate to fulfil the duties of the mission with which I was charged by the honourable the court of directors or that there may exist some defectiveness in the system of controlling power.' APAC, F/4/543/13257, pp. 988–9.

91 Referring to Moorcroft's travels, the Military Board noted that it 'could never sanction arrangements which if they had been carried into effect would have involved an expense of many lacks [*sic*] of rupees in the purchase of cattle in foreign countries in wild and romantic excursions to the banks of the Timor and the plains of Chinese Tartary or in a fanciful overland trip through Vienna to Paris for the purpose of importing into Bengal the rejected and reduced horses of the French and Austrian cavalry, measures against which the board ...considered requisite solemnly to protest.' APAC, F/4/543/13257, p. 1045.

92 In 1827, for instance, sixteen veterinary practitioners trained in Britain boarded ships for India at Gravesend. APAC, L/MIL/9/434, pp. 10–11.

93 This co-option is somewhat reflected in the fact that even purely medical procedures like post-mortems on dead cattle used to be carried out by military officials during this early phase. In 1800, Major Frazer, displaying a rather impressive knowledge of medical terminology, wrote the following report on a post mortem: 'Upon dissecting, the spleen immediately presented itself enlarged to an enormous size in the shape of a triangle upon turning it over a quantity of extravasated blood appeared and lower part of the abdomen was fill of sanguinuous serum. Upon minute observation a small aperture was observed in the splenic artery which very probably burst

from the exertion during the act of copulation and was the immediate cause of his death.' Quoted in Bhalla, *History of the Veterinary and Remount Regiments*, p. 8.

94 The Civil Veterinary Department was established only in the 1860s, which led to a divestment of military connections. This decade saw a general trend towards the shrinking of military authority in the medical field, as the medical and sanitary administration also started coming into its own during this period.

CHAPTER TWO

Beasts, murrains, and veterinary health

From our discussion in the last chapter, it becomes clear that early veterinarians were preoccupied with preserving military horses. This chapter will examine whether the late colonial state was divested of these predominantly military aims that had governed its actions during the earlier phase, at least as far as veterinary health was concerned. In other words, did the nature of colonial policy change much during the late colonial period, as the veterinary administration expanded and developed?

At the start of this chapter, it is important to note that the state's response was unquestionably quite strong, both during the early and the late colonial periods, in those cases where disease threatened to encroach into sanitised British spaces. On the other hand, cattle diseases that were quite widespread did not receive an equal degree of attention, despite leading to disastrous consequences for the rural agrarian economy. It could be argued that this neglect of cattle diseases was partly a consequence of the general neglect of village sanitation, which was a feature not only of the Indian public health administration but also of that in Britain. However, in the case of Britain, the pressure of public opinion could lead to concrete action at least in situations where epizootics assumed huge proportions, as could be seen during the great cattle plague outbreak of 1865–7.[1] In a striking contrast, much larger outbreaks that occurred in India on a sustained basis led to very little action on the part of the colonial state. The state's inaction was, therefore, much more apparent in the colonial context, and a study of the reasons behind this inactivity could possibly lead to a partial answer to the rhetorical question 'what is colonial about colonial medicine?', which has been often posed in recent times.[2] In answering this question, we will look at various aspects of veterinary medicine, while focusing specifically on developments in northern India. This will include areas such as bacteriology, veterinary training, horse breeding and the work of the Civil Veterinary Department. The overall aim of the chapter will be to study colonial veterinary policies in detail, and to point out the various ways in which these policies differed from those implemented in case of human health. It will also be argued that the lukewarm colonial response to the threat of epizootics, at least until the end of the nineteenth century, was chiefly due to a continued preoccupation with areas of military interest such as horse breeding.

Epizootics and cattle mortality

Turning our attention first to the subject of mortality due to murrains,[3] it is quite evident that many regions of the subcontinent suffered such losses to their livestock on a sustained basis as was sufficient to cripple the economy for some time to come. A series of epizootics in the Ferozepur district of Punjab in 1894–5 left, according to cautious official estimates, nearly 84,000 animals debilitated and unfit for ploughing, while killing more than 20,000.[4] Another massive scourge that had visited the Manbhum district in Bengal a few decades earlier carried away large numbers of livestock for three years in a row, peaking at the figure of 73,000 deaths in 1863, though even this is quite likely to be an underestimate.[5] There was, in fact, a general tendency to under-report these figures, partly owing to a lack of personnel and partly due to the veterinarian's preoccupation with horse breeding, a subject that we will discuss in detail later.[6] This is acknowledged with disarming frankness in official reports, and the same report that contains the numbers quoted above on the Ferozepur outbreak also notes that:

> [It can be stated] with certainty that the statistics are, in the great majority of cases, absolutely unreliable and misleading. My own experience, of the reports received from district officers, is that they are practically value-less as a rule, and the number of deaths would have to be *multiplied by many thousands* to reach a figure representing the true total.[7]

Referring again to this tendency to under-report, the Inspector General also made very pessimistic remarks as late as 1896, going so far as to say that he had 'given up all hope of ever getting reports of disease which can be of any value'.[8] However, though mortality figures were in most cases gross underestimates, they nevertheless point towards the huge scale of deaths and losses. To put them into perspective, mortality figures for single districts like Manbhum compared favourably with those for the whole of Great Britain during its greatest-ever outbreak of cattle plague in 1865: whereas 278,943 heads of cattle fell to the outbreak in Britain (1865–7), nearly 130,000 deaths occurred in

Manbhum over a similar duration.[9] Such pestilential outbreaks within a relatively small territory, without doubt, spelled nothing short of a major disaster for livestock owners from which they took years, if not decades, to recover. The price of the meanest cattle in the wake of these episodes reached such levels as to turn them into items of luxury affordable only to the wealthiest.[10] What followed was a 'cattle famine' leading, in many cases, to a food famine due to the intimate link between cattle and cultivation. In certain exceptionally bad years, when epizootics spread over larger areas, agricultural production over large tracts of the country could suffer. This was certainly the case in the year 1870, when Clive Spinage estimates that the total number of dead cattle and buffaloes within India reached the figure of nearly 1 million.[11] All-India figures for cattle mortality are difficult to obtain, but Laxman Satya has calculated from discontinuous sets of data culled from annual reports that, within the space of sixteen years at the end of the nineteenth century, the province of Berar lost nearly 11 million cattle to disease, which was almost equivalent to the total cattle population of the province.[12]

The severity of these losses is also reflected in the fact that comparisons were often made between dreaded epidemics such as cholera and epizootics. Writing of 'native' beliefs in this regard, a colonial official noted that 'they consider that what cholera is to man, *puschima* [rinderpest] is to the cattle',[13] while another official in the same year offered his considered opinion that 'the epidemic [of rinderpest] ... is as constant in its ravages as cholera amongst human beings'.[14] Since Asiatic cholera was almost unanimously seen as the ultimate scourge during these times, a comparison with it implied recognition of rinderpest's massive impact.[15] Such admission, however, did not automatically translate into concrete action: the colonial state in India failed to act promptly when faced with the question of rinderpest and other epizootics that affected the health of 'public cattle'.[16] This was apparent even at the end of the nineteenth century, by which time the colonial will to intervene into indigenous spaces due to medical reasons had supposedly intensified and strengthened.

Military authority and the halting march of veterinary medicine

Military dominance, we will argue, was one of the reasons behind the relative neglect of epizootics and animal diseases among the civilian population. This is clear even if we look at the period prior to 1860, which has been discussed in the last chapter. In fact the very foundation of veterinary science in India, in the last decade of the eighteenth century, rested upon military principles and requirements: early British veterinarians were after all recruited primarily to reduce growing debility and deaths within the incipient colonial cavalry. These initial developments were also portents of the fact that military interests – arising either in the metropolis and the colony – were to govern veterinary policies for some time to come. While the primacy of military motivations in policy formation is not a novel idea in the colonial context – this influence was quite palpable even in the case of human medicine – what is striking is the much more sustained, prolonged and intense link between the military and the veterinary. By the 1860s this had become a confirmed fact, with government passivity and inaction on the subject of animal diseases amongst the non-military cattle testifying fully to its 'enclavist' ideology.[17] This point is made even more forcefully when we look at administrative reforms (or lack of them) in the areas of animal health and compare them with the large number of reforms in the area of human health during the 1860s. In the case of the latter, this decade marked a decisive turning point, with numerous developments changing the nature, scope and reach of the medical bureaucracy. For instance, in 1864, sanitary commissions were established in three presidencies, the office of the Municipal Health Officer was set up in presidencies such as Bombay, Registration of Births and Deaths was instituted, statistical reports began to be maintained, exhaustive reports on diseases such as cholera were written, and medical issues came to be somewhat divested of their strong military connections.[18] Noting the importance of a break or dissociation between the civilian and the military John Lawrence, the viceroy, wrote in a private letter to the Secretary of State in 1867 that 'it will certainly never do to place [civilian sanitary] matters in the hands of the army sanitary commission'.[19] On the other hand, veterinary health continued to be dominated by military interests, and no noteworthy regulation was adopted during this decade for the protection of 'public cattle'. The only major attempt to examine the state of cattle disease in India was made in 1869, when the Indian Cattle Plague Commission was appointed.[20] However, in a telling commentary upon the degree of significance attached to cattle mortality within India, even this commission was partly created in a response to the great cattle plague outbreak of 1865–7 in Britain. Quite apart from these initial metropolitan motivations, when the commission did finally painstakingly produce a massive report containing several sweeping recommendations for strengthening the veterinary establishment, few if any of them even began to be implemented before a decade or two had elapsed. The commission's frenetic activities and extensive surveys succeeded, in this sense, only in papering over the inertness and immobility that characterised veterinary policy.

While the colonial government displayed a marked degree of unwillingness in implementing the much-needed veterinary measures, it sprang into action when reforms were needed within military quarters. Stirred by the numerous complaints made by officers on deputation from the British army, who constituted the bulk of the Indian veterinary contingent at any given point, questions related to salaries, emoluments, and promotions were discussed frequently and extensively.[21] Other more substantive issues connected to the efficiency of army veterinary services were also raised: a letter written by Lieutenant Colonel E. Seager in 1860 on the subject of abuses of the 'contract system' for shoeing and purchase of medicines, for instance, caused a major splash in government circles and was referred to for long afterwards.[22] Under this system, troop officers were made solely responsible for ordering purchases or allocating contracts for their regiments, thereby bypassing the authority not only of the regimental veterinary surgeon, but also of the medical department. Apart from causing myriad ills, which were pointed out by Seager, this system reflected the more general trend that we have been discussing – that of complete subordination of the veterinary officer to his military superior while carrying out both his healing and breeding functions.[23] Some attempts were made to blunt the edges of this overbearing military authority. Sir W. Mansfield, for example, initiated a debate in 1860 on the abolition of the remount agency for Bombay, which had been staffed exclusively by military personnel, and recommended the assumption of its functions by army veterinary officers led by a Principal Veterinary Surgeon for the province.[24] Using his own proposals as the blueprint, Mansfield exerted his considerable influence to create what became informally known as the 'Bombay system'; in concrete terms this meant the abolition of both the remount agency and the contract system and the appointment of J. H. B. Hallen – later to become the president of the Indian Cattle Plague Commission – as both the Principal Veterinary Surgeon and the Principal of the newly established Army Veterinary School in Pune (1862).[25] While these measures came into force only within the Bombay presidency, larger reforms for the entire Indian cavalry establishment were also implemented. Inspecting veterinary surgeons were, for instance, appointed in all presidencies in 1865 with the hope that they would lead to more effective medical supervision.[26] Further, a consensus appears to have been evolving gradually at the highest levels about the need to secure effective treatment for British cavalry regiments. The viceroy himself was reported to have been 'penetrated with conviction' that the 'astonishing mortality' among horses would be reduced if veterinarians were suitably employed by the army.[27]

These debates, discussions and reforms, however, focused exclusively on the subject of military animals, more specifically horses; the matter of general veterinary reforms in the subcontinent was continuously sidestepped by the highest authorities. No legislation was, for example, ever passed on the subject of cattle disease despite the massive annual mortalities which we have referred to above. In Britain, on the other hand, the cattle plague epidemic of 1865–7 was immediately followed by sweeping regulation in the shape of the Contagious Diseases (Animals) Act, passed in 1869.[28] In fact, the policy of segregating and slaughtering diseased livestock, which was followed rigorously during the cattle plague years, was almost single-handedly responsible for strengthening the principle of 'stamping out' epidemic diseases. It also led to greater restrictions over imported livestock and meat, while simultaneously fuelling a new interest in the aetiology of rinderpest and in the field of experimental pathology in general.[29] These changes were understandable as the epidemic was often seen as the most dramatic episode in nineteenth-century British agricultural history; in fact Fisher goes so far as to say that 'no other single event has had the same impact on public consciousness'.[30] What is more, legislation did not dry up in Britain once the immediate outrage over the 1865 outbreak had been somewhat dissipated – the pace actually quickened in the next decade when several significant developments occurred.[31] Despite all these measures, there was still a sense of outcry in Britain, reflected in the cartoon shown in Figure 1, published in the *Punch*, which criticised the government not doing enough.[32]

This stark difference between a sense of outcry and urgency on the one hand, and relative placidity on the other, points towards the colonial foundations of veterinary health in India. One can only conclude that, whereas in the metropolis considerable value was attached to the health of the nation's livestock, in India the focus came to rest on the question of protecting military livestock owned by the state.

Not surprisingly, within such a context, the only general measures that were ever implemented in India pertained exclusively to epizootics like glanders that threatened the health of horses. Colonial response to glanders, in fact, presents a classic example of fears winning over facts.[33] The briefest of surveys would immediately reveal that mortality figures related to the disease were on the lower side, being confined in most presidencies to a few dozen cases, even during periods when other epizootics had broken out on a large scale.[34] None of the annual civil veterinary reports, either for the presidencies or the country as a whole, mention any major outbreak of glanders, yet

THE POLITICAL COW-DOCTORS.

Figure 1 Cartoon regarding the cattle plague in Britain
The Patient says: 'Oh, if they'd only leave off quarrelling,
and just try "United Action", it might be the saving of me!'

these same reports also describe immediate segregation, observation, and treatment of glandered horses. Additionally, while the Glanders and Farcy Act of 1879 had made provisions for quarantine and similar measures, these were strengthened and multiplied manifold in the amended Act of 1899, which also gave an unprecedented degree of intrusive and interventionist powers to implementing authorities. It permitted disease inspectors to:

> Enter and search any field, building or any place for the purpose of ascertaining whether there is therein any horse which is diseased, and [did] away with the limitations heretofore placed upon entry and search. The revised act also provide[d] for the use of tests and isolation of horses subjected thereto, and for the recovery of the expense of detaining, isolating and testing horses from owners or persons in charge.[35]

These were indeed stupendous powers and were comparable to an extent with the authority of the plague inspector during this same period.[36] However, in the case of glanders, opportunities to implement regulations arose but rarely and therefore the likelihood of resistance or a general disquiet was rather limited. Also, in the Indian context, horses were of little or no use from an agrarian perspective and were not therefore preferred as domesticated beasts of choice, except in military situations or in situations where rapid transportation was needed.[37]

It must be mentioned here, though, that in arguing this we do not wish to underestimate the threat represented by diseases such as glanders. The disease had a very fearsome quality during these times, partly due to the fact that the absence of any cure effectively turned the disease into a death sentence for horses. It was also dreaded because it could potentially be passed on to other mammals. Extreme measures against the disease were therefore partly justified; what is surprising, though, is the complete mismatch between the attention lavished upon glanders and the relative silence or inertness on the question of epizootics affecting cattle. It could be argued that colonial reticence on the subject of cattle mortality was partly a product of its fear of encroaching into areas that affected the lives of a large number of peasants. It is equally likely, however, that the overall horse-centric character of the veterinary administration, which was fashioned out of intensely military preoccupations, led to prompt action against diseases such as glanders and a simultaneous neglect of cattle disease. This is also reflected in the great attention paid to other equine diseases, such as surra, which was the chief subject of bacteriological investigations for quite a few of years – a subject that we will deal with in detail in the next chapter.[38] Also, colonial inaction cannot be completely explained by referring to the fear of encroaching into 'native' spaces, especially when we recall that similar or stronger apprehensions did not prevent the state from devising extremely intrusive and interventionist measures in case of human diseases such as plague.

Cattle disease and civil veterinary departments

The clearest proof of colonial inaction in case of diseases affecting 'public cattle' is provided by the extremely delayed formation of the Civil Veterinary Department, which came into existence only in 1892, quite a few decades after the Sanitary Department had already been established. The idea for the creation of this department had been first mooted and unequivocally endorsed as early as 1883[39] and in fact even the Cattle Plague Commission had, in 1871, underlined the great need for such wider veterinary reforms.[40] The extreme severity or 'abnormality' – as one colonial official put it – of epizootic outbreaks also occasionally forced the question of 'public cattle' upon the consciousness of officials, and in these cases they acquiesced in despatching some unfortunate junior army veterinary officer on a short and desultory expedition to the site of the outbreak.[41] A few enlightened officials also spoke freely against such prevalent attitudes, including Hallen and George Fleming, who was the Principal Veterinary Surgeon in the army. Drawing a strong connection between 'civilized governments' and protection of a nation's cattle wealth, Fleming noted rather emphatically in 1885 that:

> The institution of such a department for India is an absolute necessity, and it is astonishing it was not created at least half a century ago. I know of no country in the world under a civilized government, which has been, and is now, so severely scourged by the most deadly, though preventable animal diseases and yet in which so little has been done in the way of prevention or suppression.[42]

Fleming's open and bold indictment of the Raj invited the ire of senior-most bureaucrats,[43] but there was almost a tacit acceptance of the fact that government attention and resources were not to be squandered away on preserving 'public cattle'. In fact, apart from a few stray instances such as the Cattle Plague Commission, the question of preserving non-military and non-equine beasts was not even discussed seriously.

Such reticence or neglect was no doubt motivated partly by financial arguments; after all, even though murrains caused huge annual losses to agriculture, these appeared to have little direct impact on the state of the colonial coffers as long as the mortality did not spread to military animals.[44] Strengthening this financial logic was the fact that, unlike the case with human diseases, large-scale cattle deaths were very rarely linked directly to the larger question of a civilised, improving colonial government. Even public posturing was therefore not necessary, nor was there any need to devise token measures to appease ruffled sentiments. Within such a context, account books were the final arbiter on policy decisions, and though epizootics raging within localised territories could reduce peasants' ability to pay revenues, the expenses involved in controlling such outbreaks would perhaps have far outweighed the losses they caused to the treasury. The Dutch colonial settlements in India, for instance, spent 3 million florins in connection with epizootics in the year 1881–2, which comprised nearly one-third of their total budgetary deficits for the financial year.[45] Already heavily encumbered with the considerable annual costs involved in breeding and purchasing horses, the British Indian government was understandably a little reluctant to add such huge expenses to its financial ledger.

Motivated partly by the desire to obviate such huge costs, even the Civil Veterinary Department focused largely on horse-breeding operations until the end of the nineteenth century, though it was ostensibly established with the aim of reducing mortality within the civilian cattle stock. This was true not just for the central department but also for its provincial counterparts in Punjab or the North West Frontier Province, both of which laboured under the strong shadow of long-standing horse-breeding departments that immediately preceded them.[46] Even J. H. B. Hallen, when appointed as the first Inspector General of the Civil Veterinary Department in 1892, became almost entirely preoccupied with horse-breeding issues despite his passionate and strong views on the subject of cattle murrains. His horse-breeding duties were so extensive that it was impossible – his personal inclinations or opinions notwithstanding – to devote the slightest attention to other questions. The Inspector General was, as part of his duties, expected to be extraordinarily mobile during the course of an ordinary year: he visited horse fairs in the most distant regions, branded mares, inspected stallions, purchased remounts, and travelled, on an average, nearly 20,000 miles.[47] His provincial colleagues followed a similar pattern, travelling comparable, if not equal distances, to ensure effective breeding and purchase arrangements.[48] Within such a scenario, cattle health was quite obviously relegated to the position of secondary significance, with veterinary officials admitting freely that the colonial obsession with breeding and remounts left no space for disease control. The annual report for 1893–4, for instance, stated clearly that 'not much progress has been made under this head [of cattle disease]' and also reproduced a statement made by the Veterinary Superintendent of North Punjab to the effect that 'during the official year under report I have had absolutely no time to investigate outbreaks of cattle disease', though he also offered the assurance that he had made arrangements to rectify this situation.[49] In the following year, though, he finally admitted defeat, stating rather baldly that:

> I have found my time so fully occupied in the horse and mule breeding industry that I have no leisure to stop and investigate outbreaks, even should I meet with them on tour, and until arrangements are made for additional help, I fear this will continue to be the case.[50]

Similar statements were made by him in succeeding years as well, and no reprimand was ever issued either to him or to other provincial authorities for insufficiently fulfilling their duties with regard to disease prevention.[51] From provinces like Madras came even clearer expressions of disinterest or defeat, with the report for the province noting frankly that 'no action was taken as regards the treatment of cattle as the government have given up at present all efforts in that direction'.[52] Though a short didactic discussion about the general benefits of disease control measures for the hapless peasants followed this unusually forthright admission, the Inspector General was himself fully aware, through his mammoth tours, of the huge burden of breeding operations. In this sense the creation of the Civil Veterinary Department made little concrete difference, at least during the initial years, to the manner in which cattle diseases were treated. What made the situation worse was that, since the department was ostensibly formed in the larger interest of the cultivators, the latter were expected to make certain financial contributions to it. The inherent unfairness of this arrangement was admitted to by the more conscientious veterinary officials, who pointed out that resources garnered through such measures were being diverted entirely towards military ends.[53]

What is interesting to note is that, while in India veterinarians had to work under military authority while performing their duties, in Britain it was the practitioners of human medicine that stole the limelight from farriers.[54] Veterinary medicine was therefore constantly sandwiched between either the military or the medical and failed to develop its professional identity at any considerable pace; this was especially true of the Indian context, where colonial exigencies twisted the profession out of shape to such an extent that even its primary functions and tasks were completely redefined. Budgetary allocations and expenditure patterns in the Civil Veterinary Department affirm this fact, with nearly one-third of the total amount being earmarked for importing stallions from abroad.[55] Add to this the cost involved in supervising, encouraging, and conducting breeding operations, and we are left with very little for other expenses such as treatment of 'public cattle' or prevention of epizootics.

The behemoth of breeding therefore appears to have sucked in substantial resources, leaving little for other, equally essential, services. What is paradoxical in this context is that, though numerous measures had been tried to reduce or transfer the cost of breeding since the earliest days of the colonial cavalry, all of them ended up doing the exact opposite. As we have seen in the last chapter, autonomous government studs failed to produce horses in the quantities needed, and were still supported for a number of years at considerable expense to the treasury. In another failed experiment, horse fairs and shows were encouraged in several districts and prizes were offered to stimulate small independent breeders, yet these fairs, in many instances, ended up becoming hot spots for powerful horse dealers and their conglomerates.[56] Large tracts of land in the Punjab were also distributed among cavalry men in the hope that they would encourage breeding practices, but the primary motivation of these land-hungry 'peasants in uniforms' was at complete variance with those of their colonial masters, leading to inadequate returns and a rather feudalistic system of fines and punishments.[57] As a result of these failed measures, the Civil Veterinary Department was forced to spend a major slice of its budget on importing stallions in a bid to kick-start internal breeding operations. What it failed to reckon with was the fundamental issue of Indian peasants being cattle rather than equine dependent, and unless this fact was altered no substantial breakthrough was possible. However, an obsession with immediate horse-breeding measures precluded the possibility of considering the larger picture, of which cattle preservation and agrarian production were a part.

Cattle upkeep was, in fact, so far removed from colonial concerns that it hardly ever received a passing mention: the Army Veterinary College at Poona, quite understandably, focused solely and exclusively on equine illnesses, while veterinary officials themselves showed little interest in diseases such as rinderpest, even though their contagiousness was fully and unreservedly accepted by most practitioners.[58] Such was the lack of discussion on the subject that the Punjab government decided, in 1883, to create awareness by publishing and circulating a short compilation of remedies that had been tried within the province at some point.[59] However, this tract only succeeded in highlighting the existing confusion on the subject by carrying conflicting opinions about the usefulness of disease control measures; it also did not dwell for long on the subject of effective and authoritative treatments for diseases.[60] Some officials did, indeed, appear to have countenanced a reformist ideology and advocated wide-ranging measures such as quarantines or strict segregation, but their arguments were invariably defeated through appeals to either metropolitan science or Hindu superstition. It was argued, on the one hand, that any measure which fell short of the policy of destroying infected cattle – the predominant method of dealing with cattle plague in Britain – would be inadequate and useless; on the other hand, it was feared that strict measures for infected cattle would militate against Hindu beliefs, leading to widespread disquiet. While it is certainly rather ironical that these two seemingly opposite poles of scientific rationality were evoked for a common cause in such discussions, together they served to perpetuate the inertness that already defined colonial veterinary policies.[61] In this context, it is hardly surprising to see that, even in the first decade of the twentieth century, pamphlets issued on the subject of cattle diseases only mentioned basic precautions such as segregation, disinfection, regulation of the infected cattle's diet, and proper burial of carcasses.[62]

In writing about colonial neglect of epizootics, we do not wish to present a picture of the peasant as the supine victim of colonial policies.

Indeed, partly due to the absence of state provisions for curing cattle disease, cattle owners all over north India continued to use various extremely popular indigenous remedies and preventive measures. For instance, the most common treatment for foot-and-mouth disease involved keeping the cattle standing in muddy water, which prevented flies from hovering over the blisters or wounds. Various astringent barks such as babool (Acacia Nilotica) were also applied in some places.[63] Similarly, in case of a rinderpest infection, though the disease was widely perceived as being incurable, cattle were fed rice gruel or soft food and their shelter was fumigated with resins. In fact cultivators also adopted several sanitary precautions on their own, without the benefit of any helpful advice from state authorities. Richer cultivators or landlords, for instance, did not allow their cattle to graze in the open fields due to the likelihood that they could acquire rinderpest from other animals in their vicinity.[64] In case of diseases such as quarter-ill too, cattle were constantly moved from place to place with a view to giving them exercise and preventing the onset of lameness. There was, therefore, a distinct awareness of the various varieties of cattle disease and the cures for them, so much so that cattle were bred selectively not only keeping in mind their potential size, strength and productivity, but also their resistance to diseases.[65]

A new breed of farriers: training veterinarians for India

Besides these notions, there was also a belief in the protective power of the first disease attack, especially in case of rinderpest. In India, official sources tell us, there was apparently a widespread and strong 'native' belief that 'salted' animals were blessed with future immunity.[66] Similar beliefs existed in other parts of the world, and it has been reported that animals were sometimes deliberately exposed to disease in order to confer immunity upon them.[67] Even the Cattle Plague Commission accepted the fact that such beliefs were based on sound principles, noting that 'there can be no doubt about the protective power of one attack of rinderpest'; what the commissioners were far more sceptical of was whether a deliberate attempt to induce a mild form of the disease would necessarily succeed in all instances.[68] Despite the commission's doubts, it is quite possible that on occasion the practice of non-segregation of animals during epizootics, repeatedly and quite vehemently criticised by colonial officials as a symptom of 'native' ignorance and apathy, was actually a calculated strategy to protect cattle against future scourges. In this sense Indian peasants showed the way to frontline colonial scientists, who began to accept the concept of immunity for animals as a viable strategy only at the

[48]

very end of the nineteenth century, by which time 'bacteriomania' had already gripped Britain and continental Europe.[69]

While the question of bacteriological research into cattle disease in India will be the focus of our discussion in the next chapter, it must be mentioned here that this research also showed traces of military influence, at least during the initial years. This section will examine whether similar influences were at work in determining the nature of veterinary training in India. In this context, one of the first points that needs to be mentioned is that the major chunk of army veterinarians in India was supplied through the 'British quota system'. There was also a negligible demand for experts in purely civilian posts and, as a result, training and producing new recruits in large numbers was not at the top of the colonial agenda. The situation was not radically transformed with the creation of the Civil Veterinary Department, as all its senior staff were recruited from the army.[70] Subordinate officers were also not in great demand, except perhaps in Burma which stood out for having a substantial staff of veterinary assistants working directly under the supervision of the provincial veterinary officer.[71] Burma, in fact, was such an exception that each instalment of the annual report of the Civil Veterinary Department carried extensive quotes and statements from the provincial officer, which partly served the function of camouflaging the striking degree of inactivity in other provinces. In such a scenario, employment opportunities for 'native' farriers were obviously limited, which in turn led to a lack of demand for whatever training opportunities were available in India. Making a note of this unabashedly employment-seeking behaviour of 'natives', the first report of the Bombay Veterinary College in 1886 identified it as a major obstacle in the advancement of colonial science.[72] It was quite another matter, of course, that the question of emoluments for British veterinarians serving in India was raised and debated almost every year.

In his subsequent reports J. H. Steel showed greater sympathy for his students – perhaps this was the result of a greater familiarity with their economic situation. He even went to the extent of criticising the government for not providing suitable opportunities, and expressed his dissatisfaction with the degree of change wrought by the creation of the Civil Veterinary Department, noting that:

> Unfortunately, the prospects held out to the graduates are too poor to attract the better class of men in larger numbers than at present. The organisation of the Civil Veterinary Department was looked forward to by the graduates and the students as a means of bettering their prospects and improving their status…but these hopes are not likely to be realised.[73]

Despite these initial hiccups, the employment situation for graduates began to show some signs of improvement in the mid 1890s. This was primarily due to the growing number of rather rudimentary veterinary dispensaries in Punjab and Bombay, where veterinary assistants were absorbed at a nominal salary.[74] What is equally interesting is the growing demand for Indian veterinary graduates in other colonies, which must have added considerably to the lucrativeness of the profession. By the year 1900, for instance, more than seventy graduates of the Lahore veterinary College – which was established exactly half a decade before its counterpart in Bombay and imparted training in the vernacular – were employed all over the empire.[75]

In spite of this gradual amelioration in employment prospects, though, there was little corresponding expansion in training facilities, except perhaps for the creation of the Calcutta Veterinary College in 1893 – a measure that had been contemplated for nearly a decade before it was eventually approved.[76] A committee headed by J. H. B. Hallen had strongly advocated for this college as early as 1883 but the idea had been turned down citing certain financial constraints, which is somewhat strange considering that these same financial constraints had been conspicuously absent just two years previously when the Lahore Veterinary College was created. Perhaps the key to this riddle lies in the originary impulses behind both proposals: while Lahore was a response to the huge losses suffered by the cavalry during the Second Afghan War, the Calcutta proposal was motivated by larger philanthropic ideas aimed at the general public.[77] Both veterinary training and research were, in this sense, closely aligned with military interests until the end of our period, and this reflects some of the general trends that we have discussed in the previous sections. Taken together, the various strands of this broad survey of veterinary developments suggest certain modifications in the existing historiographical consensus about the nature of colonial medicine in India in the late nineteenth century.

Conclusion

This chapter has broadened the definition of colonial medicine to include veterinary medicine within its fold – an area that has been largely ignored by historians of medicine. Roy Porter, writing in the context of British veterinary medicine, has made the significant observation that 'in the academic world, it is automatically assumed that a "historian of medicine" is a person who works on the history of human medicine...One unhappy aspect of this is an appalling dearth of significant writings on the history of British veterinary medicine'.[78]

This observation is equally true nearly two decades after it was first made, and holds greater validity in the South Asian context where no full-length study of the subject exists. This chapter has questioned this trend and shown that a change in perspective could lead to several fresh observations which could potentially reformulate existing hypotheses about colonial medicine that have been arrived at solely through studies of human diseases.

The first conclusion that could be safely derived from this study is that public health – if we broaden the definition of public health to include animal diseases and epizootics within it – does not appear to have assumed great importance even at the end of the nineteenth century. While strict and authoritarian measures might have been applied in the case of epidemics such as plague, this was not really true for epizootics that broke out among 'public cattle'. In his extensive study of colonial medical policies, David Arnold has shown that the 1890s might have seen a transition from 'enclavism' to public health with the establishment of a new 'tropical medicine' which was based on the germ theory of disease, and a corresponding intensification in state medical intervention in India.[79] At first glance, this appears to have held true for veterinary medicine as well, as the 1890s saw the establishment or growth of new institutions like the Imperial Bacteriological Laboratory, which laid new emphasis on the germ theory of disease. Similarly, it might be argued that state intervention into veterinary medicine increased during this decade through the establishment of the Civil Veterinary Department. However, these new institutions did not mark a decisive break with the immediate past – for instance the Civil Veterinary Department merely took over and streamlined pre-existing horse-breeding structures, and paid very little attention to the question of epizootics among 'public cattle'. Also, purely in terms of budgetary allotments, the department spent very little towards disease prevention and invested most of its resources on horse-breeding measures. Keeping all these qualifications in mind, it would appear that the measures taken for preventing cattle diseases did not reflect the larger trend towards greater investment in public health during the last two decades of the nineteenth century.[80]

Military and economic compulsions were the two major forces that drove veterinary administration into the direction that it took. Already overburdened by the massive weight of military duties and breeding expenses, veterinarians were left with little appetite to venture into medical issues of fundamental importance to peasants. In this sense, despite the various changes that occurred throughout the period of this study, the department retained the contours that had been drawn during its foundational years in the last decade of the eighteenth century. From the days of Moorcroft to those of Hallen and Lingard, veterinarians constantly struggled to broaden their operations but were met with obstacles in the shape of military dictates and financial ledgers. The autonomous expansion of the department was also hindered through association with the mother country, though counterparts in Britain argued that metropolitan association was of absolute essence if Indian experts were to make use of the latest breakthroughs in the field.[81] These issues were, of course, not specific to veterinary medicine – they did, indeed, make the presence felt within other areas of colonial administration. However, what lends a degree of uniqueness to the history of veterinary medicine in India is the much more prolonged impact of these issues, leading to developments that were not in perfect synchrony with those in closely allied fields.

The trends outlined in this chapter, however, were more strongly visible until the end of the nineteenth century – the nature of veterinary medicine in India changed considerably during the early part of the next century due to several historical circumstances. The first of these was the declining usefulness of the cavalry, especially in the wake of the First World War, as a result of which veterinary officials became less preoccupied with horses.[82] Equally importantly, the Civil Veterinary Department was forced to focus much more on cattle health as, in 1903, horse-breeding functions were taken away from it, and were handed over to a newly created Horse Breeding Commission.[83] This shift away from the military was also aided by several autonomous trends within India, including the association of the Civil Veterinary Department with the Agricultural Department, the formation of several bacteriological laboratories (like the Pasteur Institutes in Shillong, Coonoor, and other places, or the laboratory at Sohawa) and the introduction of inoculation programmes.[84] The increasing emphasis on treating epizootics and cattle diseases is reflected in the appointment, by 1911, of five inspectors, sixty-two veterinary assistants, and twenty-six veterinary dispensaries at district headquarters in the province of Bengal alone.[85] Any future inquiry into late veterinary developments would need to take these trends into account, and we would argue that a decisive break in the nature of Indian veterinary administration took place only in the early part of the twentieth century.

Notes

1 Cattle plague was an amorphous term that was often used to denote a variety of diseases, but in most cases it was used to describe outbreaks of rinderpest.

2 See for instance Shula Marks, 'What Is Colonial about Colonial Medicine? And What Has Happened to Imperialism and Health?', *Social History of Medicine*, 10(2) (1997), 205–19.

3 The term 'murrain' was used widely in the nineteenth century to refer to epizootics.

4 *Provincial Report of the Civil Veterinary Department of Punjab for the year 1894–5* (Lahore: Civil and Military Gazette Press, 1885), p. 18.

5 These numbers include both cows and buffaloes. The figure was closer to 30,000 for both 1861 and 1862. *Papers Relating to Cattle Disease, from the Records of the Government of Bengal*, XLIII (Calcutta: Central Press Company Limited, 1869), p. 46.

6 The lack of personnel was particularly acute before the formation of the Civil Veterinary Department in 1892, when the responsibility for reporting on cattle mortality fell on the shoulders of the district officials.

7 *Provincial Report of the Civil Veterinary Department of Punjab for the year 1894–5*, p. 116 (italics added).

8 *Annual Administration Report of the Civil Veterinary Department in India, 1895–6*, p. 155.

9 For mortality figures for Britain, see John R. Fisher, 'Cattle Plagues Past and Present: The Mystery of Mad Cow Disease', *Journal of Contemporary History*, 33(2) (1998), 215–28. In terms of percentages, while Britain lost nearly 6 per cent of its national herd due to the epizootic, districts like Manbhum lost nearly one-quarter. S. A. Hall, 'The Cattle Plague of 1865', *Proceedings of the Royal Society of Medicine*, 58(10) (Oct. 1965), 799–801.

10 The Commissioner of the Nuddea Division in Bengal noted that 'during the last few years, a great diminution in the number of cattle has taken place, and the price of cattle is now almost ten times higher than it was formerly, and this appears to be principally owing to many cattle having been swept away by this disease, called *puschima*'. *Papers Relating to Cattle Disease, from the Records of the Government of Bengal*, XLIII, pp. 44–5.

11 Clive A. Spinage, *Cattle Plague: A History* (New York: Kluwer, 2003), p. 471.

12 He calculates the mortality for the years between 1872 and 1877, and again between 1889 and 1901. *Ecology, Colonialism and Cattle: Central India in the Nineteenth Century* (Delhi: Oxford University Press, 2004), p. 147.

13 From the Commissioner of the Nuddea Division, dated 9 March 1864, *Papers Relating to Cattle Disease*, p. 44. The term *puschima*, official reports note, was used interchangeably for several diseases, but in this particular instance it referred to rinderpest.

14 Proceedings of the board of revenue, dated 17 June 1864, *Records of the Government of India, Papers Relating to Cattle Diseases*, vol. LXIX (Calcutta: Government of India Press, 1868), p. 12.

15 Writing about rinderpest in Southern Africa, Pule Phoofolo in fact notes that 'the rinderpest crisis [was] even more ominous than the European cholera...While cholera attacked people, who died and left their property behind, rinderpest spared the people to watch with utter shock and suspicion as their most valued means of livelihood perished dramatically.' In 'Epidemics and Revolutions: The Rinderpest Epidemic in Late Nineteenth-Century Southern Africa', *Past and Present*, 138 (Feb. 1993), 112–43.

16 This term was often used in government reports to refer to cattle owned by the public at large.

17 The term 'enclavist' was first used by Radhika Ramasubban and referred to the fact that colonial medicine was characterised by racial segregation and prompt action on medical issues that had a direct impact on the health of Europeans. *Public Health and Medical Research in India: Their Origins under the Impact of British Colonial Policy* (Stockholm: SAREC, 1982).

18 Deepak Kumar, 'Health and Medicine in British India and Dutch Indies: A Comparative Study', in Joseph Alter (ed.), *Asian Medicine and Globalization* (Pennsylvania: University of Pennsylvania Press, 2005), pp. 78–87.
19 Letter dated 4 October 1867, APAC, John Lawrence Collection, Mss Eur/F90 32B.
20 The report of the Cattle Plague Commission was published only in 1871. Its members included J. H. B. Hallen (President), Kenneth McLeod, Mr. A. C. Mangles, and Baboo Hem Chunder Kerr.
21 Warrants were, for instance, issued to raise salaries of these officials in 1859, 1866, and 1878.
22 Letter dated 2 October 1860, from Lieutenant Colonel E. Seager, commanding 8th Hussars, to the Deputy Adjutant General, Her Majesty's Forces (Bombay), APAC, L/MIL/7/902.
23 Seager also pointed out this complete subordination, noting that 'A veterinary surgeon, single handed, cannot afford to fight the commanding officer and other officers.' Letter from Colonel E. Seager, dated 2 October 1860, APAC, L/MIL/7/902.
24 Minutes by His Excellency the Commander-in-Chief on the Military veterinary system of the Bombay Presidency, APAC, L/MIL/7/902. Mansfield held the command of the Bombay presidency, with the local rank of lieutenant-general, from 18 May 1860 to 14 March 1865. He was subsequently appointed the commander-in-chief in India and became a military member of the executive council. T. R. Moreman, 'Mansfield, William Rose, first Baron Sandhurst (1819–1876)', *Oxford Dictionary of National Biography* (Oxford: Oxford University Press, September 2004).
25 Letter from W. R Mansfield, dated 28 January 1864, APAC, L/MIL/7/897, n.p.
26 Letter from the India Office, dated 15 December 1865, APAC, L/MIL/7/903, n. p.
27 Letter from Colonel E. Haythorne, dated 3 September 1864, APAC, L/MIL/7/897.
28 Michael Worboys, *Spreading Germs: Disease Theories and Medical Practice in Britain, 1865–1900* (Cambridge: Cambridge University Press, 2000), p. 56.
29 Keir Waddington, *The Bovine Scourge: Meat, Tuberculosis and Public Health, 1850–1914* (Woodbridge: Boydell Press, 2006), pp. 27–8.
30 Fisher, 'Cattle Plagues Past and Present', 215.
31 Anne Hardy notes that 'the 1870s were a propitious decade for launching such a campaign. The widening of the franchise under the 1867 Reform Act had stimulated the political interests of a wide section of the middle classes; the Public Health Act 1872 imposed a public health organization on local government throughout England and Wales; and the 1875 Public Health Act redefined and set out their responsibilities in this regard. In 1878 the Contagious Diseases of Animals Act required all local authorities to appoint suitably qualified veterinary inspectors.' In 'Pioneers in the Victorian Provinces: Veterinarians, Public Health and the Urban Animal Economy', *Urban History*, 29(3) (2003), 381.
32 *Punch, or the London Charivari*, 17 Feb. 1866.
33 It could be argued that these acts were passed in order to control zoonoses – diseases that could be transmitted from animals to humans – but this was not accurate, as other similar diseases such as anthrax, which were not perceived to be fatal in horses, were not brought under the purview of these acts.
34 For example in the year 1895–6, while more than 17,000 deaths occurred due to rinderpest, only twelve cases of glanders were reported. *Annual Administration Report of the Civil Veterinary Department in the Presidency of Bombay, 1895–6* (Bombay: Government of India Press, 1896), pp. 13–14.
35 'Review of Report by the Commissioner and Director, Land Records and Agriculture', in *Annual Administration Report of the Civil Veterinary Department in the Bombay Presidency, 1898–9*, p. 3.
36 The act also stipulated that a set of inspectors could be specially appointed during outbreaks of glanders and that these inspectors could, in fact, have uniforms of their own. For details on plague measures, see David Arnold's *Colonizing the Body: State Medicine and Epidemic Disease in Nineteenth-Century India* (Berkeley, CA: University of California Press, 1989), especially pp. 200–39; Rajnarayan Chandravarkar, 'Plague Panic and Epidemic Politics in India, 1896–1914', in Terence Ranger

and Paul Slack (eds.), *Epidemics and Ideas: Essays on the Historical Perception of Pestilence* (Cambridge: Cambridge University Press, 1992), pp. 203–40; Mark Harrison, *Public Health in British India: Anglo-Indian Preventive Medicine, 1859–1914* (Cambridge: Cambridge University Press, 1994), especially pp. 139–65.

37 The instruction farm at Babugarh, where J. H. B Hallen worked for a number of years, tried to convince local peasants that horses could be more efficient in doing agrarian tasks, but these appeals appear to have had little or no impact. *Annual Administration Report of the Horse-Breeding Department of the Bengal and Bombay Presidencies, 1891–2* (Calcutta: Government of India Press, 1892), p. 52.

38 Though surra was communicable to other species, it was primarily a disease of horses and camels.

39 The idea was first proposed by a committee formed to inquire into the institution of a veterinary college in Calcutta. Letter dated 10 July 1886, APAC, L/MIL/7/845, n. p.

40 Referring to the huge losses that occurred on a regular basis due to murrains, the Commission noted that 'whenever attention has been directed to the diseases of horned stock, murrain has been found carrying off hundreds of cattle or has been ascertained to have recently done so and the natives have with one voice declared that this is nothing new – has been told them by their fathers and grandfathers – has indeed become such a feature of rural life that it occasions neither surprise not complaint.' *Report of the Commissioners Appointed to Inquire into the Origin, Nature, etc of Indian Cattle Plagues* (Calcutta: Government of India Press, 1871), p. 37.

41 Letter dated 10 July 1886, APAC, L/MIL/7/845, n. p.

42 Letter dated 28 January, APAC, L/MIL/7/839, n. p.

43 It was in fact considered unnecessary to reply to Mr. Fleming's letter which contained several other criticisms of the veterinary establishment. An official noted that 'it will not be necessary to reply to Mr Fleming's question…Responsible authorities in India are satisfied that the present system as respects the native cavalry works well and that there is no intention of departing from it.' Dated 21 February 1885, APAC, L/MIL/7/839, n. p.

44 Noting the huge loss to agriculture, the inspector general noted that 'the vast mortality shown to have occurred proves the enormous losses which the agricultural community suffers annually…the loss from such cases as can be proved amounts to the large sum of Rs. 7,48,570'. *Annual Administration Report of the Civil Veterinary Department in India, 1893–4*, p. 84.

45 'City Notes', *Pall Mall Gazette*, 5381 (30 May 1882).

46 The first report for the Civil Veterinary Department in the North West Frontier Province was published in 1902 whereas the first report in Punjab came out in 1895.

47 The report for 1892–3 notes that Hallen travelled 17,676 miles by rail, 685 miles by road, attended eleven horse fairs and shows and 'spent 55 days under canvas'. During the course of the year he even visited Hungary to purchase stallions for breeding purposes. *Annual Administration Report of the Civil Veterinary Department in India for the Official Year 1892–3*, p. 34.

48 The provincial head for Punjab for instance travelled 10,169 miles, visited fourteen districts and twelve fairs in 1894. *Provincial Report of the Civil Veterinary Department of Punjab for the year 1894–5*, p. 23.

49 *Annual Administration Report of the Civil Veterinary Department in India, 1893–4*, p. 81.

50 *Annual Administration Report of the Civil Veterinary Department in India, 1894–5*, p. 115. See also the *Provincial Report of the Civil Veterinary Department of Punjab, 1894–5*, p. 36.

51 In his report of 1894–5, for example, the superintendent for North Punjab noted that 'beyond collecting and compiling statistics on the various forms of cattle disease in the North Punjab, I have done little with regard to the actual direction of the numerous measures taken to suppress cattle disease, any time being wholly taken up in horse-breeding' *Annual Administration Report of the Civil veterinary Department of India, 1895–6*, p. 137.

52 *Annual Administration Report of the Civil Veterinary Department of India, 1894–5,* p. 120.

53 The superintendent of the Civil Veterinary Department in Punjab noted in 1898 that 'from the standpoint of the people of Punjab horse-breeding is of very secondary interest compared with the vitally important question of ... cattle disease. They contribute through the District Boards no inconsiderable sum for Veterinary Boards and when the Civil Veterinary Department was first constituted hopes were raised that at last the agricultural stock of the province would receive some care and attention. These hopes have been fulfilled to only a small extent as the time of the superintendents has been fully taken up...with horse and mule breeding.' *Annual Report of the Civil Veterinary Department of Punjab for the year 1897–8,* p. 5.

54 Worboys notes that 'aspersions about learning and competence [of veterinarians] were often made by medical practitioners, who would distance themselves from the "horse doctors"...While medical men vigorously policed the encroachment of veterinarians into human medicine, they made many incursions the other way, for example during the cattle plague'. In 'Germ Theories of Disease and British Veterinary Medicine, 1860–1890', *Medical History,* 35(3) (Jul. 1991), 308–27.

55 In 1895 for instance, out of a total budget of rupees 4,31,229 for the Civil Veterinary Department, rupees 1,37,479 was spent on importing stallions. *Annual Administration Report of the Civil Veterinary Department in India, 1895–6,* p. 97.

56 When these fairs and shows grew to a substantial size, they were sometimes besieged by horse dealers. At Batesar, for example, nearly 10,000 horses were brought annually and it acquired such an infamous reputation as a 'dealer's fair' that other fairs, which appeared to be following the same trend, were sometimes called the 'Batesar of the province'. *Annual Administration Report of the Civil Veterinary Department of India, 1894–5,* p. 32.

57 Imran Ali discusses this measure extensively and notes that 'in Jhelum colony, military interest was much more obtrusive. The dominant factor in colonisation here was the horse-breeding scheme. Military grantees ... [obtained] about 18 per cent of the total allotted land. Initially, an area of 44,000 acres was allocated for them, but this was raised to 80,000 acres with the adoption of horse breeding. The increase went largely to cavalry-men, who were expected to do well as horse breeders.' *The Punjab under Imperialism, 1885–1947* (Princeton: Princeton University Press, 1988), p. 113.

58 As early as 1871, the Cattle Plague Commission noted in the context of rinderpest that 'diseased animals are the principal agency of the propagation of this disease'. *Report of the Cattle Plague Commission,* p. xix.

59 *Selections from the Records of the Government of the Punjab and its Dependencies: Treatment of Cattle Disease in the Punjab,* new series, no. 20 (Lahore: Punjab Government Secretariat Press, 1883).

60 The only remedy prescribed for rinderpest was the following: 'Whilst ill, an animal should be given as much *sattoo* gruel in lieu of water as he will drink. When in a weak condition he should be given:- native wine – 2 ozs, chiretta – 2 drs, Gruel – 1 pint.' In circular entitled 'Treatment of Cattle Diseases in Punjab', dated 16 June 1879, *Selections from the Records of the Government of the Punjab,* p. 1.

61 These two arguments were often put together, for example the secretary to the government of Punjab argued that 'the experience gained in western countries shows that nothing short of the extermination of the diseased cattle is sufficient to eradicate the disease in its virulent forms. The lieutenant governor is unable to propose so stringent a measure for adoption in the Punjab. The prejudices of the people would be an effectual hindrance to the adoption of such a measure', Report dated 2 March 1882, *Selections from the Records of the Government of the Punjab,* p. 11.

62 Eastern Bengal and Assam, veterinary leaflets no. 1–4 (1909), APAC, V/25/541/29, p. 2.

63 *Report of the Cattle Plague Commission,* p. xiv.

64 *Report of the Cattle Plague Commission,* p. 168.

65 Nitya S. Ghotge, *Livestocks and Livelihoods: The Indian Context* (Delhi: Foundation Books, 2004), p. 25.

66 *Report of the Cattle Plague Commission*, p. xxiii.

67 See for instance Richard Waller, '"Clean and "Dirty": Cattle Disease and Control Policy in Colonial Kenya, 1900–40', *Journal of African History*, 45 (2004), 49.

68 The report asked rather rhetorically: 'can the practice of vaccination be initiated, and a trivial non-fatal disease be induced preventing against the serious and more fatal one? To this we must reply emphatically in the negative.' *Report of the Cattle Plague Commission*, p. xxiii.

69 The term 'bacteriomania' was coined by Abraham A. Jacobi, an American practitioner who was opposed to the new craze for discovering germs. Carla Bittel, *Mary Putnam Jacobi and the Politics of Medicine in Nineteenth-century America* (North Carolina: University of North Carolina Press, 2009), p. 186. See also Nancy K. Tomes, 'American Attitudes towards the Germ Theory of Disease: Phyllis Allen Richmond Revisited', *Journal of the History of Medicine*, 52 (Jan. 1997), 42; Michael Worboys, 'Was there a Bacteriological Revolution in late Nineteenth-century Medicine?', *Studies in the History and Philosophy of Biology and Biomedical Science*, 38 (2007), 27.

70 The initial sanctioned strength of the Civil Veterinary Department in 1892 was only eighteen, all of whom were recruited from among army veterinary officers serving in the subcontinent. APAC, L/MIL/7/862. Recruits from the army were preferred as there was a consensus within the Indian establishment that the British recruits were invariably young and inexperienced and therefore not very useful. Lieutenant Seager, for instance, noted in his letter in 1860 that 'at home, almost anyone is considered good enough to export to India'. Letter dated 5 October 1864, APAC, L/MIL/7/902, n. p.

71 *Annual Administration Report of the Civil Veterinary Department in India, 1894–5*, p. 110.

72 He noted that 'I am sorry to say that very few have entered through any special liking either for their future profession or for domesticated animals but almost all because they consider the profession will give fair prospects of employment.' *Report of the Bombay Veterinary College, 1886* (Bombay: Government Central Press, 1887), p. 3.

73 The likelihood of greater employment in the Civil Veterinary Department was low because, noted Steel 'the government have been pleased to decide...that the graduates to be employed in the Civil Veterinary Department will not be enrolled as servants of Government entitled to the privilege of pension, &c., but will be considered as employees of the Local Boards concerned' *Report of the Bombay Veterinary College, 1890* (Bombay: Government Central Press, 1891), p. 2.

74 In 1894 there were a mere 5 veterinary dispensaries in Punjab, in 1897 the number grew to 7, in 1898 it had reached the figure of 10, and by 1900 there were 13 dispensaries in all of Punjab. *Provincial Reports of the Civil Veterinary Department, Punjab.*

75 By the end of this year 50 men had been sent to Transvaal, 20 to China and some had been sent to Uganda as well. *Provincial Report of the Civil Veterinary Department, Punjab, 1900–01* (Lahore: Civil and Military Gazette Press, 1901), p. 4.

76 Letter from P. Nolan, dated 25 May 1886, APAC, L/MIL/7/845.

77 An official noted that 'the establishment of a veterinary college at Lahore was the first serious attempt made in north India to train natives in veterinary science. This project...was brought to a practical issue by the experience of the Afghan campaigns, in which the security of trained farriers proved a serious inconvenience to the transport service.' Letter dated 10 July 1886, to the Secretary of State for India, APAC, L/MIL/7/845, n. p.

78 R. Porter, 'Man, Animals and Medicine at the Time of the Founding of the Royal Veterinary College', in A. R. Mitchell (ed.), *History of Healing Professions*, vol. III (Cambridge: Cambridge University Press, 1993), p. 19.

79 *Colonizing the Body*, p. 13.

80 Mark Harrison notes in this connection that 'in the late-1880s, government expenditure of public health began to rise as expenditure on other public works began to fall'. *Public Health in British India*, p. 201.

81 J. Collins, the Principal Veterinary Surgeon in Britain noted in 1881 that 'it is a fact that all discoveries with regard to special Indian [bovine] diseases…have either originated in England, or have been carried out by men fresh from England…It was only the other day that a well known disease peculiar to India, viz. "bussatti" was clearly demonstrated by a young veterinary surgeon who had never been in India at all!' Letter dated 17 November 1881, APAC, L/MIL/7/832, n. p.

82 In the wake of the First World War, larger cavalry regiments in India were amalgamated into single units in 1922. Thought the last of the cavalry charges took place during the Second World War, the usefulness of these regiments had started to decline earlier.

83 *Proceedings of the First Meeting of Veterinary Officers in India* (Calcutta: Superintendent Government Printing, 1919), p. 17.

84 *British Medical Journal*, 2(3480) (17 Sept. 1927), 514.

85 'The Bengal Veterinary Department', *British Medical Journal*, 1(2625) (22 Apr. 1911), 964.

CHAPTER THREE

Ticks, germs, and bacteriological research

From our account until now, it appears that the veterinary administration in India was a somewhat stunted version of its full-blooded British and European counterparts. This, we have argued, was the result of military and financial dictates that dogged it at every step. Yet this is a rather stark picture: after all, did the colonies not witness, in the late nineteenth century, significant investments into burgeoning new fields such as bacteriology? This certainly seems to be the case if we look at laboratories such as the Onderstepoort Veterinary Institute in South Africa, which spearheaded cutting-edge research that set the agenda for metropolitan organisations.[1] We need to ask whether the research carried out at institutes in India, such as the Imperial Bacteriological Laboratory at Muktesar, was of a similar nature. Simultaneously, this chapter will also explore other issues such as the relationship between the scientific core and its peripheries, the autonomy (or otherwise) of colonial laboratories, and the impact of the colonial context on the nature of scientific research. In doing this, we will focus mostly on the Muktesar laboratory, though Pasteur Institutes will also be discussed in order to provide a broader picture of bacteriological developments.

Muktesar, at the time, was a small settlement nestled in the Kumaon hills at the height of 7,500 feet. In terms of its location, it boasted of absolutely no special attributes that could make it the preferred choice for bacteriological research. What worked in its favour was its location in the hills, as it was felt that laboratory experiments could not be carried out in a controlled fashion in the hot and humid plains. Several technical explanations were offered in support of this conviction: gelatine could not be used for cultures in the plains; thick glass vessels might crack due to the heat; sera might deteriorate if constantly exposed to high temperatures, and so forth.[2] However, at the same time as these doubts were being expressed, there were several senior researchers and 'old Indian hands', such as D. D. Cunningham and E. H. Hankin, who saw climatic conditions as having absolutely no bearing at all on bacteriological investigations. In fact, they argued that the plains might be a more suitable location for such institutes, as there would be greater access to patients of all kinds from large, established hospitals.[3] The fact that the hills were chosen despite this could be ascribed to two interrelated developments, both of which became quite discernible in the second half of the nineteenth century: one of these was the growing consensus regarding the virtues of hills and their climate, and the other was the strengthening of popular European fears regarding the 'tropics'.[4] Born out of such ideas and fears, with little emphasis on practical matters, institutes in places such as Muktesar would later face several huge obstacles: for example, cattle for preparing vaccines would be difficult to obtain, field operations would become difficult to carry out, and fodder would have to be obtained from the plains.[5] Despite all this, however, colonial faith in the suitability of the hills remained unshaken.

The shift from the plains to the hills was especially striking in the case of the Imperial Bacteriological Laboratory. Halfway through the construction of its building in Poona, Dr Alfred Lingard – soon to be appointed as the first head of the institute – was asked to offer his opinion on the suitability of the project's location. In a brave departure from the previous official decision on the issue, he advocated an immediate abandonment of Poona buildings and a move up the hills, citing adverse climatic conditions as the chief reason. Officials acted promptly upon his judgement, leading to a loss of nearly 32,000 rupees to the exchequer.[6] The laboratory's contents were subsequently packed and sent away on the long trek up the country and into Muktesar, where it took nearly a year to reassemble everything.[7] As mentioned before, though, Muktesar was not the only example of this preference for the hills. In fact the idea of the tropics as antithetical to laboratory research had become so strong that nearly all such institutes that were established in India were situated in the hills (apart from the one in Calcutta). Thus, the first institute was established in Kasauli (1900), and subsequently others in Coonoor, Rangoon, and Shillong.[8] It is interesting to note, in this context, that whereas Patrick Manson and others extolled the benefits of conducting research in the 'Tropics', where one could find 'a wealth of pathogenic organisms', within India itself researchers were keen to move away from the heat and dust of the tropics and into the temperate hills.[9] The history of bacteriology in India is replete with such peculiarities, some of which will be explored in this chapter.

Metropolitan influences and colonial laboratories

Some of these peculiarities were inevitable in a colonial situation, where a wide range of ideas, compulsions, and motives acted together to twist official policies out of shape. One of these was the need to respond to public opinion on the subject of animal experimentation back home. Another was the criticism received from anti-vivisectionist quarters within India, led by organisations such as the SPCA (Society for Prevention of Cruelty against Animals).[10] These obstacles, however, were not powerful enough to derail the pro-bacteriology movement in India, which had gathered significant momentum by the 1890s.

Curiously, the opposition to laboratories from the larger public in India was slightly muted, though the bogey of 'Hindu sentiments' was often raised by the officials themselves while discussing this question. One of these officials expressed a widely-held colonial sentiment that 'we govern an enormous population who have peculiar religious prejudices regarding animals, and we must be very careful not to rouse those prejudices unnecessarily'.[11] Colonial perceptions notwithstanding, the urban middle-class in India was, in fact, remarkably amenable to the idea of laboratories, and saw them as powerful symbols of modernity. Reflecting the high estimation in which scientific research was held, a Bengali health periodical berated practitioners of indigenous medicine for showing 'no commitment to experimentation through research work'. These practitioners, it went on to observe in a mocking tone, were 'like lumps of clay...not capable of radiating the light of knowledge on [their] own'.[12] The fact that this 'light of knowledge' was being produced at the cost of numerous animal lives did not appear to cause much consternation for these writers. Even colonial officials noted that 'native' opposition against laboratories had been exaggerated earlier, and that the strongest criticism offered by the 'native press' was on the grounds that these institutions conducted research only for the benefit of Europeans.[13] Also, contrary to what has often been assumed, poorer peasants and other cattle owners were, by no means, unreflexively opposed to the drugs and vaccines being produced by Muktesar. In fact the rinderpest serum had already won wide acceptance only a few years after it was first introduced. A report noted that:

> at first there was strong prejudice against inoculation, but...cattle owners are beginning to look upon it with great favour, and consider it the only satisfactory measure to be adopted against rinderpest.[14]

Laboratories did not merely receive verbal support: they were also the objects of great financial munificence by wealthy Indians. Even before the first Pasteur Institute had been set up, a sum of 100,000 rupees had already been offered by a Parsi donor.[15] All subsequent Pasteur Institutes were also established through private donations, partly because it was feared that the state's involvement in these projects would lead to vehement attacks from anti-vivisectionists.[16] Also, indigenous approval was nowhere as clearly evident as in the actions of princely rulers, some of whom adopted laboratories with much greater gusto than the British. There is, for instance, the striking example of the Nawab of Hyderabad, who approved the killing of 500 animals by the Chloroform Commission of 1889 within the short space of fifty-six days.[17] Explaining this enthusiasm among princely rulers for new kinds of sciences, David Arnold notes that this was prompted by considerations of political legitimacy and financial gain.[18] Investments into laboratories also allowed the princely rulers, often portrayed as conservative 'oriental despots',[19] to project a progressive, modern image of themselves.

Interestingly, while the urban middle class and the princely rulers clamoured to adopt the latest scientific ideas and principles, colonial scientists and officials often took a rather disparaging view of the former's muddled attempts at appearing modern. It was frequently noted, both by officials and colonial scientists, that cutting-edge sciences such as bacteriology were beyond the intellectual ken of the 'natives'. Even if they were to be trained in bacteriology, an official noted, one failed to see how they could become proficient in a science 'which only a few men in the civilized world [were] competent to undertake'.[20] Another official recounted stories regarding his 'native' assistant's blundering ways in the laboratory: apparently, in one case he mistook the mistaking sealing wax for blood stains; in another, he diagnosed a cow as having been poisoned by a substance that was simply not available in India.[21] Despite this disparaging attitude though, there is hardly any doubt that most laboratories and institutes could not have existed without 'native' support, be it support in terms of manpower, expertise, or funds.[22]

In fact the sharpest criticism of laboratories in India did not emerge from within the country at all, but from the metropolis, where the anti-vivisectionist lobby was quite strong. The strength of this movement is reflected in the use of colourful words and phrases that were employed by officials to describe its adherents: activists were, for example, often described as 'fanatics', 'those people who have a disproportionate influence over politics', 'those who fan the fire of ignorance', and so forth.[23] Despite this dismissive attitude, the government thought it prudent to exercise extreme caution and restraint, so as to avoid showing 'the red rag to the fanatics'.[24] Pasteur Institutes, as mentioned earlier, were therefore established through private donations, though the government found indirect strategies for controlling them. This included the strategy of appointing government officials as members of the committees that ran these institutes. Such control was assumed in return for substantial government subsidies, such as the free allotment of land, the granting of liberal fees for treating every British patient, and the payment of the salary of the IMS official who was appointed the head of the institute.[25] Other measures that were taken in order to avoid or deflect criticism included renaming bacteriologists as 'Special Health Officers', and even the move up the hills was sometimes justified on the grounds of greater isolation and freedom to experiment.[26] All this showed great receptivity to opinions and ideas back home.

Such receptivity towards ideas and movements back home could be seen not just in the case of the anti-vivisectionist movement. In fact the metropolitan influence could be strongly detected in the fact that the new science of bacteriology itself was taken up seriously by colonial scientists. Colonies such as India could not, after all, remain immune from the influence of major breakthroughs in bacteriology that were achieved by Robert Koch, Louis Pasteur, and others, starting from the late 1870s onwards.[27] These breakthroughs inaugurated a new trend, which was picked up by numerous others, leading to the discovery of the aetiology of several diseases such as anthrax, tuberculosis, rabies, cholera, plague, diphtheria, typhoid, among others. In the colonies these trends were reflected in the fact that, when the bacteriological institute was initially opened, it began its career by carrying out investigations on anthrax, the disease that had given Pasteur his finest hour. Not just this, the fact that Pasteur Institutes in India focused almost completely on rabies and hydrophobia despite the negligible mortality caused by the disease, was partly as a result of the great interest in the disease in Paris and Berlin.[28]

A much stronger example of slavish imitation of metropolitan agendas was provided during Koch's visit to the laboratory in 1897, when he tried to conclusively prove his own bile treatment for rinderpest.[29] Koch had, by this time, become the definitive authority on all things bacteriological, and received a suitably deferential treatment in India, with the entire staff of the laboratory devoting nearly six weeks exclusively towards organising and conducting his trip.[30] Lingard's conversations with Koch also became the basis for demanding an expansion of the laboratory premises and facilities, which was granted by the colonial government.[31] Such episodes make it clear that the authority and opinion of an acknowledged expert from the 'core' was valued immensely in the 'peripheries'. The authority of these experts was reflected not just in the deference accorded to them but also in the adherence to their methods and hypotheses.[32] Not only this, every single instrument, chemical, or dye had to be imported all the way from Europe, which slowed down the pace of research massively.[33] An official noted in this connection that several articles, which had been requested for Muktesar in the summer of 1900, had not reached the laboratory even a year later. This, he noted, had a 'paralysing effect', and 'the whole of the work of the laboratory [had been] brought to a stand-still owing to the stock of certain necessaries of culture media being exhausted'.[34] Muktesar was also run completely by experts or scientists trained in Europe, despite the fact that many of them quickly deserted the station due to the isolated nature of the spot.[35] This, again, inevitably interfered with the research, as did the fact that these scientists were not very well adapted to the exigencies of research in India due to a 'prolonged experience of work...in the modern laboratories of large European towns, with all their elaborate appliances and facilities'.[36]

Yet, despite these instances, it would be misleading to present such a one-sided view of overwhelming dependence on the metropolis. In fact, Koch's celebrated India trip – though it received a huge amount of attention and publicity – was not hugely successful in expanding the number of Indian adherents to his bile theory of treating rinderpest. Lingard filed a negative report on his experiments at Muktesar,[37] while the Principal of the Lahore Veterinary College made the guarded comment that 'it is, perhaps, too early yet to give an opinion; in its present form it is rather unwieldy, and would only be applicable to certain cases, in which, however, it might be extremely useful should it prove efficacious.'[38] Such negative assessments might partly have been occasioned by the inconclusive nature of the experiments themselves, but they also reflect a degree of confidence and self-assuredness among Indian researchers.[39]

Further, despite the stellar reputation that bacteriology enjoyed within Europe, the colonial establishment in India was quite slow to capitulate to its charms. In the wake of Koch's stunning demonstration of the tubercle bacillus in Germany on 24 March 1882, colonial officials did show a sneaking interest in the new science of bacteriology, as a result of which J. H. B. Hallen – the most trusted and influential veterinarian in India – was sent on a trip to Pasteur's famed laboratory in Paris to learn the art of producing vaccines.[40] However, even though he returned to India a fully converted man, eager to preach the gospel to his colleagues and the government, his glowing reports and enthusiastic endorsements did not lead to immediate measures.[41] Pasteur himself was quite keen to expand his sphere of influence within India, and showed a great proselytising zeal in his correspondences with the

India Office. In a letter to them he noted that he was even 'prepared to bear the expense of establishing suitable works in India, and to find properly qualified officials altogether at his own cost until the remedy is well established in the several presidencies'.[42] However, despite such proposals from Pasteur, and in spite of the colonial government's own initial interest in the new science, the latter was quite circumspect in adopting measures that had been widely endorsed within Europe. Such developments show a separation, or at least a divergence, between metropolitan and colonial trends, which goes against old Basalla-esque models regarding the unidirectional flow of science.[43]

However, though Basalla's model has been justifiably critiqued for its tendency to see the colonies as completely dependent on metropolitan knowledge and expertise, we still need to ask ourselves whether indigenous peoples were really equal partners in a 'global scientific enterprise'. Also, was science, as practiced in the colonies, merely a slightly under-confident younger sibling of its feisty metropolitan counterpart? Or was it an altogether different species, following a different law of creation, and a different life cycle? The next section will move beyond the question of autonomy of colonial institutes, and show that at least the bacteriological institutes in India followed an entirely divergent path that was governed by specifically colonial circumstances.

The 'incredible scientific destitution': bacteriology as a colonial science

As argued in previous chapters, one question that rendered the colonial situation especially unique was the constant insistence on the question of finances. This is not to say, of course, that the question of finances was irrelevant in the metropolis, but in the colonial situation it appeared to have a much greater influence on policy making. In fact, it was because of the centrality of the question of finances and potential savings that the state agreed to establish certain scientific institutes in the first place. Pasteur Institutes, for example, held the prospect of a possible reduction in medical expenses by providing antirabic treatment for European patients, who had earlier to be sent all the way to Paris to receive treatment at considerable government expenses.[44] This was, by no means, a small expenditure: it could cost nearly 22,000 rupees every year to send patients away to Paris for treatment, roughly equivalent to the cost of setting up three Pasteur Institutes in India.[45] An official noted that 'it [was] a great scandal that we should have to send all these poor soldiers and other dog-bitten persons *every* year –at a great cost – when it is quite easy to start an institution for their treatment in India.[46]

However, despite the advantages of treating rabies within India, the state did not provide full funding to the Pasteur Institutes, and preferred to rely on private subscriptions. Muktesar was in this sense more fortunate, as the funding from government sources was approved without much debate or controversy. One of the prominent factors behind the greater financial liberality of the colonial government in the case of Muktesar was the desire to compensate for the lack of investment into cattle disease in general, which we have discussed in the earlier chapters. Also, it was felt that bacteriological research into animal diseases could potentially lead to great cost-saving discoveries such as cheap vaccines. The veterinary head for Punjab, for instance, despaired of any immediate hope of suppressing rinderpest outbreaks through public health measures and looked towards colonial bacteriologists for a magic cure that would eradicate the disease. Writing in 1899 with a sense of anticipation of some impending discovery, he noted that:

> I have been informed that before long an immunising agent for inoculation will be ready for use and, if successful, given a sufficient staff, an incalculable amount of good should follow its use, but, until then, I hope you will see that the effects of this disease in this country as in other countries are practically out of our hands.[47]

He was perhaps referring to the new 'anti-serum' for the disease which Alfred Lingard, the Imperial Bacteriologist, had discovered at the Muktesar laboratory in 1899 (see Figure 2).[48] The central government had already approved Lingard's claims and had shown considerable promptness in producing the prophylactic, so that within a decade of its introduction nearly half a million doses were being issued annually.[49] However, though the vaccine was initially distributed free of cost, a decision was soon made to sell it at a reasonable cost. The year in which this charge was introduced (1911–12), the income from selling rinderpest sera jumped from Rs. 5,000 to Rs. 74,000.[50] The income obtained from this, and other products, kept increasing every year, until it reached the figure of Rs. 1.55 million in 1929–30. In fact, throughout this period, the institute posted a net profit of nearly 0.8 million every year.[51] The trend was strengthened in 1922–3, when the Inchcape Committee deliberated the fate of Muktesar and decided that the institute should become entirely self-supporting.[52] The order of the Inchcape Committee was rescinded, but only much later, and by then the institute had already acquired a huge establishment for the manufacture and sale of sera. Also, when the serum was eventually declared free, this did not come as a huge relief to cattle owners, as the cost of its manufacture had already fallen to an absolute minimum due to the use of goats, instead of bulls, in the production process.

Figure 2 The Muktesar Laboratory

It is therefore safe to say that, though the institute was initially set up using government grants, it was by no means solely concerned with the question of 'public good'. What this meant, in effect, was that the laboratory was forced to churn out as many doses of the serum as possible in order to maximise its income. Muktesar was, as a result, reduced to a manufactory rather than a research institute. The Acting Imperial Bacteriologist noted in this connection in 1927 that:

> Ever since the beginning most of the staff at Muktesar has been employed on manufacture, and ...though there is a long list of publications relating to the work done at Muktesar, a great deal of it is in connection with research into production, and it is not what I would call pure research.[53]

In another place, he noted that the amount allotted to research, apart from research connected with the manufacture of biological products, was almost negligible.[54] These statements were, no doubt, very strong indictments of government policies, but they were by no means announcing a startling new fact – even officials at the highest rungs quite often freely admitted to the lack of funding for research. In fact, no less a personage than the director of the Indian Medical Service himself plainly admitted that 'officers have been expected to work miracles with a test-tube, and they have been subjected to unmerited abuse because they have failed'.[55] That very little was done despite

[67]

this points towards the colonial roots of scientific policies in India. To an extent, this 'incredible scientific destitution'[56] – as Ernest Hart of the *British Medical Journal* chose to call it – was understandable as colonial governments chose to place a greater emphasis on 'practical matters', and much less on abstract theoretical issues.[57]

There were numerous indicators of this scientific destitution, especially in the field of laboratory research, some of which have already been outlined above. Some half-formed attempts were made to organise research on a sound footing, especially through the establishment of the centralised Bacteriological Department in 1905. However, the department – already quite small and rather inconsequential – failed to attract and retain sufficient talent. There were several reasons for this, one of the most prominent of which was the smallness of the department (it employed a total of mere thirteen officers seven years after it was established), which meant that very few permanent positions were created for existing temporary staff.[58] Besides this, a rather curious set of rules were imposed on officers of the bacteriological department. For example, though other medical officers were allowed to carry out private practice, those in the bacteriological department were asked to hand over half their private earnings to the government. Also, the salary and pay conditions in the department were quite poor: officers on the same grade in other medical departments could earn as much as Rs. 550 a year more in the way of salaries and allowances.[59] All this reflected the fact that the government was not too keen to invest the funds required to attract the best talent into this newly created department.[60] As a result of this lack of personnel, there was very little frontline research being produced in the colony. One indicator of this was the closure of the *Journal of Tropical Veterinary Science*, which was published for a few years from India, on the grounds that 'it would be difficult to obtain material for a journal'.[61] Instead, a bulletin called the *Tropical Veterinary Bulletin* was started, which simply culled new information and abstracts regarding relevant research from elsewhere in the world.

Another way in which the organisation of veterinary research showed colonial characteristics was in its emphasis on investigating diseases that affected the colonial cavalry. We have already discussed this overbearing military influence in other contexts, but this influence was discernible even in the case of bacteriology, at least in its early days. In the specific case of Muktesar, though the institute was eventually reduced to being a manufactory for rinderpest sera, in its initial years there was a lot of emphasis on investigating surra – the disease was, in fact, Lingard's pet project until Koch's visit brought rinderpest into sharp focus.[62] In fact, Lingard was not the only scientist interested in investigating surra, and it was another veterinarian called Griffith Evans who achieved a major breakthrough in discovering the causal organism for the disease. Evans, a Welshman, had been deeply inspired by Pasteur's anthrax demonstration in 1876, and had earlier wished to investigate anthrax in horses. However, when the Second Afghan War broke out in 1880, and British cavalry regiments suffered huge losses through surra, Evans immediately sought permission to study this disease instead.[63] He appears to have seen this as a rare and career-defining moment, and threw himself energetically into the task of collecting blood samples and studying them under his microscope. Soon enough he made the triumphant announcement that he had discovered the microbe responsible for surra and even claimed success in transferring the disease into healthy horses,[64] thereby satisfying Koch's postulates even before they had been explicitly formulated.[65] That one of the major breakthroughs achieved by colonial scientists concerned an equine disease should not surprise us – especially if we keep in mind the great influence of the military over veterinary policies until at least the end of the nineteenth century. However, at least in the case of bacteriological research, the emphasis does appear to have shifted to cattle diseases later.

Conclusion

The final word in this story of bacteriology in India must go to the Director of the Muktesar institute who was asked by an Indian member of the Royal Commission for Agriculture (1927) whether, in a country like India, which was mostly agricultural, the government had paid adequate attention to veterinary research and education. His short reply to this was: 'No, I think, speaking generally, they certainly have not.'[66] This is certainly the impression one gathers from a survey of the Muktesar laboratory. In fact, it is perhaps fair to say that the state was slightly more prepared to make investments where vaccination for human diseases such as cholera was concerned. A clear example of this was furnished in 1893 when Haffkine arrived in Calcutta and was immediately given permission to try out his anti-cholera vaccination. Subsequently, within the space of three years, he was able to vaccinate nearly 40,000 people, even though the efficacy of his vaccine had, by no means, been conclusively proved.[67] Another instance was the swift government response against the outbreak of the plague, which was the first major crisis that led to a consolidation of the 'bacteriological era' not just in India, but also in the rest of the world.[68] Pratik Chakrabarti describes how the plague outbreak attracted researchers from everywhere in the world, so that a 'great experimental theatre' unfolded in Bombay.[69] Compared to this, epizootics did not receive adequate attention, and it was arguably Koch's visit, rather than a single outbreak of the disease, that led to focused research on it.

How did this relative paucity of research into veterinary issues square with the notion of the 'civilising mission' that colonialism was imbued with? After all, though there were a lot of continuities between older disease theories and the new germ theory (and perhaps, in this sense, it is better to talk of several germ theories rather than one), it is clear that bacteriology had come to be seen as path-breaking and innovative.[70] It was a new science that most European states and governments were eager to invest in, partly in order to gain some legitimacy for themselves. In the colonial situation, the state could afford to behave in a slightly different fashion. This was especially so in case of cattle disease, which did not attract the same amount of attention back home, or even among 'enlightened sections' in India. As a result, the question of finances and funds seems to have triumphed over the civilizing or philanthropic impulse of the colonisers. This seems to tie in with some of the developments in connection with the veterinary department that we have discussed in detail in earlier chapters.

Notes

1 Karen Brown, 'Tropical Medicine and Animal Diseases: Onderstepoort and the Development of Veterinary Science in South Africa 1908–1950', *Journal of Southern African Studies*, 3(3) (2005), 513–29.
2 National Archives of India (hereafter NAI), Home Department, Medical-A, nos. 26–30, August 1904, p. 12.
3 NAI, Home Department, Medical-A, February 1901, nos. 39–43, pp. 4–11; NAI, Home Department, Medical Branch, November 1898, nos. 118–23, pp. 24–8.
4 There has been a substantial amount of research on the idea of the tropics. See, for instance, David Arnold, *Tropics and the Travelling Gaze: India, Landscape and Science, 1800–1856* (Washington, DC: University of Washington Press, 2006); Mark Harrison, '"The Tender Frame of Man": Disease, Climate and Racial Difference in India and the West Indies, 1760–1860', *Bulletin of the History of Medicine*, 70(1) (spring 1996), 68–93; Warwick Anderson, 'Climates of Opinion: Acclimatization in Nineteenth-Century France and England', *Victorian Studies*, 35(2) (1992), 135–57; E. M. Collingham, *Imperial Bodies: The Physical Experience of the Raj* (Cambridge: Polity, 2001); Karen Ordahl Kupperman, 'Fear of Hot Climates in the Anglo-American Colonial Experience', *William and Mary Quarterly*, 41 (1984), 213–40. On hill stations, see Dane Kennedy, *The Magic Mountains: Hill Stations and the British Raj* (California: University of California Press, 1996); Pamela Kanwar, *Imperial Simla: The Political Culture of the Raj* (Delhi: Oxford University Press, 1990); Judith T. Kenny, 'Climate, Race, and Imperial Authority: The Symbolic Landscape of the British Hill Station in India', *Annals of the Association of American Geographers*, 85(4) (Dec., 1995), 694–714; Pamela Kanwar, 'The Changing Profile of the Summer Capital of British India: Simla 1864–1947', *Modern Asian Studies*, 18(2) (1984), 215–36; Robert R. Reed, 'The Colonial Genesis of Hill Stations: The Genting Exception', *Geographical Review*, 69(4) (1979), 463–8; Nandini Bhattacharya, *Contagion and Enclaves: Tropical Medicine in Colonial India* (Liverpool: Liverpool University Press, 2012).

5 For details on these operational difficulties, see annual reports of the imperial bacteriologist.

6 Letter from T. Cooke (Principal, College of Science, Poona) to the Director of Public Instruction, dated 9 July 1892, NAI, Home Department, Medical Branch, August 1893, nos. 79–87, p. 15. It was also noted that 'those buildings have to date cost some Rs. 32,000 to apparently no purpose' (p. 13).

7 Dr Lingard found that the 'climate of the plains rendered laboratory research work extremely difficult and was also little suitable for the manufacture and preservation of vaccines and serums. Consequently, in 1893, it was decided to remove the laboratory to a suitable site in the hills, and Muktesar was selected for this purpose.' J. D. E. Holmes, *A Description of the Imperial Bacteriological Laboratory, Muktesar: Its Works and Products* (Calcutta: Superintendent Government Printing, 1913), p. 1.

8 For a detailed discussion of Pasteur Institutes, see Pratik Chakrabarti, *Bacteriology in British India: Laboratory Medicine and the Tropics* (Rochester: University of Rochester Press, 2012).

9 Patrick Manson, *Tropical Diseases: A Manual of the Diseases of Warm Climates* (London: Cassell, 1900), p. xxiv.

10 SPCA was established in India in 1861, before it was established in America. Pratik Chakrabarti, 'Beasts of Burden: Animals and Laboratory Research in Colonial India', *History of Science*, 48(2) (Jun. 2010), 130.

11 Letter from M. D. Chalmers, dated 5 March 1897, NAI, Home Department, Sanitary Branch, March 1897, nos. 388–424, n. p.

12 From an article by Shri Jadunath Gangopadhyay, *Chikitsa Sammilani* (April–June 1889), translated in Pradip Kumar Bose (ed.), *Health and Society in Bengal: A Selection from Late 19th-Century Bengali Periodicals* (Delhi: Sage, 2006), p. 260.

13 NAI, Home Department, Medical-A, June 1903, nos. 22–4, p. 3.

14 'Veterinary Work in India', *Journal for the Royal Society of Arts*, 63(3280) (1 Oct. 1915), 945.

15 NAI, Home Department, Medical Branch, August 1892, nos. 76–84.

16 Pasteur Institutes offered anti-rabic treatment, which involved using a preparation from the spinal cord of rabbits which had been inoculated with rabies. This inoculation involved pain to the animal, and could therefore become special targets of attack by anti-vivisectionist sections. NAI, Home Department, Medical-A, June 1903, nos. 22–4, p. 2.

17 Chakrabarti, 'Beasts of Burden', 137–8.

18 *Science, Technology and Medicine in Colonial India* (Cambridge: Cambridge University Press, 2000), p. 160.

19 Waltraud Ernst and Biswamoy Pati (eds.), *India's Princely States: People, Princes and Colonialism* (London: Routledge, 2007). See especially chapter by Indrani Sen, pp. 30–48.

20 Letter from Sir E. C. Buck, dated 7 June 1893, NAI, Home Department, Medical Branch, August 1893, nos. 79–87.

21 NAI, Home Department, Sanitary Branch, December 1895, nos. 46–59, p. 42.

22 In one case an official talked about one Raj Tara Prosonno Rai Bahadar, who officiated temporarily on a post with distinction, and was thought worthy of holding the position permanently. NAI, Home Department, Sanitary Proceedings, December 1895, nos. 46–95, p. 59.

23 See for instance NAI, Home Department, Sanitary Branch, March 1897, nos. 388–424; NAI, Home Department, Medical-A, May 1900, nos. 79–88; NAI, Home Department, Medical-A, August 1899, no. 100.

24 NAI, Home Department, Sanitary Proceedings, March 1897, nos. 388–424.

25 In this respect, it did not really make much difference whether the institute was controlled directly by the government or through a committee, as the committee was constituted purely in order to keep anti-vivisectionist criticism at bay. An official noted that the difference between the two was 'not much more than that between tweedledum and tweedledee'. NAI, Government of India, Home Department, Medical-A, July 1900, nos. 125–36, p. 8.

26 NAI, Home, Medical-A, August 1899, no. 100.
27 In fact, not only was the influence of the metropolis clearly discernible, the rivalry between metropolitan scientists was, in some cases, replayed in the colonies. A. Cunningham, 'Transforming the Plague: The Laboratory and the Identity of Infectious Disease', in A. Cunningham and P. Williams (eds.), *The Laboratory Revolution in Medicine* (Cambridge: Cambridge University Press, 1992), 209–44.
28 In fact, an official noted that 'horrible though death from hydrophobia is, the deaths in India from this cause are not very numerous, and hardly concern us as a government'. Letter from M. D. Chalmers, dated 5 March 1897, NAI, Home Department, Sanitary Branch, March 1897, nos. 388–424, n. p.
29 This treatment involved injection of bile from an infected animal to a healthy one in order to confer immunity. Koch had claimed great success with this method during the course of extensive trials that were conducted in the Cape Colony, and his trip to India followed quick on the heels of his experiments in Cape Colony. In *Friend of India and Statesman*, dated 20 October 1897. See also Daniel Gilfoyle, 'Veterinary Research and the African Rinderpest Epizootic: The Cape Colony, 1896–1898', *Journal of Southern African Studies*, 29(1) (2003), 133–54. Also, in 1897 the laboratory was not just visited by Koch, but also by other European researchers such as Pfeiffer and Gaffky.
30 Lingard, 'Preliminary Note on Rinderpest', APAC, V/27/541/20, p. 1.
31 Lingard, 'Preliminary Note on Rinderpest', p. 10.
32 Paul Cranefield shows a striking instance of this in the case of East Coast Fever where Koch's claims led to a derailment of local investigations despite doubts to the contrary. *Science and Empire: East Coast Fever in Rhodesia and the Transvaal* (Cambridge: Cambridge University Press, 1991), pp. 22–51. See also Brown, 'Tropical Medicine and Animal Diseases', where she argues that, while peripheral scientists were very deferential during the initial years of bacteriological investigations in the region, they had become far more confident and independent about four decades later.
33 NAI, Home Department, Medical-A, October 1901, nos. 93–5.
34 NAI, Home Department, Medical-A, October 1901, nos. 93–5, p. 6.
35 Between 1914 and 1926, thirteen Imperial Service Officers held appointments at the institute, out of which eight resigned and left. *Royal Commission of Agriculture in India, vol. I, Part I: Evidence of Officers Serving under the Government of India* (Calcutta: Government of India Publications, 1927) p. 210. In his deposition before the Royal Agriculture Commission in 1926, the Acting Imperial Bacteriologist noted that prolonged isolation at the hilltop 'made officers cranky', leading them to 'fall out with their brother officers' (p. 230).
36 D. D. Cunningham, letter dated 12 May 1897, NAI, Home Department, Sanitary Branch, July 1897, no. 269.
37 After detailing all the experiments carried out by Koch in his report, Lingard reached the conclusion that 'the experiments commenced at Muktesar, under the supervision of Professor Koch to ascertain the value of rinderpest bile as a protective agent against that disease in India, have up to the present proved very little'. 'Preliminary Note on Rinderpest', p. 10.
38 *Friend of India and Statesman*, Calcutta, dated 20 October 1897.
39 Koch faced many practical difficulties during the course of his experiments in India, chief among which was his inability to find and preserve infected rinderpest blood.
40 Hallen notes that 'while in England I received instruction from the Indian Office explaining to me that before returning to my duties I should visit Monsieur Pasteur's laboratory in Paris, with the view of learning the method of vaccinating cattle...I proceeded there on the 5th September 1884, on the visit of enquiry.' Letter dated 6 December 1884, APAC, L/MIL/7/840, n. p.
41 In his report Hallen noted that 'animals duly vaccinated with the attenuated virus, as prepared in professor Pasteur's laboratory...become protected from anthrax. This boon should now be extended to India, where anthrax in many forms attacks animals.' Letter dated 6 December 1884, APAC, L/MIL/7/840, n. p.

42 Letter dated 11 October 1886, APAC, L/MIL/7/840.

43 George Basalla, 'The Spread of Western Science', *Science*, 156(3775) (5 May 1967): 611–22.

44 NAI, Home Department, Medical-B, September 1900, no. 46, p. 4.

45 According to a government estimate, it took nearly 8000 rupees to set up a new Pasteur Institute, whereas the new laboratory at Liverpool cost £60,000 to set up. Another proposed laboratory in Netley was estimated to cost £20,000. NAI, Home Department, Medical-A, February 1901, nos. 39–43, p. 1.

46 Letter dated 20 February 1900, NAI, Home Department, Medical-A, July 1900, nos. 125–36 (italics in original).

47 *Provincial Report for the Civil Veterinary Department of Punjab for 1898–9* (Lahore: Civil and Military Gazette Press, 1899), p. 4.

48 Dr Lingard was a Welshman who was appointed as the Imperial Bacteriologist in 1890 at the Imperial Bacteriological Laboratory. He acted as the head of the laboratory until 1908. Major J. D. E Holmes, *A Description of the Imperial Bacteriological Laboratory, Muktesar: Its Works and Products* (Calcutta: Superintendent Government Printing, 1913).

49 Percival Hartley, 'The Imperial Bacteriological Laboratory, Muktesar, India', *Nature*, 9 April 1914, pp. 137–8; Holmes, *Description of the Imperial Bacteriological Laboratory*, pp. 25–6.

50 S. Dutta, 'Indian Veterinary Research Institute, 1890–1950', *Indian Veterinary Research Institute, Diamond Jubilee, 1890–1950, Indian Farming: Special Number* (Delhi: Government of India Printing, 1950), p. 15.

51 Dutta, 'Indian Veterinary Research Institute', p. 15.

52 *Royal Commission on Agriculture in India*, vol. I, pt I, p. 214.

53 *Report of the Royal Commission for Agriculture* (Calcutta: Government of India Press, 1927), p. 234. Another report, written much later, recounted the history of the institute, and noted that the decision to cover the institute's expenditure through the sale of sera led to a focus on the cheap production of sera, and 'with the staff available, it was not possible to carry out the immense amount of research which was needed into diseases other then fatal plagues such as rinderpest and surra'. Arthur Olver, 'Animal Husbandry in India', *Journal of the Royal Society of Arts* (29 May 1942), p. 439.

54 *Royal Commission on Agriculture in India*, vol. I, pt I, p. 216. In making this statement, he also took into account the research taking place at the provincial veterinary colleges.

55 Letter dated 9 June 1897, NAI, Home Department, Sanitary-A, July 1897, no. 269, p. 2. Cleghorn went on to note, in the same report, that 'if these officers were treated in the same liberal manner and sympathetic spirit, as specialists are in other countries, the results would undoubtedly be different. The Germans, for example, have become famous as specialists, chiefly because of the liberal way in which they are treated' (p. 2).

56 NAI, Home Department, Medical Branch, December 1895, nos. 15–18, p. 23.

57 The Inspector General of Civil Hospitals in Bengal noted, while discussing the poor research infrastructure in India, that 'the medical profession in India is perforce a practical one'. NAI, Home Department, Medical Branch, November 1898, nos. 118–23, p. 27.

58 NAI, Home Department, Medical-A, July 1912, nos. 4–5, p. 5.

59 NAI, Home Department, Medical-A, July 1912, nos. 4–5, p. 10.

60 Officers working in the bacteriology department had other complaints as well. For instance, though they nominally worked for the central government, those located in the provinces found themselves occupied with routine duties that were imposed upon them by the local governments. NAI, Home Department, Sanitary-A, July 1908, nos. 285–90, p. 3.

61 *Proceedings of the First Meeting of Veterinary Officers in India* (Calcutta: Superintendent Government Printing, 1919), p. 14.

62 The report of the imperial bacteriologist for 1895–6, for instance, was occupied

exclusively with the investigation of surra, and did not even mention rinderpest once. *Annual Report of the Imperial Bacteriologist, 1895–6* (Government of India Press, 1896).

63 A. Murray Fallis, 'Griffith Evans 1835–1935: Discoverer of the First Pathogenic Trypanosome', *Canadian Veterinary Journal*, 27 (1986), 336–8. See also 'Presentation of the Mary Kingsley Medal to Dr. Griffith Evans', *Annals of Tropical Medicine and Parasitology*, 12 (1918), 1–16.

64 Murray Fallis, 'Griffith Evans 1835–1935', 337.

65 Koch came up with his four postulates in 1884 in the wake of his tuberculosis demonstration, and these postulates quickly became the touchstone with which any new claim of a discovery was tested. See Cunningham, 'Transforming the Plague'.

66 Evidence of Mr F. Ware, Officiating Director, Imperial Institute of Veterinary Research, in *Royal Commission on Agriculture in India*, vol. I, pt I, p. 213.

67 Ilana Lowy, 'From Guinea Pigs to Man: The Development of Haffkine's Anticholera Vaccine', *Journal of the History of Medicine and Allied Sciences*, 47 (1992), 271.

68 Mark Harrison, *Disease and the Modern World, 1500 to the Present Day* (Cambridge: Polity, 2004), p. 129.

69 Pratik Chakrabarti, *Bacteriology in British India: Laboratory Medicine and the Tropics* (Rochester: University of Rochester Press, 2012), p. 52.

70 Michael Worboys, *Spreading Germs: Disease Theories and Medical Practice in Britain, 1865–1900* (Cambridge: Cambridge University Press, 2000); see also his article 'Was there a Bacteriological Revolution in Late Nineteenth-Century Medicine?', *Studies in History and Philosophy of Biology and Biomedical Sciences*, 38(1) (2007), 20–42.

PART II

Caste, class, and cattle

CHAPTER FOUR

Cattle, famines, and the colonial state

In our discussion on livestock until now, we have looked mostly at the nature of the colonial state, while touching briefly upon the reactions of various indigenous sections to government policies. In the present chapter, we will look much more closely at indigenous reactions to government policies, especially in the context of famine relief. These reactions are easier to locate in the case of famines as there is an extensive body of government correspondence, reports, and files on the theme, but more importantly, the relief measures that were organised by the state in the case of famines were more extensive than the measures that were adopted during the times of epizootics. As a result, indigenous reactions against them are easier to examine. Simultaneously, though, this chapter will also look at famine relief policies, and examine the ways in which they were shaped due to the influence of the reigning doctrines of free trade and Malthusianism.

Equally important, this chapter will shift the focus away from the human cost of famines and bring it to bear on the impact of scarcity on the livestock economy of rural India.[1] This is not to belittle the human cost of famines, but an attempt to add another dimension to our understanding of them. Cattle mortality during famines had an obvious impact on rural livelihoods from which it took quite a few years, if not decades, to recover. It is therefore surprising that very few studies of Indian famines have paid adequate attention to an issue that had such a direct bearing on agricultural productivity and economic recovery. The period chosen for this study saw two major famines (1896–7 and 1899–1900), both of which had a unique character as they involved large-scale fodder famines that added to the already severe scarcity conditions.[2] They were also temporally close enough to be virtually indistinguishable and will provide ideal conditions to examine the issues noted above.[3]

Famines and cattle mortality

The severity and uniqueness of the famine in 1896–7 was noted by F. H. S. Merewether, a reporter with Reuters who made a grand tour of the famine districts in Northern and Western India. Starting his tour in the Satara district of Bombay presidency, he was disappointed at not being immediately presented with 'the horrors of the Indian famine' that his British public expected him to serve up.[4] His patience was, however, soon rewarded so fulsomely that his initial curiosity gave way to a sense of fatigue and distress. The death of human beings caused him the greatest consternation, but he also noted the striking loss of livestock in most of the areas he visited. Writing about his visit to Hissar he described how, on his way out of the district courthouse, he saw 'frameworks of cattle in the wayside…burrowing in the ground, like pigs, to get at roots'.[5]

This was indeed a scene that one was most likely to encounter upon entering most famine-affected districts. In fact, cattle mortality was significantly great even during famines that were not particularly known for scarcity of fodder. An official noted in the context of the famine in Orissa in 1866, for example, that:

" THE LAST OF THE HERD "

THE FAMINE IN INDIA—SCENES IN THE BELLARY DISTRICT, MADRAS PRESIDENCY

Figure 3 Sketch depicting the famine in Bellary district

[78]

The cattle are mere moving skeletons; [I have] seen wretched beings, with hardly a rag on them, eating the fruit of the prickly-pear and berries from trees; every night hundreds of poor wretches skulk about the streets of Caroor picking up what wretched garbage they will collect.[6]

The impact of famines on cattle was also, quite often, depicted visually. For instance, Figure 3, published in *The Graphic* of 6 October 1877, showed the plight of both men and their cattle during these calamities.

These impressionistic evidences can be corroborated using statistical data. Though no overall figures for the total cattle mortality during these famines are available, certain indicative figures allow us to grasp the scale of devastation. Berar, for example, lost more than half-a-million heads of cattle in the famine of 1899–1900,[7] and this is matched by equally striking examples of mortality from other regions. Officials noted that certain regions, such as the Radhanpur estate in Western India, experienced almost a complete decimation of livestock.[8] Generally speaking, however, most regions that were affected by the fodder famine lost between one-third and half of their most valuable cattle.[9] This is illustrated in Table 1, which shows the proportion of deaths among plough cattle in the Delhi region during the famine of 1899–1900.

Table 1 Mortality among plough cattle, Delhi (1899–1900)

Districts	Number of deaths	Percentage of the total number before commencement of the famine
Gurgaon	176,000	41
Karnal	154,360	21
Delhi	47,876	33
Shahpur	66,216	41
Gujrat	100,144	25
Hissar	192,449	43

These figures would jump substantially if we were to discuss overall mortality, as it was common knowledge that, while plough cattle were kept alive at huge costs to the cultivator, other less useful cattle were either sold off or allowed to perish and die. Indeed scholars have often talked about how, during these famines, 'cattle ate cattle' – in other words the absolute necessity of preserving valuable stock meant that their survival had to be funded by selling off the less useful cattle.[10]

One of the surest indicators of overall cattle mortality was the figure for hide export, which registered a sharp increase during famine years. Colonial officials noted that Chamars and other 'menial castes' benefited greatly from the overabundance of cattle during famines, as it allowed them to obtain both meat and leather in prodigious quantities.[11] From their hands the raw hide travelled to factories and subsequently into the export channels, and this trade network showed an astonishing growth during the second half of the nineteenth century. From being valued at Rs. 5 million in 1859, the export trade in hides and skins swelled to reach the figure of nearly Rs. 115 million in 1901, an increase that was remarkable by any standards.[12] In another, more regional, example exports from five divisions of the Central Provinces nearly quadrupled within the space of a single year between 1898 and 1899. This was quite obviously due to the intensification of the famine during the latter year.[13] Examples of this kind could be multiplied, and these computations based on leather exports were considered more trustworthy than the figures for cattle mortality returned by village officials, who were considered to be inefficient, lazy, and corrupt.[14]

Mortality on this scale was bound to leave a serious dent on the economy, and for the cultivator 'there were few misfortunes so difficult to contend against as loss of cattle'. It not only affected the current economic situation but was also 'destructive of hopes for the future'.[15] In fact, to officials steeped in Malthusian doctrines the loss of cattle appeared to be a bigger blow than the loss of human life. A report on famines made a classic Malthusian statement when it noted that:

> In its influence on agriculture, [cattle mortality] is perhaps more serious and lasting evil than the loss of population. As a rule, those who die of hunger must be old or helpless, whereas the able-bodied and useful escape. But if the cattle perish, cultivation is almost impossible.[16]

Indeed, cultivators who had lost a majority of their plough cattle found it exceedingly difficult to re-attain pre-famine productivity levels.[17] The optimum ratio between plough and cattle was one yoke for every 5–6 acres of land, and in the years following a famine it was sometimes difficult to bring more than one-quarter of the land under cultivation.[18] Those who could still muster some funds attempted to meet the deficit by hiring cattle at very high rates – sometimes for as much as Rs. 2 per cattle per day.[19] Dealers made the most of this situation by driving their herds through the affected districts, renting them out wherever a demand for them existed. Hiring was preferred not just by the poorer cultivators but also by the more affluent ones, who found it difficult to find good quality cattle on the market even though they were willing to offer inflated prices for them. The Famine Charitable Relief Committee also found this to be the case when it tried to procure cattle for distribution among the poorer ryots.[20] In fact, realising the fact that cattle was an extremely prized commodity in times of scarcity, the Committee decided to distribute all its available stock on short-term loans rather than on a permanent basis. This allowed it to help a larger number of cultivators, and also ensured that the cattle did not immediately pass out of the hands of debt-ridden peasants.[21]

One of the more desperate measures that the peasant adopted in order to emerge out of this dire situation was to draw the plough using his own or his family's labour. Also, many smallholders who had become landless due to the famine tried to earn some livelihood by pulling small hand-drawn carts, and these carts acted as replacements for bullock carts for many years following the famine.[22] Such scenes evoked a sense of pathos within colonial onlookers, some of whom admitted that it was 'painful in the extreme to see men, women, and children dragging, like beasts of burden, heavy loads through miry roads';[23] however, all that could be done in the absence of the necessary commitment and funds was to circulate advisory circulars and notices, one of which contained detailed instructions and diagrams for developing a new lighter plough which could be more easily drawn by hand.[24] Such government publications were almost an admission of official inability or reluctance to alleviate the situation.

All this meant that recovery from fodder famines was often a very long-drawn-out process. In the specific context of the two famines we are looking at, the process of recovery was slowed down even further due to the impact of the plague epidemic during these years.[25] The combined effect of all this was extremely severe, and led to long-term changes such as a switch in the cropping patterns. Due to the lack of cattle, cultivators preferred to grow less labour-intensive subsistence crops such as *jowar* while avoiding crops such as wheat which required numerous ploughings.[26] Not only this, cattle mortalities also had a significant impact on the pattern of wealth distribution, with those losing most of their cattle getting 'locked into a subordinate position', while those who had sufficient resources to maintain their cattle stock through the period of famine further strengthened their competitive position within the local economy.[27]

Cattle, famine relief, and the Raj

Combating or reversing the full impact of such famines would have required a huge financial and administrative commitment, and the state was reluctant to do so especially after the financially ruinous experience of the 1874 famine in Bengal, when an unprecedented Rs. 67.5 million was spent on relief.[28] Also, the scale of disasters was quite often so huge that, even if the state had opened its coffers generously, it would still have been difficult to undo the full effects of the famine. For instance, if we estimate the average district-wide loss of cattle during our period at a modest 15,000 heads, replacing these within a single district would have cost nearly Rs. 250,000.[29] However, the state's evident reluctance to intervene was not fuelled by a sense of helplessness. With respect to the issue of protection of livestock, at least, the state justified its relative inactivity using the threefold logic of free trade, Malthusianism, and financial prudence. This section will examine the practical fallouts of these arguments while looking, in particular, at certain key measures such as the construction of cattle camps, distribution of grass/fodder, and other provisions such as forest-grazing and *tacavi* loans.[30]

The first response of the state to any news of a fodder famine was, more often than not, to open up the local forest areas to cattle – this was seen as a quick redressal of the problem at very little financial outlay and was therefore preferred over other measures.[31] The policy was first discussed and implemented in the 1880s, and by the end of the century it had become the first line of defence against cattle losses.[32] Officials soon realised, though, that the response to this was not as overwhelming as they would have expected, and this was put down to inadequate advertising and to the 'inherently suspicious' or 'irrational' temperament of peasants. Various incentives were therefore devised to induce greater acceptance of the plan, including reducing grazing fees and subsidising the cost of transporting cattle by train to the forests, but they did not appear to have any great impact.[33] In districts like Hissar, which bore the full brunt of the two famines, an extremely large proportion of the cattle stock perished despite the policy of open forests.[34] Part of the reason behind this was the ambivalence of local officials towards this directive, with many of them showing great reluctance to allow free access to the forests for weak, undernourished, or disease-susceptible cattle. A district official expressed the opinion of many of his colleagues when he 'strongly objected to [forests] being opened to promiscuous grazing by all cattle during [the] famine year'.[35] Together with the divisional commissioner, he successfully managed to preserve forest areas for the 'really valuable plough cattle'. Similar discretionary powers were exerted by officials in other districts to prevent the entry of cattle belonging to poorer cultivators.

This reluctance to provide for the weaker cattle was, in fact, the most striking feature of relief policies, and it was nowhere as evident as in the case of cattle camps which absolutely refused to admit them under any circumstance. Contrary to the case with relief camps for humans, where even a colonial regime was forced to demonstrate

its benevolent intentions, it was much easier to ignore the interests of the poorest cultivators in the case of cattle camps. Officials
could insist much more strongly on the need to run cattle camps
on 'scientific principles', which meant that weaker animals had to
be carefully 'weeded out' before admitting the more useful ones; in
fact, on occasion experts were appointed to regulate admissions on
the basis of criteria such as breed, age, and health.[36] Such indifference
towards the fate of weaker cattle had, for long, been the basic premise
of relief policies, and is reflected clearly in an official statement made
in 1877 which noted rather coldly that 'such animals must take their
chance; they are of no use or value, and would only consume the [avail-
able] grazing'.[37] These sentiments were informed to a large extent by
Malthusian principles, so that the loss of such cattle was seen not
only as unavoidable but also, to some extent, desirable.[38] As a result,
officials felt extremely exasperated with 'native philanthropists', who
stubbornly continued their practice of feeding and protecting all kinds
of cattle, thus obstructing the course of 'natural laws'. This remarkable
failure to take rational decisions was once again attributed to 'religious
scruples' and a certain peculiar imperviousness to the call of reason.[39]

These Malthusian impulses were bolstered to a large extent by
the tenet of financial prudence, so that even when cattle camps were
created, the aim was to keep their expenses to a bare minimum. Costs
were recovered using a variety of strategies, including private chari-
ties, sale of cattle, and admission fees. For example, though nine
camps were established in the Bombay presidency during the famine
of 1899–1900 at the total cost of Rs. 1,54,120, nearly 75 per cent of
these expenses were recovered using the above-mentioned strategies.[40]
Despite these recoveries, the expenses involved were considered to be
too prohibitive for a fully-fledged reliance on relief camps. An official
report in fact noted in 1897 that the policy had already been abandoned
as 'utterly impracticable'. The fact that it was brought back again on a
limited scale in 1899 points towards the severity of the fodder crisis in
this year.[41] However, looking at the short and inconsistent life of this
policy, it is quite clear that cattle camps never really won a significant
degree of favour within administrative circles. In fact, whenever the
relative efficacy of camps and forest-grazing was debated, the latter
won comprehensively, and the clinching argument was often based on
financial and budgetary calculations.[42]

These financial arguments derived great strength from the doctrine of
free trade, which had formed the bedrock of relief policies for a long time.
Even before the first instance of modern famine relief policies occurred
in 1837–8,[43] free trade had always been cited as the reason behind
official reluctance to intervene – a reluctance that became unshakably

entrenched by the time Lord Lytton issued his 'semi-theological orders' prohibiting any reduction in the price of food'.[44] Lytton's pronouncements were also noteworthy for combining non-intervention with a unique aversion to 'cheap sentiment'. He accused his British critics of indulging in 'humanitarian hysterics', and rather acerbically invited them to foot the bill if they wanted to save Indian lives.[45] True to his resolve to encourage fiscal economy, he despatched Richard Temple to Madras during the famine of 1876–7 with the brief to reduce the cost of relief measures, and this was achieved with great success and with little regard for the condition of the suffering populace.[46] Temple, the architect of liberal relief policies in 1874, quickly swung to the other extreme just two years later in a bid to salvage his damaged reputation. The most significant legacy of his new-found faith in the virtues of financial judiciousness was the 'Temple wage' which, as Mike Davis notes, 'provided less sustenance for hard labour than the infamous Buchenwald concentration camp'.[47]

If relief for humans was affected to such an extent by the tenets of free trade and financial prudence, cattle relief was quite understandably affected by them to a far greater extent. This was reflected clearly in the policy of distribution of pressed grass, which was a subject that led to much introspection and debate among officials. This measure was introduced for the first time on a limited scale in India in 1876, when it was declared to be a complete failure.[48] However, it was reintroduced in a modified form in the early 1890s, by when many advances had already taken place in pressing, transporting, and preserving grass. This included the relatively new technique of 'ensilage', which allowed the preservation of green fodder for long periods.[49] Such methods were initially used for military purposes – more specifically to feed the cavalry during times of war – but were also applied on an experimental basis in India during periods of scarcity in the 1890s.

On the face of it, the policy of distributing fodder stood in stark contrast to the existing consensus around the virtues of non-intervention and free trade. However, its implementation was made possible only due to the notion that it might be cheaper to take the fodder to the cattle rather than the other way round.[50] After all, moving cattle to distant forests could also prove to be very expensive, especially when railway companies had to be paid heavy subsidies for transferring them.[51] Also, it must be mentioned here that fodder was never distributed free of cost – the aim was always to recover at least the expenses incurred in cutting, pressing and transferring it. The government also attempted to further reduce its responsibilities by inviting private traders to buy fodder from them and resell it to cultivators at market prices.[52] It is quite another matter altogether that there were not too many takers for this offer, and private dealers, in fact, turned around and offered their own fodder stocks to the government at reduced prices.[53] The reality was that, though the need for fodder was felt severely, famines also drastically reduced the purchasing power of poorer cultivators, thus effectively reducing the demand for fodder and other necessities.[54] This is a clear example of how market forces became so skewed in scarcity conditions that the 'laws' of supply and demand ceased to function normally.[55] The official report on the famine of 1866 in Orissa made a very significant remark in this connection when it observed that 'all questions of interfering with private trade are set to rest with the simple fact that there was at this time none to interfere with'.[56] Perhaps the argument of non-interference and free trade was, in some cases at least, a ruse to avoid further expenditure on famine relief. An official made an insinuation to this effect in 1899 when he noted that:

> The importation of grass by government is said to be interference with private trade and therefore as unjustifiable as would be importation of grain. The argument would have more force if there existed an organized trade in grass in touch with the great body of consumers. As a matter of fact there were no grass merchants except for the supply of the townspeople, and it was pretty certain that none would spring up.[57]

To the government's credit, it was slightly more amenable to the policy of importing grass during the extreme fodder scarcity of 1899–1900, despite encountering stiff opposition from proponents of the non-interference doctrine. During the famine of 1896–7, for example, the total expenditure on fodder in the province of Bombay was only Rs. 216,000, whereas just two years later it increased nearly fivefold to reach the figure of more than Rs. 1.1 million.[58] However, even these seemingly large sums proved to be woefully inadequate in addressing the scale on which the problem of fodder scarcity was faced. In fact, the total stock of fodder collected under the scheme in 1899–1900 could only feed 40,000 bullocks for a period of two months, and this was clearly only a very small proportion of the total requirements.[59] What is more, a sizeable portion of this stock went unused, as the poorest cultivators were unable to buy fodder even at reduced prices. The colonial government had, quite obviously, targeted this policy at the most prosperous section, and it was stubborn in its refusal to indulge in anything that could be remotely construed as 'imprudent charity', even if it meant unused or wasted resources.

The only truly charitable measures that the government allowed were, in fact, implemented by the Indian Charitable Relief Fund, but this fund was only semi-official in nature, though it was managed at the provincial level by government officials.[60] The fund targeted the 'poorest classes' and made the largest number of grants towards the purchase of seeds and cattle.[61] Crucially, donations were made in perpetuity, and no interest or fee was expected in return. Such magnanimity was completely unexpected, especially as the government had otherwise displayed great unwillingness in making free grants towards agricultural recovery. This is reflected in the circulation of numerous rumours about the 'real' motivation behind these grants, one of which conjectured that the Amir of Kabul was planning to invade India and the government was anxious to turn public opinion in its own favour. Another rumour had it that a rich Bombay merchant and his entire family had succumbed to the plague, and the government had decided to donate his property towards public charity.[62] Though a sense of surprise at government generosity is quite discernible in such rumours, this surprise was soon to be diluted by the realisation that it was extremely difficult to benefit from such charitable policies. Those who tried to make their way into the list of potential recipients found this to be an extremely difficult process. The screening process was extremely long, and officials were advised that they 'must not be unduly hurried and must [allow] plenty of time to decide who were the persons best entitled to receive gifts from the charitable fund'.[63] Additionally, the total amount disbursed through the fund was quite meagre, and could hardly be expected to leave any substantial mark on a famine-stricken landscape.[64]

Much more substantial funds were distributed by the government in the form of *tacavi* loans, the biggest share of which went towards purchase of seeds and cattle. These loans were institutionalised after the passing of two government acts: the Land Improvement Act of 1883, and the Agriculturists Loans Act of 1884. Though the practice of granting loans was started immediately afterwards, it was not till the fag end of the century that any significant amount of loans was disbursed under these schemes. In 1900–1, for instance, *tacavi* loans worth nearly Rs. 10 million were made, which was nearly twelve times the total volume of lending in 1891–2.[65] What was peculiar about these loans was the fact that they were targeted quite unabashedly at the more prosperous sections, and were advanced only after ascertaining the ability of the cultivator to return the full amount within a stipulated period. Such was the consensus against propping up the 'lazy, idle, unproductive classes' that officials not only reserved these loans exclusively for those with existing assets, but also spoke in favour of levying an interest on top in order to further weed out undesirable elements.[66] The overall official attitude towards these loans is reflected in the proud declaration made in 1912 by the Collector of

Ahmedabad, who noted that 'not a pie was given for "maintenance". This year the *tacavi* was taken in the true sense of the word, viz., a loan which supports the industrious, not the idle, raiyat.'[67] Indeed, these industrious or prosperous classes were seen as being more likely to return borrowed money, as it was supposed to be 'Imaan Ki Baat' (a matter of personal honour) for them.[68]

Famine relief policy was, in fact, quite frequently informed by colonial deference to the question of honour of the 'respectable classes'. Georgina Brewis notes that doles of food or money were sometimes secretly delivered by volunteers of the Famine Charitable Relief Fund to members of the 'respectable classes', as they showed reluctance in presenting themselves at the relief camps. In some cases they also received 'a more liberal allowance' than the labouring classes, while *purdanashin* women received special consideration from officials.[69] Such preferential treatment was even more clearly evident in the case of relief for cattle, where the state refused outrightly to 'waste' its precious funds on weak and 'useless' cattle – most of which quite obviously belonged to the poorest cultivators. This holds true for all government measures that we have examined in this section, be it the case of cattle camps, grass distribution, forest grazing, or *tacavi* loans. Even in those cases where cattle were considered worthy of protection, the government was adamant in its resolve to not indulge in old-fashioned charity. This meant that often the relatively prosperous cattle owners also found themselves unable to avail of government schemes during seasons of extreme scarcity, as these schemes invariably demanded considerable expenses on the part of the beneficiaries. One major fallout of this was a great deal of dependence on non-official sources of charity, which riled officials no end as they saw such charitable donations as indiscriminate alms-giving and an unacceptable wastage of limited resources. However, there was very little the state could do to control this, as it was part of the overall coping strategy adopted by indigenous sections in the absence of adequate government relief. The next section will focus on these coping strategies and will also examine the reasons behind the lukewarm response to government relief policies.

Famine relief and the 'irrational peasant'

These coping strategies, we will argue, were based on a careful appraisal of all available options, and took into account past experiences of famines. In this sense, they were well-considered decisions and were not simply knee-jerk reactions against official dictates. However, for officials involved in famine relief, indigenous responses to these disasters appeared illogical and even counter-productive. Officials often argued that peasants were incapable of comprehending their own situation, as a result of which they failed to take advantage of government schemes and measures. How else, asked officials, could one explain the fact that *tacavi* loans went unused, while peasants continued to borrow from merchants and moneylenders at ruinous rates?[70] How could one explain the reluctance to send cattle to government forests, even though the fee charged was minimal and the cost of railway tickets heavily subsidised? How could one explain the lukewarm response of the relatively prosperous peasants, who could afford the small costs that were involved? Though these responses to colonial policies and to the threat of famines in general appeared perplexing to colonial officials, we will argue that they could be explained using mundane, practical, or economic interpretations.[71]

This comes across most clearly in case of *tacavi* loans. Though officials were perplexed at the 'native' reluctance to take advantage of this scheme, this reluctance appears more than a little justified if one digs below the surface. To begin with, the availability of these loans was advertised poorly by officials, and in those cases where a substantial number of applications were received, they were followed by a 'minute and troublesome inquiry' into the suitability of the applicant.[72] A sizeable amount of security – reaching up to nearly one-quarter of the total amount borrowed – was also demanded, while repayments had to be made within three years or slightly more. A report on the famine of 1899–1900 noted in this connection that 'people should clearly understand that punctual and early repayment of the loans will be insisted upon, and no confusion must be allowed between the charitable grants and *tacavi* loans'.[73] Bearing these points in mind, one is inclined to agree with the conclusion reached by David Hall-Matthews, that *tacavi* was in fact 'as mean in principle as the worse marwari bond, and much less readily given'.[74] It is not surprising at all, therefore, to find that peasants preferred to obtain loans from those with far less coercive power than the colonial state.

Peasants' reluctance to take advantage of other relief measures can also be explained in a similar way. With respect to the policy of sending cattle to forests for grazing – which appeared, at first sight, to be a perfectly legitimate response to fodder scarcity – the unwillingness arose out of a history of disastrous experiences in the past. It was common knowledge among cattle owners that fodder had to be selected with great care and that indiscriminate feeding could prove counter-productive and cause illness and mortality. For example, when 60,000 cattle were taken from Bijapur to forests in the western hilly portions of Dharwar, 42,000 of them failed to return, and this was primarily due to the fact that they overfed on fodder that they were not used to.[75] In fact, not only cattle but also their owners were susceptible to mortality in unknown terrains due to the combined effect of disease, fatigue and exposure to unfamiliar climates.[76] Understandably, these experiences instilled fear of unfamiliar fodder and terrains, and this was also responsible for the outright rejection of government's suggestion that fodder substitutes such as prickly pear should be used during famines.[77] Forest-grazing was accepted much more readily where it did not entail inordinately long treks into unfamiliar regions. It was also more acceptable for cattle owners who were used to the practice of transferring cattle to regions with abundant pastures during hot summer months.[78] The response to the measure was therefore a finely calibrated one, based not just on the reality of fodder scarcity but also on past experiences and a careful calculation of possible benefits. Far from being irrational, peasants were quite alive to the reality of their own situation and weighed every decision carefully before acting on them. Christopher Hill also makes a similar observation in his study of famine migration and resettlement in Bihar, noting that 'the rational peasant in India explored and adapted his options in conformity with his own environment'. The choices the peasant exercised have, therefore, to be seen in this light.[79]

This is also clear in case of the policy of fodder distribution, which did not evoke the kind of exuberant response that was expected by officials. In this case, however, the response could be understood much more easily, and it was conditioned to a large extent by official stubbornness on the issue of prices. A clear directive had been issued on this subject, and officials were left in no doubt that 'when adequate price was not achieved at the auction for bales of grass, they were [to be] reheld till adequate price, covering manufacturing and transport expenses, were covered'.[80] Such was the official firmness in this regard that no compromise was ever made despite regular destruction of stored grass through fire outbreaks at government depots. It is clear that this strong unwillingness to lower prices was the only obstacle preventing a quick sale of stock – in the few instances where prices were lowered, it had such a 'magical effect' that 'crowds gathered and grass was bought immediately'.[81] Quite obviously, then, there was no inherent and inexplicable antipathy towards government measures; rather, the response was determined by much more practical and mundane issues of prices and future prospects. An official expressed this fact rather clearly when he noted with regards to the fodder scheme that 'ryots who stood in need of fodder were too poor to buy, whereas those who could afford to buy had a small stock of fodder in their backyards'.[82]

Though these explanations pointed towards the reasons behind the reluctance to accept government measures, officials continued to see peasant responses as an outcome of their inherently irrational temperament. This, according to them, was reflected clearly in their inordinate attachment to cattle due to the depth of religious sentiments. Officials noted frequently, and with great amazement, that 'the Hindoo peasant [preferred to] perish by hunger beside his fat bullock'.[83] Similar conjectures about supposed prejudices have also been made by scholars writing on the subject, with Simoons making the observation that men were compelled, as a result, 'to overlook food that are abundant locally and are of a high nutritive value, and to use other scarcer foods of less value'.[84] While these references to the practice of beef-eating might be partly true for high-caste Hindus and for those aspiring towards greater Sanskritization, such overemphasis on religious questions serves to eclipse the purely economic significance of cattle ownership.[85] Put simply, cows or bullocks were assets that set a smallholder or share-cropper apart from a landless labourer. As mentioned earlier, they also conferred a certain respectability upon the owner, which he was obviously quite reluctant to lose. Sarat Chandra's moving story about a poor peasant's struggle to keep his family and his bullock alive through a season of extreme drought brings this out clearly, though it focuses to a greater extent on the strong emotional attachment between man and beast.[86] The story inevitably ends with the tragic death of Mahesh (the bullock) and with Gafoor's reluctant departure for the city, as he could no longer hope to sustain his former position in the village. Interspersed throughout the story are numerous depictions of Gafoor's desperate attempts to keep Mahesh alive – feeding him straw pulled out of the roof of his hut, begging the zamindar and the village priest for fodder, and even feeding him his own meagre meals. These literary references are substantiated by official sources, some of which talk directly about the massive efforts that were made towards ensuring the survival of cattle. The Famine Commission of 1901, for example, observed that:

> In their efforts to save their cattle the Gujarat agriculturists expended all their savings, themselves enduring great privations; they sold their jewels and even the doors and rafters of their houses, we were told, in order to purchase fodder. Their efforts failed, their cattle died, and with their cattle all their accumulated wealth disappeared.[87]

These were indeed desperate measures, but they were no doubt needed during desperate times. Contrary to official assertions about the numerous unclaimed government benefits, peasants were forced to adopt these measures due to a lack of credible policies that aimed

[90]

to alleviate their misery. As a result, the cultivator had no option but to try everything within his powers to ensure the survival of his cattle, even if it meant migration to distant lands. In discussing the phenomenon of famine migration, the Famine Commission of 1880 made a distinction between various kinds of migration during periods of scarcity: migration with cattle in search of pasture; migration to find food and employment; and the 'aimless wandering' of the destitute.[88] The last two choices were arguably made in relatively more extreme situations, after assets, property and hope for future recovery had been lost.[89] Movement for the sake of cattle was, in this sense, a more hopeful case of migration, as it was aimed at ensuring the maintenance of assets and social position. These hopes, however, were not justified in most cases as the consequences of migration were often quite disheartening. We have already seen the outcome of cattle migration to government forest reserves, but even other non-official forms of migration had little positive impact. This was primarily because fodder scarcity, at least between 1896 and 1901, was quite widespread and the situation was only marginally different in neighbouring regions. In such a scenario there was but little choice other than to let the cattle feed on 'famine fodder' – on leaves from mango, neem, and other trees, on the roots of the *hariali* grass that were painstakingly dug out, on jowar stalks which often led to poisoning, and so on.[90] These too, an official noted, were soon 'stripped clean as though a flight of locusts had passed over them'.[91]

Given such a context, and given the lack of government support, the only reliable method of obtaining sustenance for cattle was through 'native' charity and munificence. This was much more readily available than government relief, did not involve a series of 'tests' or screenings to determine eligibility, and did not require trekking over very long distances. In fact some amount of charitable relief was available from the village zamindar himself, who was thought to have been bound by a 'moral contract' to rescue his ryots during times of distress.[92] Scholars like Scarlett Epstein have in fact gone to the extent of arguing that the *raison d'être* for the 'jajmani system' in the South Asian villages was that it provided a kind of insurance for artisans during times of scarcity or famine.[93] However, the significance of relief through this channel should not be exaggerated, as famines also seriously depleted the zamindar's coffers and made him alive to the virtues of hoarding and storing valuable resources. In this sense the mahajan, who was able to make some speculative gains during conditions of scarcity, was in the best position to dole out charity, and peasants thronged the nearest town or city with their cattle in order to benefit from his largesse.[94] Officials noted that mahajans were providing an 'excellent service' by importing thousands of maunds of pressed fodder and distributing them freely and without restrictions.[95] In certain cases the beneficiaries were expected to pay for the fodder at reasonable rates, but this could be stalled till such a time as prosperity and good times returned to the villages.[96] Private cattle camps were also opened in several towns by mahajan bodies through individual subscriptions. The relief provided through these means was so widespread and unconditional that officials often complained of wasteful extravagance and indiscriminate alms-giving. Every word of praise about the mahajans' charitable acts was immediately followed by sharp remarks about the 'native tendency' to treat all kinds of cattle on the same scale, and an official noted in despair that 'the chief difficulty is to persuade [well-to-do Hindus of the town] to exclude old and worthless stock. The possibility of such action on any considerable scale seems doubtful'.[97]

Similar criticisms were also made of pinjrapoles, which were animal sanctuaries set up mostly by wealthy individuals, but sometimes also at the behest of organisations such as the Society of Prevention of Cruelty against Animals.[98] Though they functioned differently during normal times, they were effectively turned into cattle camps during famines and provided relief to the 'castaways' from government cattle camps. In a sense official criticism of them was somewhat unjustified, as it was the government itself which, by carefully weeding out 'worthless cattle' from its relief system, forced owners to seek sanctuary in pinjrapoles.[99] During famines the number of weak, undernourished cattle was obviously quite high, and pinjrapoles were understandably swamped with hordes of cattle that had nowhere else to go. In fact, the pinjrapole in Ahmedabad city alone sheltered as many as 21,500 cattle during the famine of 1899–1900, out of which nearly 16,500 perished.[100] Such mortality rates provided further ammunition for those arguing for the elimination of undeserving cattle. Katherine Mayo, though writing in 1927, echoed the general official sentiment about pinjrapoles when she noted after visiting one such institution that '[its] description...need not be inflicted upon the reader's sensibilities. I hope that every animal that I saw in it is safely dead'.[101] Isabel Burton also noted after a similar visit that 'I should think it is far better to put a bullet through their head', though she was quite impressed with the charitable impulses of 'natives'.[102]

Clearly, then, officials were quite dismissive of both 'native' charitable efforts and of the various individual strategies adopted by peasants to keep the livestock alive. At the same time, as we have seen throughout this chapter, they were quite reluctant to invest into cattle relief. In such a scenario, the only possible solution from the official perspective was to wait patiently for the famine to disappear, and this was indeed what some officials advocated openly. A report on the fodder famine in Ajmer-Marwara in 1899–1900 noted, for example, in an extremely fatalistic tone that the famine would eventually 'right itself' if one waited long enough.[103] Though famines did indeed 'right themselves' sooner or later, such an attitude meant that disasters of this kind continued to occur on a frequent basis.

Conclusion

While most scholarly literature has focused on the human cost of famines, this chapter has evaluated their impact on the cattle wealth and livestock of affected regions. This had a direct impact on agricultural productivity which took several years, if not decades, to reach pre-famine levels. Such losses affected the less prosperous cultivators to a greater extent, as they ran the great risk of losing their social and economic position. Ironically, however, it was the livestock owned by these sections which was most rigorously excluded from official relief policies. The inherent inequity of these policies was justified on the basis of the doctrines of Malthusianism, free trade, and non-interference, though the need to minimise relief expenses was, of course, another major determinant.

One point that emerges clearly is the official incomprehension of peasant needs and responses. This is in some ways reminiscent of the manner in which E. P. Thompson described the reaction of authorities towards food riots in Britain. Indignant and astonished, they saw the riots as being 'symptomatic of the "frantic" and distempered humours of people whose brain was inflamed by hunger'.[104] Similar opinions were also expressed by colonial officials in India during famines, when peasants were quite obviously stricken by scarcity and hunger. Yet, as Thompson asks rhetorically a few sentences later, 'were the poor really so silly'?[105] The answer to this is of course in the negative, but this still leaves a much larger issue hanging in the balance: the question of characterising the nature of peasant responses. In other words, could peasant responses be understood within a well-defined framework that gives primacy to certain overriding imperatives or influences? Here, as we noted earlier, we have several choices, ranging from Theodore Schultz's 'rational' peasant who was preoccupied with maximising his profits, to James C. Scott's peasant who was guided by a subsistence ethic.

Between these two ends, the findings of this chapter incline us to favour Scott's conclusions. Scott's hypothesis is based on a study of the poorest class of peasants, who formed a substantial chunk of the population in countries like India. Eking out an existence in the most difficult circumstances, these sections were heavily in debt and were preoccupied with the question of stability and survival. This becomes especially evident while carrying out a study of famines in India. The notion of profits and margins was, in many cases, of secondary importance to famine-stricken peasants in the subcontinent as they were much more concerned with surviving from one famine to the next. Also, since these disasters had become a regular visitor to the countryside, they had to be meticulously planned for, and strategies had to be developed to ensure the survival of the entire household.[106]

This frequent experience of dealing with famines led to a preference for certain conventional or familiar relief strategies over others, and peasant responses have to be understood within this framework rather than by referring to an abstract 'market-driven rationality' or to their 'inherently suspicious character'.[107] We have therefore avoided the temptation to characterise peasant responses as 'rational' or otherwise; wherever the term 'rational' has been used, it is intended to refer to a certain practical approach towards dealing with crisis situations. Peasants did not act at the spur of the moment, without premeditation or discussion. In fact, as Ranajit Guha shows, even in situations of insurgency when tempers were obviously running high, the preparation was marked by 'much temporization and weighing of pros and cons', which could go on for weeks and even months.[108] This was true even for famine situations: the failure of famine relief policies was less a knee-jerk or spontaneous reaction against official dictates, and more the outcome of a deliberate decision-making process that took into account various factors and conditions.

Notes

1 A substantial amount of historical work has been done on the question of the human cost of famines in India. Noteworthy among these are B. M. Bhatia, *Famines in India: A Study in Some Aspects of the Economic History of India, 1860–1965* (London: Asia Publishing House, 1967); Michelle Burge McAlpin, *Subject to Famine: Food Crises and Economic Change in Western India, 1860–1920* (Princeton: Princeton University Press, 1983); Tim Dyson (ed.), *India's Historic Demography: Studies in Famine, Disease and Society* (London: Curzon, 1989); David Hall-Matthews, *Peasants, Famine and the State in Colonial Western India* (Hampshire: Palgrave Macmillan, 2005); Sanjay Sharma, *Famine, Philanthropy, and the Colonial State: North India in the Early Nineteenth Century* (Delhi: Oxford University Press, 2001); Mike Davis, *Late Victorian Holocausts: El Nino Famines and the Making of the Third World* (London: Verso, 2001); David Hardiman, 'Usury, Dearth and Famine in Western India', *Past and Present*, 152 (Aug. 1996), 113–56; David Arnold, 'Social Crisis and Epidemic Disease in the Famines of Nineteenth-century India', *Social History of Medicine*, 6 (1993), 385–404; Ira Klein, 'When the Rains Failed: Famine, Relief, and Mortality in British India', *Indian Economic Social History Review*,

21(2) (1984), 185–214; Vinita Damodaran, 'Famine in Bengal: A Comparison of the 1770 Famine in Bengal and the 1897 Famine in Chotanagpur', *Medieval History Journal*, 10(1 and 2) (2007), 143–81; Georgina Brewis, 'Fill Full the Mouth of Famine: Voluntary Action in Famine Relief in India 1896–1901', *Modern Asian Studies*, 44(4) (2010), 887–918.

2 It was noted that 'the great feature that distinguishes this [1899–1900] famine from all which have preceded it is the enormous destruction of cattle which has gone side by side with the failure of the crops – the destruction, in other words, of the capital and much of the material wealth of the cultivating classes'. *Report of the Central Executive Committee, Indian Famine Charitable Relief Fund, 1900* (Calcutta: Government Press, 1901), p. 37.

3 The report of the Indian Famine Charitable Committee noted that 'the years in which there has been widespread distress through a failure of the seasonal rains have been generally separated by considerable intervals, but the close of the nineteenth century has been marked by one great famine being succeeded by another and greater one within a short span'. *Report of the Indian Famine Charitable Relief Fund, 1900*, p. 1. The half-decade when these two famines occurred has been called the 'famine era'.

4 *A Tour through Famine Districts in India* (London: A. D. Innes, 1898), p. 20.

5 *Tour through Famine Districts in India*, p. 234.

6 Parliamentary Papers: Papers and Correspondence relative to the Famine in Bengal and Orissa, Including the Report of the Famine Commission and the Minutes of the Lieutenant Governor of Bengal and the Governor General in India (House of Commons, 31 May 1867), p. 35.

7 Laxman Satya, *Ecology, Colonialism and Cattle: Central India in the Nineteenth Century* (Delhi: Oxford University Press, 2004), p. 127.

8 APAC, R/673(m)/44, p. 62.

9 For example, Palanpur lost nearly 79 per cent of its cattle. APAC, R/2/673(m)/44, p. 82.

10 Alula Pankhurst, *Resettlement and Famine in Ethiopia: The Villagers' Experience* (Manchester: Manchester University Press, 1992), p. 34.

11 *The Punjab Famine of 1899–1900*, vol. I, p. 12. Chamars had almost become synonymous with leather-work by the end of the nineteenth century, and official alleged that much of the cattle mortality during famines and epizootics was in fact caused by Chamar cattle poisoners who would stoop to any level to obtain leather. We will discuss this in detail in Chapter 6.

12 Dharma Kumar and Tapan Raychaudhuri (eds.), *Cambridge Economic History of India, vol. II, c.1757–c.1970* (Cambridge: Cambridge University Press, 1983), pp. 439–40.

13 These included Nagpur, Nerbudda, Nimar, Jubbulpore, and Chattisgarh: *Report on the Famine in the Central Provinces in 1899–1900*, vol. I (Nagpur: Secretariat Press, 1901), p. 31.

14 A report noted in this connection that 'the district reports contain figures of cattle mortality, for the most part obtained from special returns made by Patwaris. Even if carefully compiled these returns can hardly ever be accurate.' *Report on the Famine in the Central Provinces in 1899–1900*, vol. I, p. 30.

15 J. C. Geddes, *Administrative Experience Recorded in Former Famines: Extracts from Official Papers Containing Instructions for Dealing with Famine* (Calcutta: Bengal Secretariat Press, 1874), p. 230.

16 Geddes, *Administrative Experience Recorded in Former Famines*, p. 350. Another official noted that 'a loss that is likely to fall more heavily on the farmers than even the temporary loss of manual labour, is the loss by death of their plough and well bullocks'. Parliamentary Papers: *Report of Colonel Baird Smith to the Indian government, dated 8 May 1861, on the Commercial Condition of the North West Province of India; and Report of the Same Officer to the Indian Government on the Recent Famine in the Same Province* (London: George Edward Eyre and William Spottiswoode, 1862), p. 39.

17 It was recognised as early as 1792 that 'the whole effect of the famine is not considered as confined to that alone but as there has evidently been a prodigious loss of inhabitants of cattle the effects of this calamity must be continued to be felt for a succession of years and the revenue necessarily be diminished'. Letter from Anthony Sadlier, Masulipatam, dated 19 November 1792, APAC, F/4/12/738, n. p.

18 *Report of Colonel Baird Smith*, p. 49. Merewether also notes that when he asked someone 'what the villagers would do for plough-cattle?' he replied submissively, 'god knows there weren't any – the land would have to go untilled'. *Tour through Famine Districts*, p. 54.

19 APAC, P/5439, p. 29.

20 It was noted in the report that 'the most difficult part of the work was the supply of cattle. It was obviously impossible to purchase any in the district or in any part of the country which had suffered from the famine.' *Report of the Indian Famine Charitable Relief Fund, 1900*, p. 106.

21 Report of the Central Executive Committee, Indian Famine Charitable Relief Fund, 1897, vol. II (Calcutta: Government Printing, 1898), p. 208.

22 Report of the Indian Famine Charitable Relief Fund, 1900, p. 36.

23 Report of the Indian Famine Charitable Relief Fund, 1900, p. 36.

24 The circular also noted that 'many of your work cattle have died through unavoidable starvation. Many of those that have been kept alive are weak. In many villages you cannot hope to get all the fields prepared by your work cattle in proper season for sowing. If men or women or boys do part of the work ordinarily done by work cattle, you may expect to get most of your fields sown in good time.' In R. C. Wroughton, *Famine in the Bombay Presidency, 1899–1902, vol. II – Appendices* (Bombay: Government Central Press, 1902), p. 174.

25 Tim Dyson, 'On the Demography of South Asian Famines: Part I', *Population Studies*, 45(1) (Mar. 1991), 17.

26 Kumar and Raychaudhuri, Cambridge Economic History of India, p. 75.

27 Gregory Maddox, 'Mtunya: Famine in Central Tanzania, 1917–20', *Journal of African History*, 21 (1990), 181–97.

28 *The Imperial Gazetteer of India: The Indian Empire*, vol. III (Oxford: Clarendon Press, 1907), p. 488. Ira Klein summarises the extraordinary relief efforts during the 1874 famine in the following words: 'A highly interventionist and expensive policy of famine combat was organised. The government purchased half-a-million tons of rice in the Burmese market and took careful measures to distribute it effectively... It built steamers and flat boats, and procured all types of pack animals from as far as the Sutlej. It deployed companies of sappers and miners and a corps of regular troops...At relief works, tasks were relaxed or ignored and sufficient money or grain was allotted to "all comers who were prima facie in want". On the famine-ridden locales over 700,000 were employed on the works, almost a half million received "gratuitous relief daily for six months," and over three million were sold grain cheaply or received loans of money or food.' In 'When the Rains Failed', 193.

29 *Report of Colonel Baird Smith*, p. 49. In fact Colonel Smith also gave examples where it would cost the government nearly 1 million rupees to replace all the cattle in a single district (p. 39).

30 These measures for the protection of cattle had also been enshrined in the Famine Codes. See for example *Famine Code of the North Western Provinces and Oudh*, Revised Edition (Lucknow: Government Press, 1895), pp. viii–ix.

31 Indeed there was a potential to earn some money by opening up forests as owners sending their cattle into them were, in many cases, required to pay a fee even during times of famine.

32 In the North Western Provinces and Oudh, for example, the policy was the subject of a special enquiry in 1885: letter dated 1 August 1890 APAC, P/3906, n. p.

33 Report on the Famine in the Bombay Presidency in 1896–97 (Bombay: Government Central Press, 1897), p. 41.

34 Hissar was one of the most severely affected districts. An estimated 92 per cent of the cattle had died or been transported from Hissar by October 1897, even though

government forests had been opened for free grazing. See Deborah Guz, 'Population Dynamics of Famine in Nineteenth Century Punjab, 1896–7 and 1899–1900', in Dyson, *India's Historic Demography*, p. 200.

35 Report on the Famine in the Bombay Presidency in 1896–97, p. 146.

36 Wroughton, Famine in the Bombay Presidency, vol. II, pp. 164–5.

37 Parliamentary Papers: Copy of Correspondence between the Secretary of State for India and the Government of India on the Subject of Famine in Western and Southern India (London: George Edward Eyre and William Spottiswoode, 1877), p. 10.

38 The Governor-General of the North-Western Provinces and Oudh, for example, regretted the fact that 'a large number so useless animals that are saved from destruction by the customs and religious scruples of the people till removed by the natural process of disease or starvation'. Letter dated 3 October 1885 APAC, P/3906, n. p. Another official noted in the context of the famine of 1897 that '[it] is to a great extent the case that the famine has been productive of a certain amount of good, in getting rid of the more useless of the village stock'. *Further Papers Regarding the Famine and the Relief Operations in India during the Years 1896–97: Correspondence Regarding the Appointment of a Famine Commission* (London: Darling & Son, 1897), p. 57.

39 See for example letter from J. R. Reid, Chief Secretary to the Government of the North Western Provinces and Oudh, Revenue Department, Naini Tal, 3 October 1885, APAC, P/3906, n. p.

40 The receipts were made up of private donations (Rs. 20,613), recoveries (Rs. 50,568) from owners for the upkeep of their cattle, realisations (Rs. 35,875) from sale of cattle and other miscellaneous items. The net cost to government on account of these camps was Rs. 40,527. *Report on the Famine in the Bombay presidency, 1899–1902*, vol. I (Bombay: Government Central Press, 1903), p. 82.

41 B. M. Bhatia notes in this connection that 'this subject [of cattle preservation] had received attention in the formulation of Famine Codes in 1883 and 1893, but its gravity does not appear to have been realized till the famine of 1899–1900 which caused a terrible destruction of cattle in Gujarat, the Central Provinces, Berar, Ajmer and the Punjab.' *Famines in India*, p. 286.

42 For example, the report of the Famine Charitable Relief Fund noted that 'the real cattle camp is the forest reserves. There is no possible substitute.' *Report of the Central Executive Committee, Indian Charitable Relief Fund. 1897, vol. II* (Calcutta: Government Printing, 1898), p. 374.

43 Sanjay Sharma, 'The 1837–38 Famine in U.P.: Some Dimensions of Popular Action', *Indian Economic Social History Review*, 30(3) (1993), 341.

44 Davis, Late Victorian Holocausts, p. 31.

45 Davis, Late Victorian Holocausts, p. 31.

46 Klein, 'When the Rains Failed', 194.

47 Davis, Late Victorian Holocausts, p. 39.

48 A report noted that 'all that was tried [in 1876–7] was to provide a stock of fodder on the main lines of road along which grain had to be carried, and even this comparatively modest endeavour failed, the greater part of the grass supplied never being utilised'. *Report on the Famine in the Bombay Presidency in 1896–97*, p. 39.

49 J. F. Duthie, the director of botanical gardens in North India, noted that 'within the last few years ensilage operations have been extensively undertaken in India, and with so much success, that silage may now be considered as a safe and valuable form of food for cattle'. *The Fodder Grass of Northern India* (Roorkee: Thomason Civil Engineering College Press, 1888), p. vii.

50 APAC, P/5789, p. 7548.

51 *Papers Regarding the Famine and the Relief Operations in India during 1899–1900*, vol. I (London: George Edward Eyre and William Spottiswoode, 1900), p. 372.

52 An official noted in 1899 that 'the grass was offered for sale at a fair price, such as, if possible, will cover all charges, there being no attempt made to exclude dealers, who, on the contrary, were encouraged to take part in the distribution of grass'. APAC, P/5896, p. 655.

53 It was noted during the 1896–7 famine that 'the dealers offered their stacks of grass, at virtually cost prices, because they complained that the heavy cost of railway freight to the famine districts, as well as the uncertainty of sale when the grass landed there, prohibited them from exporting the grass themselves'. APAC, P/5439, p. xlv.

54 This was also true not just for fodder but also for food grains. C. Beadon, *Minutes of Famine in Bengal and Orissa*, 1866, APAC, V/27/830/31, p. 9.

55 However, the fact that private trade did not provide a solution to the problem of scarcity was also attributed to the 'inferior intelligence' of Indians. A comparison in this regard was made with the greater efficiency of British traders. Geddes, *Administrative Experience Recorded in Former Famines*, p. 16.

56 It also went on to note that 'the demand was far more than could be satisfied by any means'. *Report of the Commissioners Appointed to Enquire into the Famine in Bengal and Orissa in 1866*, vol. I (Calcutta: Government Printing, 1867).

57 Famine in the Bombay Presidency, 1899–1902, vol. II, Appendices, p. 168.

58 The total losses incurred in implementing this policy amounted to Rs. 72,000 in 1896–7, whereas in 1899–1900 the loss incurred was Rs. 472,000.

59 This figure has been reached on the assumption that 1,000 pounds of fodder would keep a pair of bullocks alive for a period of twenty days. Parliamentary Papers: *Papers Regarding the Famine and the Relief Operations in India during 1899–1900, vol. I: British Districts* (London: George Edward Eyre and William Spottiswoode, 1900), p. 367.

60 The fund was maintained largely through private donations from Britain and from 'eminent natives'. For more details on this, see Brewis, 'Fill Full the Mouth of Famine', 887–918.

61 Parliamentary Papers: Advances and Gifts to Agriculturists for Seed, Cattle and Subsistence at the End of the Famine (London, 1900), p. 4.

62 Parliamentary Papers: Further Papers Regarding the Famine and the Relief Operations in India during the Years 1896–97, no. V, Resolution on the Administration of Famine Relief in the North Western Provinces and Oudh (London: George Edward Eyre and William Spottiswoode, 1898), p. 59.

63 *The Punjab Famine of 1899–1900*, vol. I (Lahore: Government Press, 1901), p. 34. The process of screening included the following steps: each Patwari prepared a list of cultivators who according to him needed help. This list was checked by the Revenue Inspector on the basis of criteria like degree of destitution, possession of bullocks, duration for which land had been fallow, position of the land, amount of debt incurred, etc. The list was subsequently to be checked and verified by the Tahsildar, who would conduct an enquiry. *Report of the Indian Famine Charitable Relief Fund, 1897*, vol. II, p. 208. The report on the Punjab Famine of 1899–1900 also noted that 'district officers and local committees must not be unduly hurried and must be allowed plenty of time to decide who were the persons best entitled to receive gifts from the charitable fund'. *The Punjab Famine of 1899–1900*, vol. I, p. 33.

64 The total amount of money available to the Charitable Relief Fund in 1896–7 was nearly Rs. 15 million, which was nowhere enough considering the scale of the disaster. *The Imperial Gazetteer of India*, vol. III (Oxford: Clarendon Press, 1907), p. 492. This meant that single districts like Lohardaga (in Bengal) were entitled to, on an average, nearly 25,000 rupees. *Report of the Famine Charitable Relief Fund, 1897*, vol. II, p. 275.

65 Kumar and Raychaudhuri, *Cambridge Economic History of India*, p. 200.

66 For example, an official noted in the context of the famine of 1899–1900 that he was 'very much opposed to free gifts for the purchase of cattle and seed ... these must tend to demoralise the people and induce them to look to government instead of helping themselves'. *The Punjab Famine of 1899–1900*, vol. II (Lahore: Punjab Government Press, 1901), p. 198.

67 Cambridge Economic History of India, vol. II, p. 200.

68 The Punjab Famine of 1899–1900, vol. II, p. 198

69 'Fill Full the Mouth of Famine', 911. The report on the famine of 1899–1900 in the

Punjab also noted that one of the aims of relief policies was 'to [assist] respectable people, and especially their purdanashin women, to struggle though the present crisis'. *The Punjab Famine of 1899–1900*, vol. II, p. 198.

70 Resonating the opinion of officials, Merewether noted that 'the native is nothing if not intensely conservative, and though he does not actively resent the arbitrary measures of the sircar, yet by his masterly inactivity and generic passivity he would defeat the ends of the government, and still continue to deal, as of aforetime, with the local bania, in whose clutches he has been since he assumed the toga virilis, or took over the ancestral homestead.' *Tour through the Famine Districts of India*, p. 36.

71 Some historians working on South Asia have made a similar argument. Rajnarayan Chandravarkar, for example, has shown that many supposedly 'irrational' indigenous responses to state interventions could easily be understood easily if one adopted a more sympathetic perspective. See his *Imperial Power and Popular Politics: Class, Resistance and the State in India, c.1850–1950* (Cambridge University Press, Cambridge, 1988), especially pp. 234–66. A similar argument has also been made by Marvin Harris in the specific context of cattle in India in his article titled 'The Cultural Ecology of India's Sacred Cattle', *Cultural Anthropology*, 33(1) (Feb. 1992), 261–76.

72 Hall-Matthews, Peasants, Famine and the State, p. 117.

73 Report on the Famine in the Central Provinces in 1899–1900, vol. I, p. 117.

74 Hall-Matthews, Peasants, Famine and the State, p. 118.

75 Report on the Famine in the Bombay Presidency in 1896–97, p. 41.

76 *Famine Proceedings, Revenue and Agriculture Department*, APAC, P/5665, p. 8. David Arnold notes that 'this kind of migration strategy was hazardous for man as well as beast'. In 'Social Crisis and Epidemic Disease', 398.

77 The famine commission of 1901 noted that 'though not sufficient as the main article of diet, the leaves [of prickly pear], if carefully prepared and supplemented with oil-cake, bran, straw, pulse, &c., will serve, we understand, to keep cattle alive'. *Report of the Indian Famine Commission, 1901, and Papers Relating Thereto* (London: Darling & Son, 1901), p. 76. See also Bombay Agriculture Department Bulletin no. 14, *Prickly Pear as Fodder for Cattle during Scarcity* (Calcutta: Government Press, 1892).

78 For example, it was the custom for 'the Cattle-owning Bikaneri to emigrate even in ordinary years, as the year's rainfall [was] never sufficient to provide pasturage throughout the next hot season'. They, in fact, had to be discouraged from migrating during famine years as pasturage was not readily available even in the regions to which they usually migrated. *Papers Regarding the Famine and the Relief Operations in India during 1899–1900, vol. II: Native States*, p. 82.

79 'Philosophy and Reality in Riparian South Asia: British Famine Policy and Migration in Colonial North India', *Modern Asian Studies*, 25(2) (1991), 272.

80 APAC, P/5439, p. xl.

81 APAC, P/5439, p. xlv.

82 APAC, P/5440, p. 217.

83 Parliamentary Papers: *East India (Madras and Orissa) Famine*, 4 July 1867, Ordered by the House of Commons (London: George Edward Eyre and William Spottiswoode, July 1867), p. 44.

84 F. J. Simoons, *Eat Not this Flesh* (Madison: University of Wisconsin Press, 1961), p. 3.

85 The term 'Sanskritization' was coined by M. N. Srinivas and referred to the urge to attain higher ritual status by adopting religions practices traditionally associated with upper caste groups. See his *Religion and Society amongst the Coorgs of South India* (Oxford: Clarendon Press, 1952).

86 Sarat Chandra Chatterjee (1876–1938) was and continues to be one of the most popular novelists in Bengali. Sasadhar Sinha notes that Chatterjee 'wrote with a directness of experience and style which contrasts refreshingly with the writings of his literary forbears'. In *The Drought and Other Stories* (Delhi: Sahitya Akademi Press, 2004), p. viii. An English translation of the short story 'Mahesh' can also be found in Sinha's translated edition under the title 'The Drought'.

87 Report of the Indian Famine Commission, 1901, p. 72.
88 *Report of the Indian Famine Commission*, pt I (London: George Edward Eyre and William Spottiswoode, 1880), p. 61.
89 This was certainly the case with respect to finding employment and food at the government relief camps, as there was a great deal of prejudice against them. Bidyut Mohanty notes that the prejudice against them was such that a distinct lower caste called *chhatra-khia*, or those who ate in the relief kitchen, was created and people from all castes were subsumed under this caste. 'Orissa Famine of 1866: Demographic and Economic Consequences', *Economic and Political Weekly*, 28 (1/2) (2–9 Jan. 1993), 93.
90 It was noted that 'in the country the poorer people had for a time kept their cattle existing by digging up the roots of hariali grass, but even this supply had at last failed, and in the neighbourhood of Bijapur was completely exhausted'. Merewether, *Tour through the Famine Districts of India*, p. 46.
91 An official noted that such indiscriminate feeding on tree leaves and jowar stalks could also lead to tainting of milk, 'causing to the human consumer gastric derangements which are apt to prove fatal to children'. *Papers Regarding the Famine and the Relief Operations in India during 1899–1900, vol. II: Native States*, p. 37.
92 In fact the Lieutenant Governor of Bengal himself acknowledged the contribution made by zamindars towards famine relief when he noted in a public speech made in 1866 that 'the duty of relieving individual distress in times of great scarcity is one which devolved on all who enjoy the superfluities of life, and is peculiarly incumbent on zemindars and landed proprietors...I am happy to find that this duty has in many instances not been neglected.' Beadon, *Minutes of the Famine in Bihar and Orissa, 1866*, p. 19.
93 Scarlett Epstein, 'Productive Efficiency and Customary Systems of Rewards in Rural South India', in R. Firth (ed.), *Themes in Economic Anthropology* (London: Tavistock, 1967), pp. 229–52. The 'jajmani system' implies that 'the requirements of the rural population in certain goods and social services were met by a staff of professionals, who were remunerated not with the payment for the work done, but summarily with a fraction of gross agricultural produce and/or a parcel of land'. Tapan Raychaudhuri and Irfan Habib (eds.), *Cambridge Economic History of India, vol. I, c.1200–c.1750* (Cambridge: Cambridge University Press, 1982), p. 316.
94 The Commissioner of the Northern Division, Bombay, noted that 'large numbers of starving cattle are already coming into the town of Ahmedabad...and their preservation is even more important economically than the more direct preservation of human life'. Letter dated 4 August 1899, no. 5437, Bombay Castle, APAC, P/5665, n. p.
95 Papers Regarding the Famine and the Relief Operations in India, 1899–1900, vol. II: Native States, p. 32.
96 Papers Regarding the Famine and the Relief Operations in India, 1899–1900, vol. II: Native States, p. 27.
97 Papers Regarding the Famine and the Relief Operations in India, 1899–1900, vol. I: British Districts, p. 367.
98 See S. Muthiah's 'An Old-age Home for Cattle', *The Hindu*, 18 August 2003, www. hindu.com/thehindu/mp/2003/08/18/stories/2003081800150300.htm (accessed 25 June 2010). We find several references to pinjrapols from the early nineteenth century onwards, though they had been in existence even earlier. See for example Walter Hamilton, *A Geographical, Statistical and Historical Description of Hindoostan and the Adjacent Countries*, vol. I (London: John Murray, 1820), p. 709.
99 Out of all the cattle arriving at government camps, the weaker ones were sent away to pinjrapoles. A government report noted that nearly 2000 cattle were turned away in this manner from a single relief camp during the famine of 1899–1900. *Famine in the Bombay Presidency, 1899–1902*, vol. II (Bombay: Government Central Press, 1903), p. 164.
100 Famine in the Bombay Presidency, 1899–1902, vol. II, p. 83.
101 Mrinalini Sinha (ed.), *Selections from the Controversial 1927 Text Mother India*

(Michigan: University of Michigan Press, 2000), p. 223.

102 I. Burton, *Prevention of Cruelty, and Antivivisection, etc, [extracted from* 'Arabia, Egypt and India'*]* (London and Belfast: William Mullan, 1879), p. 3.

103 APAC, P/6134, p. 1499.

104 'The Moral Economy of the English Crowd in the Eighteenth Century', *Past and Present*, 5(1) (1971), 114.

105 'Moral Economy of the English Crowd', 115.

106 For the impact on disasters such as floods and droughts on the agricultural practices adopted by peasants, see Jiayan Zhang, 'Environment, Market, and Peasant Choice: The Ecological Relationships in the Jianghan Plainin the Qing and the Republic', *Modern China*, 32(1) (Jan. 2006), 31–63.

107 E. J. Hobsbawm noted in the inaugural issue of the *Journal of Peasant Studies* that 'traditionally peasants tended to distrust and dislike all who were not peasants, because most other people appeared to belong to a conspiracy to rob and oppress them, and stood above them in whatever social hierarchy was established'. In 'Peasants and Politics', *Journal of Peasant Studies*, 1(1) (1973), 6.

108 *Elementary Aspects of Peasant Insurgency in Colonial India* (Durham: Duke University Press, 1999), p. 9.

CHAPTER FIVE

Food adulteration, public health, and middle-class anxieties

Tell me the secret of your magic: how do you manage to extract a milk-like product out of that miserable cow-like creature to supply thirty families as you do every morning? What exactly are you, conjuror or milk-vendor?

R. K. Narayan, *The Man-Eater of Malgudi*[1]

Our narrative of the social life of cattle in India has, until now, dealt mostly with rural developments and colonial policies. However, this story must also venture into towns, cities and urbanised spaces, where the question of adulterated dairy products caused quite a few frayed tempers – as reflected in the quote above from R. K. Narayan's tale of 'simple folks' from the fictitious small town of Malgudi. The issue continues, until today, to cause such agitation that there have been frequent demands, sometimes led by responsible government agencies, to award the death penalty to those found guilty of the crime.[2] Every major festival leads to a huge spurt in demand and, inevitably, also to a spate of discoveries of counterfeit or adulterated milk and milk products.[3] Solely in terms of the importance that has been historically attached to it, therefore, the subject deserves to be examined in its own right. More importantly, it presents us with an opportunity to examine middle-class notions of health, hygiene, food and, through it, the closely related questions of modernity and urbanisation. In this sense, it also carries the story forward from the last chapter on famines, where we looked at the peasants' engagement with the colonial state.

It has been argued that one of the defining features of urbanisation is the increasing gulf or divide between the town and country, as new centres of production began to elbow out the familiar farms and agricultural lands that had hitherto enjoyed prominence. In this sense the relationship between them is assumed to be inherently antagonistic, though most scholars have also underlined the town's parasitic dependence on the countryside, from where it sucked in the nourishment that allowed it to survive. This divide has been, at least in the Indian context, overemphasised. The city was always linked, through a thousand tentacles, to the villages: migrant and seasonal workers travelled back and forth between them; a large number of people from the middle and upper classes possessed, or desired to possess, land and property in the villages; goods and services travelled in both directions; and, if nothing else, townsfolk continued to structure their life on the basis of a certain highly idealised notion of villages and village life. E. P Thompson has noted, in the context of eighteenth-century England, that the urban culture was more 'rural' (in its customary connotations), while the rural culture was more rich than we often suppose. This was certainly true of India during our period of study as well.[4] This is another aspect that the present chapter will explore, and we will look at how villages and village life was perceived by the growing middle class in rapidly urbanising cities such as Calcutta.

Of lost villages and 'magical milk'

Milk and ghee were not merely seen as healthy food items – they played a much larger role in the economy as a whole. Milk and milk products, in fact, accounted for transactions worth nearly 300 crore (or 3 billion) rupees in 1937, which was roughly equivalent to the value of India's total output of rice at the time, and three to four times the value of the output of wheat.[5] Besides this, ghee-making, as a government report noted, was a cottage industry that employed a sizeable number of people, especially women.[6] In fact nearly half of the total milk produced in the country was converted into ghee and this was, in part, due to ghee's remarkable ability to preserve its freshness and value over quite a few years.[7] If cattle, besides being a cultivation tool, also represented an investment opportunity for the landlord, ghee similarly presented an option for the small milk producer to store his savings or potential income. It was no doubt partly due to this that ghee has retained its status as a valuable commodity across centuries.[8]

Another striking feature of the trade in both milk and ghee was the fact that, though they were generally produced within rural areas, it was within the cities that they found a ready market.[9] This was understandable in the case of ghee, which was easier to transport, but one would have assumed that milk, given its perishable nature, was more likely to be consumed at its place of production.[10] What happened in reality was that satellite 'milk suburbs' began to dot the landscape next to the urban areas as the latter became more populous. According to contemporary accounts, some of these suburban villages became completely deserted in the mornings and evenings – the two time slots when milk was delivered to urban households.[11] This is hardly surprising as cities and towns grew at a much faster pace than ever before during our period of study, which naturally led also to an exponential growth in the numbers of middle-class families (or consumers) living in these areas. As a rather unique survey conducted in Lahore showed, the consumption of milk was highest among the new class of professionals (especially doctors, lawyers, and teachers), who were to be found almost exclusively in cities and towns.[12] It is no wonder, then, that milk and ghee sellers began to target this new breed of urban professionals.[13]

Why were these food items so important in terms of diet? Was it partly because milk began to be seen as the pre-eminent item of food among vegetarians due to a confluence of both traditional beliefs and modern researches into nutrition? Though one does not wish to regress into culturalist explanations regarding Indians and vegetarianism, it is perhaps true that the urban middle class was largely comprised of upper-caste Hindus who had, by the Victorian period, taken to vegetarianism with some gusto, partly as a marker of caste identities.[14] This shift towards vegetarianism is interesting, especially in the context of the larger desire to construct a new, robust image of Indian masculinity, which could counter the charges of effeminacy that the coloniser often made against the 'natives'.[15] Within this project, diet was of crucial importance, and milk no doubt received approbation from all quarters, as it was the most acceptable ingredient in a healthy diet. Everyone, including vegetarians, cow-protectionists, nationalists, medical researchers, and even wrestlers appeared to agree on the great good qualities of milk![16] The huge increase in the popularity and consumption of milk is, therefore, not at all difficult to understand.

This popularity is clearly reflected in vernacular Ayurvedic texts which, in underlining the medical qualities of milk, helped to carry its popularity further, especially among the urban middle class that had not received western education. In fact the one remedy that was often suggested in these texts for all manners of illnesses was to stop intake of all other food items and turn to a milk-only diet.[17] Milk was supposed to aid the growth of the brain, make the heart and lung stronger, treat all kinds of illnesses (including headaches, boils, epilepsy, eye diseases, asthma, and pleurisy), and even cure madness.[18] In these accounts milk almost appears to be a magic cure, though, of course, some *vaids* were more profuse in their praise than others. One author, getting carried away on a wave of hyperbole, unleashed what he thought was the final argument in favour of the potency of milk: apparently, he had received reliable information that both Hitler and Mussolini – according to him the two most powerful men in the world at the time – had been won over completely by the great good qualities of milk. Mussolini, he said, had once publicly proclaimed that his ability to work without respite was owed solely to his prodigious consumption of milk, which gave him extraordinary energy and strength.[19] Interestingly, though these tracts harped upon the time-tested virtues of milk, they also simultaneously drew affirmation from recent researches into nutrition, and used biomedical terminologies (such as vitamins, microbes, etc.) to a great extent.[20]

While Ayurveda and biomedical research were together responsible, to some extent, for the consensus around the health-giving qualities of milk, the commodity itself needed little recommendation from medical practitioners of either kind. As we have seen in earlier chapters, cattle were indispensable within an agrarian or pastoral economy, and milk had always been an important part of the rural diet. However, to what extent it was available across all classes – from the rich landlord to the poor peasant – is arguable. Government reports note that milk producers and their families consumed the product in miniscule quantities, and this is also borne out by literary sources that depict milk as a particularly valued, and valuable, commodity.[21] The value attached to milk is also reflected in the fact that the female members of a household, be they rich or poor, received much less milk than male members.[22] Perplexed by this, a colonial official asked in amazement how a mother could be partial in feeding her sons over daughters, but this was an extremely common phenomenon in both urban and rural areas.[23] Also, if milk was prized, ghee was no less so. Consumed with extreme care even in prosperous households, tales of woe regarding the soaring prices of ghee were a constant fodder for conversation, and comparisons were often made – in a sarcastic vein – between the prices of ghee and gold.[24]

Within such a context, when prices were seen as being unjustifiably high, nostalgic stories regarding the abundance of milk products in earlier times began to abound. In ancient times, it was said, milk flowed like water, with every individual possessing no less than two or three cows.[25] Others waxed lyrical about 'those times when early morning chants included the sound of cows being milked; when Aryan men and women thought it their primary duty to house and feed cattle; when, fed on a diet of milk, men and women achieved fair complexion, sharp intelligence, and optimal health.'[26] There was also a category of writers who got carried away and lost all restraint in painting a picture of striking contrast between ancient greatness and modern decadence. Acharya Chatursen Shashtri thought, for example, that in ancient times 'an ordinary householder had thousands of cows'. Perhaps recognising that this might be difficult to digest for his readers, he added that 'this might be difficult to grasp in the modern age, when a single cow costs no less than a hundred rupees', but that this was indeed true.[27] Cashing in on this palpable nostalgia for villages from an idyllic rural past, some wily merchants even hired the services of villagers and sent them to the city for hawking *ghee.* This was done in order to create the 'false impression to many consumers that the *ghee* being brought by village producers must be unadulterated'.[28]

Such was the consensus regarding this imagined ancient plenitude that some historians have also ended up swallowing the discourse in a rather uncritical manner. Kabita Ray notes, for instance, that 'Bengal in the ancient period was a land of plenty and there was an abundant supply of rice, fruits, various esculent roots, vegetable, pulses, molasses, sugar, honey, milk and the by-products of milk like butter, clarified butter, cream, casein etc.'[29] However, though it is understandable in a contemporary observer who was enmeshed in the debates of the time, this kind of nostalgia is not excusable in a historian writing with the benefit of hindsight. What is the reason behind this nostalgia, though, especially with regards to items of food? Partha Chatterjee discusses precisely this question while examining issues related to the question of colonial modernity. Citing the example of Rajnarayan Basu's book *Se Kal ar e Kal* [Those Days and These Days], written in 1873, Chatterjee notes that the tropes of food, health, plenitude, and prosperity in the distant past were indeed very prominent within texts written by Basu and his contemporaries.[30] He explains this trend by suggesting that modernity was experienced within the colonies in a vastly different way: the colonised people were forced to become mere consumers rather than producers of modernity due to the lack of a sense of autonomy or agency. Within such a context, modernity, instead of leading to a sense of liberation from the past, merely drove the colonised people further into it in search of solace and identity.[31] This appears to be a plausible explanation, but disregards the fact that colonised regions were in fact not the only places where a sense of nostalgia or romanticism existed. As Raymond Williams and others have shown in the European context, it was one of the most prominent features of modernity, as experienced in even the most industrialised and urbanised regions. Williams argues convincingly that such ideas were popular as they were a subconscious way of expressing discontent with city life – the idealised notion of the villages was, in this sense, a barely concealed critique of the modern urban condition.[32] This appears to be a much more acceptable suggestion, though it does need to be adapted to the colonial situation in the light of certain specificities that were distinctly absent in the European case. One of these, which is particularly relevant to our study, was the sense of dissatisfaction with an alien government and rule that was quite palpable within the ranks of the middle classes. Sumit Sarkar expands upon this theme in *Writing Social History*, where he notes that the *bhadralok* in late colonial Bengal – tired of being ruled by the new tyranny of the clock, and deeply dissatisfied with his humiliating lower-rung job within the colonial bureaucracy – experienced a sense of alienation and discontent like never before.[33] Within such a scenario, it is quite possible that when the *bhadralok* looked upon the past and rural life with inordinate fondness, he was in fact trying to articulate a critique of his own modern, urban lifestyle.[34]

There were several other reasons as well for the *bhadralok* to be dissatisfied with his lot, many of which were connected directly with the rapid spurt in urbanisation that was taking place during these times. Newspapers complained frequently about the rising cost of living and the rising spectre of youth unemployment; disease and epidemics appeared to occur with much greater frequency than ever before; there was a significant level of overcrowding in urban areas; and there were regular outbreaks of famines that affected not just the rural areas but also towns and cities.[35] Most importantly, there was a strong sense of uprootedness that most city dwellers experienced, as many of them were recent migrants from rural areas and still retained strong connections with their villages. No wonder, then, that a sense of crisis, or *Kaliyuga* was quite discernible among the *bhadralok*.[36] The question of adulteration of food items, in this context, became a metonym for all the various problems that plagued the middle-class existence: it became a daily reminder of all the dishonesty, corruption, and decay that one faced. The fact that the issue succeeded in kicking up a major storm should, therefore, not cause us any surprise.

Adulteration laws and the 'scandalous trade' in milk and ghee

Another huge factor that contributed towards building up the public furore around adulteration, especially of milk and milk products, was the new concern for the rising child mortality rates. Sudeshna Banerjee notes, in this context, that during these times 'the Bengali middle class developed a high strung sensitivity to the issue of child mortality', which was reflected directly in the several articles and letters published in popular periodicals.[37] Many of these articles attributed the real or supposed rise in infant mortality to the quality of milk available within cities. Dr Bardi, an Indian practitioner, made a direct link between the two in 1903, noting that much of the infant mortality in Bombay was caused by the impurities in the milk supply.[38] J. N.

Datta, an assistant analyst for the Calcutta Corporation, also noted in an article in the *Medical Reporter* that 'one of the most fruitful cases of mortality amongst infants, viz. the infantile liver, has also been attributed to faulty milk'.[39] In fact Lord Linlithgow, the Viceroy of India, was also quite concerned about the link between milk supply and the health of children, and ordered a village enquiry into milk in seven breeding tracts of India to explore this connection, though this enquiry took place after our period of study.[40]

Due to these reasons, urban lore regarding milk adulteration began to reach a critical mass by the late nineteenth century, and tales about the rapacity and dishonesty of milkmen thickened the city air. These stories were corroborated by official sources through numerous surveys and public statements, all of which expressed great concern regarding the adulteration of milk in the cities. For instance, a random examination of 989 milk samples in Bombay in 1921 revealed that nearly 65 per cent of these samples were adulterated.[41] Another exercise of a similar nature, carried out in 1913, revealed that 83.6 per cent of the milk supplied to hospitals was adulterated.[42] Again, at the third All-India Sanitary Conference in 1914, an official noted that 'the adulteration of milk with water has reached a scandalous point in Bombay ...four-fifths of milk supplied to Bombay is adulterated with water'.[43] Within such a context, where rampant adulteration was openly acknowledged even by officials, it is understandable why certain apocryphal stories regarding the legendary dishonesty of milkmen began to circulate. One such story recounted how, in ancient times, a king launched an amusing new experiment to ascertain the level of honesty among milkmen in his kingdom: he ordered all milkmen to pour a pitcher of milk anonymously (through pipes that were laid down expressly for this purpose!) into a large reservoir. Apparently, when the king arose in the morning to examine the results, he found the reservoir full of water, as all milkmen 'with the characteristic mentality of [their] caste', had poured in pitchers of water rather than milk (see Figure 4).[44]

Such anecdotes appear amusing and innocuous at first sight, but they were linked directly with larger developments regarding the stereotyping of certain caste groups that were seen as hereditary milkmen. As a result of these developments, groups like Ahirs and Gujars began to be seen as dishonest rogues – a reputation that they have still not been able to shake off completely.[45] This is reflected in popular jokes doing the rounds, one of which noted, only half in jest, that before milkmen left home to hawk milk, their wives often asked them whether they had 'made' the milk.[46] Besides this reputation for habitual and routine dishonesty, they were also seen as being notoriously unclean and unhygienic: a resolution of the government of India

noted in 1914 that it was difficult to put a complete stop to adulteration as 'in most cities the milk supply is in the hands of men ignorant
of sanitation and addicted to uncleanly practices'.[47] Also, it was not
just caste groups like Ahirs and Gujars that were being stereotyped:
immigrants from neighbouring provinces who were involved in the
milk trade were also often vilified and depicted negatively.[48]

' *Sources* of *Lahore Milk Supply.*

Figure 4 A satirical sketch depicting the 'real sources' of milk supply
in cities

Such negative depiction is surprising, considering the fact that
milkmen in India performed the very difficult task of providing milk
at extremely low prices, especially in view of the high cost of fodder. A
report surveying the potential methods of improving the milk supply
in the United Provinces minced no words in expressing amazement at
the low prices at which the milkman peddled his wares. It noted that:

> looking to the initial cost of their cattle, the interest the *gwalas* (milkmen)
> have to pay on the loans for their purchase, the cost of food, losses by
> disease, &c., the wonder is that it can be sold at such low rates.[49]

In fact, the profits connected with all aspects linked to cattle were
quite low, including the profits to be had from cattle breeding, sale
of hide, or the sale of milk. A report noted that 'profits from cattle
breeding are very small and it is adopted as an industry by the small
landowner as a means of eking out a living for himself.'[50] The situation would have been even grimmer for the landless cattle owner who
could not afford to breed and sell cattle on a large scale, and survived
purely on the profits derived from the sale of milk.

[109]

The relative poverty under which milkmen languished did not create a sense of empathy among middle-class consumers, who continued to demand the strictest penalties for those responsible for adulteration. Their suspicions regarding the pathological dishonesty and craftiness of milkmen were further strengthened due to certain public scandals that broke out from time to time. Nowhere was this more clearly apparent than in the case of the 'ghee scandal' that occurred in Calcutta in 1917. During this year, rumours began to circulate that the city had suddenly become a great centre for the trade in adulterated ghee. Though adulteration of ghee was by no means a revelation for the middle classes in Calcutta, what agitated them to a much greater extent on this occasion was the suspicion that animal fat might have been used as an adulterant. Responding to these suspicions, the Marwari Association organised the examination of random samples of ghee from all over the city, and the results showed that nearly every sample that was tested contained some animal fat. In fact, out of the sixty-seven samples tested, only seven were found to be pure and one sample contained no ghee at all.[51] This was followed by even stronger protests all across the city, led by upper-caste Hindus who demanded that all offending merchants be apprehended and punished without delay.[52] The matter acquired such importance that priests from Banaras were consulted regarding the best means of atoning for the sin of consuming animal fat. When they recommended fasting and praying on the banks of the Ganges as an acceptable solution, this was promptly followed by a large number of upper-caste Hindus who gathered by the riverside. The Governor of Bengal noted that 'the result of this edict was electrifying. Three thousand Brahmins gathered on the banks of the Hooghly forthwith ...by the morning of 19 August there was a vast concourse of between four and five thousand undergoing purification.'[53] The situation settled down only after the Marwari Association accepted responsibility and imposed a fine on the culprits.[54]

Though this episode did not, in itself, have a huge political import, it reflected the great anxiety around the question of adulterated milk and milk products that existed at the time. In the case of ghee, the problem was taken more seriously – both by colonial officials and the public at large – due to the possibility of adulteration of ghee with animal fat. To some officials, this was deeply reminiscent of the revolt of 1857, and one of them noted, much before the 'ghee scandal' occurred in 1917, that:

One of the main causes that led to the terrible events of 1857 was the belief that the government was tolerating the mixture with certain substances of cow's fat and pig's fat with which to grease cartridges, a mixture which was a defilement to every Hindu or Mahomedan who had any respect for his religion...Partly on sanitary grounds, partly to protect the people from ghee made in a disgusting way, and also because I think it would be a very impolitic thing for the masses to feel that the government pays no heed to their religious feelings, I hope the Council will proceed with this Bill.[55]

This incident was not an isolated example of its kind. In fact, much earlier, in 1886, a wide-ranging bill on adulteration had been 'hurriedly passed' in Bengal in direct response to the 'urgent cry of the native community'.[56] It was hoped that this piece of legislation would lay to rest 'the panic [that] prevailed' during the year. Apparently, fears regarding adulteration with animal fat had been so great in 1886 that wealthier sections had begun to import their ghee from Persia, while many others abstained from using ghee altogether.[57] This agitation left a deep impression on official minds and, in later years, whenever there was a discussion on the subject of tough new legislations against adulteration, the 'strength of feeling' in Bengal in 1886 was given as an example of 'native sentiments' in this regard.[58] Besides these flash-points, agitations, and public scandals that confirmed 'native senti-ments', official attention was also drawn to this subject through several petitions that were received from time to time. In one case, nearly 50,000 people in Bombay signed a petition that demanded – on religious rather than medical/health grounds – a complete stop to the sale of adulterated ghee.[59] Also, at the everyday level, many prosperous high-caste households began to make their own ghee in response to these fears.

As a result of these growing fears, a number of laws were passed on the subject of adulteration from the 1880s onwards. In fact the first bill was passed as early as 1866, but this had a limited reach and was appli-cable only within the municipalities in Calcutta. This was followed by the 1886 bill, which had a slightly wider jurisdiction; the 1886 bill, in turn, became the template for a similar bill that was passed in Bombay in 1899.[60] These new laws, argues Mark Harrison, were the direct fallout of the fact that the colonial state began to show a great deal of interest in public health issues by the end of the nineteenth century.[61] However, what is equally important is the strength of middle-class agitation on subjects such as food adulteration, which forced the colonial state to make these concessions. This was true at least in the case of the first substantial law against adulteration that was passed in Bengal in 1886.

Interestingly, though there was a rather thin trickle of legislation in the late nineteenth century, this turned into a virtual deluge by the second decade of the next century, when nearly every province passed its own bill, starting with the United Provinces Prevention of

Adulteration Act in 1912 (subsequently amended in 1916 and 1930), followed by similar bills in Madras (1918 and 1928), Central Provinces (1919 and 1928), Bengal (1919 and 1925), Bombay (1925 and 1935), and Punjab (1919 and 1929).[62] Besides this, provincial legislative councils debated the question of adulteration almost as a rule on an annual basis, reflecting the fact that it was foremost in the minds of the Indian elites who occupied these hallowed councils and committees. The next section will discuss the reasons behind this resurgence in interest on the subject.

The reincarnation of an old debate: adulteration in the 1920s and 1930s

In the second decade of the twentieth century, a completely unforeseen new development suddenly transformed the nature and intensity of all existing debate surrounding ghee adulteration. This was the introduction of *banaspati* ghee into India in 1917 by Dutch firms such as Van den Berghs, Jurgens, Verschure Creameries, and Hartogs.[63] Manufactured using vegetables, this was a completely unknown quantity in India, but the speed with which it gained a substantial market was extremely striking: in a little over a decade, the value of annual imports of *banaspati* ghee rose from nil to the figure of nearly Rs. 20 million.[64] While other novelty food items such as condensed milk only succeeded in carving out a very limited niche market for themselves, *banaspati* appeared to straightaway fill a gap in demand that had existed even before its arrival into the subcontinent.[65] In reality, this demand had very little to do with the actual acceptance of the product by middle-class consumers, who saw it (at least initially) as a poisonous or noxious substance; most of it was used to adulterate ghee as it was cheap and difficult to detect.[66] Indeed, far from being accepted, *banaspati* was detested to such an extent that there was a strong perception in Punjab that the colonial government had purposely introduced *banaspati* as part of a sinister plot to 'kill the manhood of the Punjab'.[67]

These arguments were often bolstered using scientific data and results, where possible. One of the more famous experiments, often quoted by opponents of *banaspati*, was the one that had been carried out on two cats by a provincial chemical examiner. The examiner fed one of these cats on a *banaspati*-rich diet and the other on a butter-rich one, and found that the cat that had been fed on the *banaspati* mixture lost weight quickly, and displayed the classic signs and symptoms of starvation, while the other one thrived.[68] If cats were affected to such an extent, it was argued, one could only imagine the impact it would have on the health of humans. Despite these experiments and the repeated debates though, the demand for *banaspati* remained so great that a large number of factories began to be established within India. In fact, by the late 1930s most of the *banaspati* ghee that was needed began to be manufactured within India and there was no need to import any from Holland.[69]

Banaspati's entry into the Indian market was, therefore, partly responsible for re-energising the old debate on ghee adulteration, but these concerns were also strengthened by several recent scientific discoveries regarding diet and nutrition. As Michael Worboys has noted, the inter-war period witnessed the 'discovery' of malnutrition within European laboratories, from where it spread very quickly to all parts of the British empire.[70] Although nutrition had been the subject of scientific interest from as early as the 1860s, it was only during the inter-war period that vitamins were discovered.[71] One fallout of this discovery was that malnutrition began to be linked with high mortality rates, especially with high child and infant mortality rates, which, in turn, led to a much greater emphasis on the purity of milk and milk products.

These new developments created new anxieties, and the middle class had nowhere else to turn to for redress but the colonial state. However, though the state responded to these anxieties by passing new laws, implementing these laws was a far trickier business that would have required huge investments in terms of manpower and infrastructure: appointing a few food inspectors in major cities like Calcutta could hardly be expected to satisfy consumers.[72] Also, if new laws could be devised, so could new methods of circumventing them. For example, retailers often created posters that admitted to impure ghee being sold, but these were safely tucked away into dark, invisible corners of their shops, so that they could not be noticed by customers. Again, when food inspectors paid them a visit, they admitted freely to the fact that they were selling mixed/adulterated ghee, thus gaining immunity from the law which, in most provinces, was applicable only if mixed ghee was being hawked off to unsuspecting consumers under the guise of pure ghee.[73] Finally, what scuppered any remaining chances of obtaining quick convictions was the very limited number of public analysts in each province, as it would take them several weeks to examine a sample and pass their verdict on it.[74]

When all else failed, self-help appeared to be the only available option: no wonder, then, that milk and ghee cooperatives began to mushroom all over north India during the 1930s. In fact, apart from cooperatives dealing in agricultural credit, dairy cooperatives were among the first organisations of this kind to emerge in north India.[75] These became

[113]

possible due to the wide availability of certain modern technologies such as cold storage or motorised vehicles (for quick transportation).[76] However, technological developments merely provided the means in many cases – the motives were furnished by much larger concerns regarding purity and cost. This was certainly true of ghee, which was not a perishable commodity and required no special arrangements for storage. Despite this, ghee cooperatives also registered a surge in numbers only during the 1930s, so that by 1939 the number of ghee societies had swelled to reach the substantial figure of 607 in the United Provinces alone, with a total membership of 12,579.[77] As ghee was a luxury commodity, these societies preoccupied themselves with the question of quality rather than cost, sometimes performing multiple tests on samples before putting them up for sale.[78] In doing this they were, quite clearly, responding to the demands of an incipient or new middle class, which still hankered after the 'lost purity' of rural India.

It was this obsession with purity that lent a very distinctive edge to the great Indian debate over adulteration, even though similar debates were taking place in many other parts of the world at around the same time.[79] Whereas milk-borne diseases such as diphtheria, tuberculosis, and typhoid caused great consternation elsewhere, in India it was the question of food purity that was the focal point of all discussions.[80] In fact, in all the debates and discussions that took place regularly within legislative councils and assemblies, the linkage between milk/ milk products and disease was hardly ever mentioned. The only way in which this apparent anomaly can be explained is by going back to our original discussion regarding the urban middle class, which saw commodities such as ghee and milk as an essential link with a relatively recent rural past, and adulteration as a metonym for all urban ills. Nowhere is this metonymic quality of adulteration revealed better than in the following verses by the noted Bengali poet Sukanta Bhattacharya, in a poem entitled 'Bhejal':

> Polluted and tainted lies this entire land,
> Purity here is an impossible dream;
> Impure oil, impure rice, impure honey:
> What else does one expect, when the corrupt mint money;
> Impure are people's clothes and food, impure their emotions,
> Impure is this entire realm – from Pabna to Patna.[81]

Conclusion

Such despondency and gloom notwithstanding, it is fair to suggest that the colonial state bent over backwards to accommodate the anxieties of the urban middle class whenever they became powerful. While it is true that most laws that were passed on the subject had very little impact, and the practice of adulteration continued unchecked throughout our period, yet the very fact that there were several debates and laws on the subject in itself testifies to the power of the middle-class discourse.[82] After all, as we have seen in the preceding chapters, cattle-related issues that were of immense importance to the poorer peasants did not even elicit empathetic noises from the colonial state. Millions of cattle perished during large-scale epizootics that broke out from time to time, but very few preventive rules were drafted, nor was any prompt action taken to prevent them. Similarly, relief during cattle famines was hard to come by, especially for poor cattle owners. In contrast the question of adulteration, which concerned the middle class, was repeatedly discussed, and the state appeared keen to at least be seen as taking some action.

The question of why this was so is a tricky one to answer. To an extent this was due to the greater ability of the middle class to make its voice heard. By the end of the nineteenth century, the middle class was becoming more self-aware, and began to use terms such as *madhyabitto* to refer to itself.[83] More importantly, this class had greater access to various 'tools of persuasion', such as the earliest legislative councils, newspapers, petitions, etc. But also, this class was able to make itself heard due to the simple fact that the colonial government was more willing to listen to it. While, during the early period of colonialism, the half-formed British state relied massively on the opinion of those who possessed a thorough knowledge of the scriptures, by the end of the nineteenth century it was the 'English-educated' or 'enlightened' section that began to be considered more loyal or knowledgeable.[84] But was this greater attention to this particular section also the result of a certain degree of 'class empathy' within the ranks of colonial officialdom? After all, though separated by the vast gulf of race, it cannot be denied that officials, many of whom were themselves from families of the 'middling sort', were sensitive to issues that had a resonance for the middle classes back home. They therefore appeared to be slightly more sensitive than usual to issues such as the question of female respectability/honour, food adultera-tion, and so forth.[85] Be that as it may, it seems clear from our study that the middle class had a contradictory and contested relationship with the colonial state. On the one hand, it led the emerging nationalist and anti-colonial movement and was deeply troubled by the position of relative subservience vis-à-vis colonial rulers. On the other hand, it sometimes appeared to work in close relationship with the colonial state. It is this contradictory and contested relationship that future studies of this class will have to explore more fully.

Notes

1 S. Krishnan (ed.), *A Town Called Malgudi* (Delhi: Penguin, 2002), p. 8.
2 Such a demand was, for instance, made recently by the government of Maharashtra. *The Times of India*, 19 March 2011, http://articles.timesofindia.indiatimes.com/2011-03-29/mumbai/29356984_1_milk-prices-milk-production-milk-rates (accessed 5 October 2012).
3 The cost of milk and milk products also shoots up during these festivals, and this used to happen during colonial times as well. For instance, Rai Bahadur Dr Chunilal Bose noted in 1918 that 'during the time of Hindu festivals, the price goes up very high, specially at Jorasanko, milk being sometimes sold there at eight annas per seer'. *The Milk Supply of Calcutta* (Calcutta: Central Press, 1918), p. 6. Right before the festive season, ghee sellers would start hoarding their stocks, in anticipation of a huge jump in prices. *Report on the Marketing of Ghee and Other Milk Products in India* (Calcutta: Government of India Press, 1947), p. 133.
4 *The Making of the English Working Class* (2nd edn, London: Penguin, 1968), p. 445
5 Norman C. Wright, *Report on the Development of the Cattle and Dairy Industries of India* (Simla: Government of India Press, 1937), p. 57.
6 A report noted that 'since ghee making is a remunerative cottage industry with the cultivator, he always utilizes the maximum possible quantity of milk for ghee production'. *Report on the Marketing of Ghee and Other Milk Products in India* (Delhi: Government of India Press, 1947), p. 3.
7 To be precise, 43.4 per cent of the milk produced in the country was converted into ghee. *Report on the Marketing of Ghee and Other Milk Products in India*, p. 2.
8 Irfan Habib notes that around 1660, the selling price of ghee ranged from 6.5 to 8 times the price of wheat. In *The Agrarian System of Mughal India, 1556–1707* (2nd rev. edn, Delhi: Oxford University Press, 1999), p. 60.
9 A report noted that 'milk products are prepared and consumed in large quantities only in cities and towns'. *Report on the Marketing of Ghee and Other Milk Products in India*, p. 29.
10 It was due to this perishable nature that there was practically no inter-provincial trade in milk or milk products (other than ghee). *Report on the Marketing of Ghee and Other Milk Products in India*, p. 151.
11 In fact there was a vernacular saying in Lahore that Handu (a village near the city) was well inhabited during the night, but a deserted place during the day. Roshan Lal Anand, *The Milk Supply of Lahore* (Lahore: Civil and Military Gazette Press, 1933), p. 21.
12 This was the report on the milk supply of Lahore, quoted above (n. 11), which was set up by the Board of Economic Enquiry (Punjab).
13 Another report linked higher consumption of milk with greater prosperity in urban areas, noting that 'owing to a higher standard of living, a demand had arisen from classes among whom milk had not been an article of regular consumption'. H. R. C. Hailey, *The Improvement of the Milk Supply in the Towns of the United Provinces of Agra and Oudh* (Allahabad: Government Press, 1913), p. 2.
14 In an anthropological survey in a 'vegetarian Brahmin village' carried out by McKim Marriott in 1968, he noted how certain dietary contrasts constituted differential attributes of castes: eggs and certain meats were, for example, publicly proclaimed as desirable foods only by the four Muslim castes. See 'Caste Ranking and Food Transactions: A Matrix Analysis', in Bernard S. Cohn and Milton Singer (eds.), *Structure and Change in Indian Society* (Chicago: Aldine, 1968), p. 135. Ibbetson, the colonial ethnographer, also saw vegetarianism as an 'artificial' marker due to its recent inclusion as a high-caste attribute. Quoted in Susan Bayly, *Caste, Society and Politics in India: From the Eighteenth Century to the Modern Age* (Cambridge: Cambridge University Press, 1999), p. 139. Kancha Illiah links vegetarianism explicitly with the period of nationalism, which 'aimed at constructing the vegetarianism of Brahmins and Baniyas as the superior food culture'. In *Buffalo Nationalism: A Critique of Spiritual Fascism* (Kolkata: Samya, 2004), p. xviii.

15 For a detailed study of the colonial discourse around 'native effeminacy', see Mrinalini Sinha, *Colonial Masculinity: The 'Many Englishman' and the 'Effeminate Bengali' in Late Nineteenth Century* (Manchester: Manchester University Press, 1995).

16 Joseph Alter notes that wrestlers believed that 'Milk builds up [the] semen reserve, but it also cools [their] passion, just as milk neutralizes poison'. *The Wrestler's Body: Identity and Ideology in North India* (Berkley, CA: University of California Press, 1992), p. 151.

17 See, for instance, Acharya Shri Chatursen Shashtri, *Arogya Shashtra* (Delhi: Sanjeevni Institute, 1932), p. 238; Ganpati Verma Singh, *Dugdh Gun Vidhan* (Bikaner, 1934, publisher not mentioned), pp. 19–26; Tarachandra Doshi, *Dugdhopchar aur Dugdh ka Khana* (Sirohi, 1918, publisher not mentioned). Cure of diseases through the intake of milk is the sole subject of Tarachandra's treatise, and he deals with it in great detail.

18 Singh, *Dugdh Gun Vidhaan*, pp. 34–65; Kaviraj Harnamdas, *Keval Bhojan Dwara Swasthya-Prapti* (Lahore: Madan Mohan Printing Press, 1944), pp. 196–9; Babu Hanumandas Goyal, *Doodh Hi Amrit Hai* (Prayag: Nagri Press, 1937), pp. 175–85.

19 Goyal, *Doodh Hi Amrit Hai*, p. 13.

20 See for example Chandreshekhar Shastri, *Sharir Vigyan* (Delhi, 1937, publisher not mentioned), p. 230.

21 In Premchand's *Godan*, neither Hori nor the rest of his family get to drink the milk of the cow that he bought. The cow remained a liability and was only expected to produce enough milk to pay for its fodder.

22 Even within middle-class households, it was often a luxury that was only made available to women during their pregnancies. In Manju Kapur's novel *Difficult Daughters*, when the protagonist Virmati falls pregnant, her mother-in-law 'substituted [her] morning cup of tea with a glass of hot milk, with either almonds or honey added to it. Then, almost every day there was a milk sweet with the evening meal, kheer, rubri, rasgulla, shrikhand, rasmalai...There was even talk of keeping a cow.' Kapur, *Difficult Daughters* (London: Faber and Faber, 1998), p. 242.

23 He noted that 'it is difficult to conceive that any mother would discriminate against her baby girl in the distribution of the milk she has in the household'. *Report on a Village Enquiry regarding Cattle and the Production and Consumption of Milk in Seven Breeding Tracts of India* (Simla: Government of India Press, 1939), p. 15.

24 In fact even vernacular newspapers regularly carried not just the prices of gold, but also that of ghee in the regional and national markets.

25 *Doodh hi Amrit hai*, p. 1. In fact, members of legislative councils also made similar statements. For instance, during one such debate in Assam in 1931, Maulvi Abual Mazid Ziaoshshams noted that 'sir, we hear that our forefathers were very able bodied persons, and centenarians amongst them were not rare. But now, Sir, we are crippled by disease and are short-lived. One reason may be that we do not get pure things to eat.' APAC, L/E/7/1450.

26 Singh, *Dugdh Gun Vidhan*, p. 1.

27 *Arogya Shashtra* (Delhi: Sanjivni Institute, 1932), p. 238.

28 *Report on the Marketing of Ghee and Other Milk Products in India* (Delhi: Government of India Press, 1947), p. 73.

29 *Food for Thought: Food Adulteration in Bengal, 1836–1947* (Calcutta: Papyrus, 2003), p. 1.

30 See also Jayanta Sengupta's article, which also discusses Basu's text, 'Nation on a Platter: The Culture and Politics of Food and Cuisine in Colonial Bengal', *Modern Asian Studies*, 44(1) (Jan. 2010), 81–98.

31 Partha Chatterjee, *Our Modernity* (Rotterdam: SEPHIS, 1997).

32 Raymond Williams, *The Country and the City* (Oxford: Oxford University Press, 1973).

33 See Sumit Sarkar's articles on *Kaliyuga*: 'Renaissance and Kaliyuga: Time, Myth and History in Colonial Bengal', and 'Kaliyuga, Chakri and Bhakti: Ramakrishna and His Times', in *Writing Social History* (Delhi: Oxford University Press, 1997).

34 Srirupa Prasad also makes the same point, noting that 'many of [the *bhadralok*], who were working as educated professionals or clerks or in mercantile establishments under the British in Calcutta, were recent immigrants to the city (after the disintegration of the *zamindari* system) and still had families in the villages. Moored in nostalgia, village life became a sign, which made up for everything that the city dwelling *bhadralok* yearned for.' In 'Crisis, Identity, and Social Distinction: Cultural Politics of Food, Taste, and Consumption in Late Colonial Bengal', *Journal of Historical Sociology*, 19(3) (Sept. 2006), 247.

35 In this context it must be noted that the population of Calcutta increased rapidly in the thirty years between 1891 and 1921 and it became the first city in India to attain the 'million mark'. Prasad, 'Crisis, Identity, and Social Distinction', p. 246

36 Sumit Sarkar notes that this sense of disenchantment and *kaliyuga* was stronger in Calcutta than anywhere else in Bengal. According to him, 'it is difficult to think of any extended descriptions of Calcutta written by a Bengali that is not satirical ... Calcutta, rather, was often portrayed as the heart of *kaliyuga*, the last and the most degenerate of eras in the traditional upper-caste Hindu notion of cyclical time.' 'The City Imagined: Calcutta of the Nineteenth and Early Twentieth Centuries', in *Writing Social History* (Delhi: Oxford University Press, 1997), p. 177.

37 Sudeshna Banerjee, '"Non-Bengali" Icons of Malevolence: Middle Class Representation of an "Other" in Interwar Calcutta', in Himadri Banerjee *et al.* (eds.), *Calcutta Mosaic: Essays and Interviews on the Minority Communities of Calcutta* (Delhi: Anthem, 2009), p. 235.

38 'Sufficient improvement in the state of affairs', he noted, 'could hardly be expected when those guilty of flagrant misdeeds in connection with the milk supply are allowed to ply their dangerous trade without any controls or checks'. Quoted in Harrison, in *Public Health in British India*, p. 188.

39 'Food Adulteration', *Medical Reporter, a Fortnightly Journal of Medicine, Surgery, Public Health, and of General Medical Intelligence*, 5 (Jan.–Jun. 1895), Calcutta, p. 12. The Dairy Superintendent of the Bombay municipality also noted that 'the fearful child mortality of Bombay is an eloquent testimony to the imperfect method of production, distribution and supervision of the city's milk supply'. *Proceedings of the Cattle Conference Held at Bangalore on 22nd and 23rd January, 1924* (Calcutta: Government of India Press, 1924), p. 52.

40 *Report on a Village Enquiry Regarding Cattle and the Production and Consumption of Milk in Seven Breeding Tracts of India* (Delhi: Government of India Press, 1939). Linlithgow is supposed to have said that 'any race of men must be below par in direct ratio as the consumption of milk by the children and to a great extent by the adults falls below the effective optimum' (p. 1).

41 Report by Zal R. Kothawala, in *Proceedings of the Cattle Conference* (Calcutta: Government of India Press, 1924), p. 52.

42 Rai Bahadur Dr Chunilal Bose, *The Milk Supply of Calcutta* (Calcutta: Central Press, 1918), p. 4. The problem of adulteration, in fact, continued even after all the legislation on adulteration had been passed. For example, a report noted that 26.7 per cent of the total samples examined all over the country in 1937 was adulterated. Orissa topped the chart with nearly 70 per cent of adulterated samples, with Punjab coming a close second. *Report of the Committee Appointed by the Central Advisory Board of Health to Investigate the question of Food Adulteration in India with Particular Reference to Legislation now in Force in Difference Provinces and to the Varying Standards which are in Force* (Simla: Government of India Press, 1940), p. 4.

43 *Proceedings of the Third All-India Sanitary Conference held at Lucknow in January 1914* (London, 1914), p. 91. Another report noted that, after examining 1,400 samples in Bombay, it was found that nearly 90 per cent of the milk was adulterated. Lemuel Lucas Joshi, *Milk Supply of Indian Cities – with Reference to Bombay* (Bombay: Tarporewala, 1916), p. 4.

44 Bose, *Milk Supply of Calcutta*, p. 3.

45 R. V. Russell noted that Ahirs 'according to the proverbs, [are] held to be treacher-

ous and false to engagements. They are also regarded as stupid because they seldom get any education, retain their rustic and half-aboriginal dialect, and on account of their solitary life are dull and slow-witted in company.' *The Tribes and Castes of the Central Provinces of India*, vol. II (London: Macmillan, 1916), p. 20.

46 Anand, *Milk Supply of Lahore*, p. 23.

47 Joshi, *Milk Supply of Indian Cities*, pp. 4–5. The Dairy Superintendent of the Bombay municipality also noted that 'progress must of necessity be very slow... where we have to deal with a class of people of so backward a type as the *gowlis* (milkmen)'. *Proceedings of the Calcutta Conference*, p. 54.

48 Banerjee notes in this connection that 'the icon of the Hindustani [or non-Bengali] *goala*, allegedly capable of killing infants with cholera-diluted milk is a particularly prominent stereotype that came to permeate the world of Bengali print in the inter-war period'. '"Non-Bengali" Icons of Malevolence', p. 234.

49 Hailey, *Improvement of the Milk Supply*, p. 5.

50 *Village Enquiry Regarding Cattle*, p. 77.

51 Anne Hardgrove, 'The Politics of Ghee Adulteration and its Public Resolutions in Calcutta, c.1917', in Susan Strasser (ed.), *Commodifying Everything: Relationships of the Market* (New York: Routledge, 2003), p. 204.

52 'Brahmin's hunger strike', *Singapore Free Press and Mercantile Advertiser*, 4 September 1917, p. 8.

53 Quoted in Geoffrey Moorhouse, *Calcutta: The City Revealed* (4th edn, Delhi: Penguin, 1994), p. 184.

54 Apparently the Darbhanga Maharaj also visited those fasting on the banks of the Ganges and convinced them to give up their penance ('Brahmin's hunger strike', p. 8).

55 *Extract from the Proceedings of the Council of the Governor of Bombay Assembled for the Purpose of Making Laws and Regulations, under the Provisions of the 'Indian Council Acts, 1861 and 1892', on Saturday the 20th August 1898*, in APAC, L/PJ/6/511, n. p.

56 'Affairs in India', *Belfast Newsletter* (Belfast, Ireland), 22233, 28 September 1886, p. 5.

57 'Affairs in India', *Belfast Newsletter*. The Advocate-General also noted that this had produced 'great, I may say wild, excitement, dismay, and disgust among the native inhabitants of Calcutta, both Hindu and Muhammadan, who naturally regard the admixture of such substances as I have mentioned with the pure article us an outrage on their religious tenets and feelings, and justly consider it prejudicial to their health. I have reason to believe that thousands of persons, especially the Marwaris, than whom a more peaceful and industrious race scarcely exists in India, have left the use of ghee and are now living upon dry rations, with a view to atone for the sin they have committed, though unconsciously, by using the adulterated article. The richer classes of Muhummadans and Hindus have been subjected to great expense and inconvenience in importing ghee from distant places, while the poorer classes have been obliged to abstain from using an article of food so essential to their daily wants. Under these circumstances, it cannot but appear to the Council that the adulteration of ghee in the manner I have described is an abominable malpractice, an evil of the most serious kind.' *Index to the Proceedings of the Council of the Lieut.-Governor of Bengal for the Purpose of Making Laws and Regulations for the Year 1886* (Government of India Press, Calcutta, 1887), p. 83.

58 In certain cases (like the one that occurred in Bombay in 1889), however, legislation could be deferred as the 'strength of feeling' was nowhere close to what prevailed in Calcutta in 1886. NAI, *Home Department, Judicial Branch*, nos. 54–7, January 1890, n. p.

59 NAI, *Home Department, Judicial-B*, March 1899, nos. 64–7, n. p. Officials also agreed that the adulteration of ghee was 'not a commercial but a religious matter', and it was recommended that great circumspection must be exercised in dealing with the matter. In letter from J. Woodburn, dated 4 February 1896.

60 The 1886 bill was based on the British Food and Drug Act, 1872. Also, though the Bombay bill was eventually passed more than a decade after its equivalent in Bengal

had come into effect, there had been several previous attempts during the interven-
ing decade to pass the bill. The first such attempt was made in 1889, though it had
to be dropped due to legal objections raised by the government of India. The subject
was raised gain in 1892, 1894, and 1897. *Extract from the Proceedings of the Council
of the Governor of Bombay*, APAC, L/PJ/6/511, n. p.

61 Harrison notes that 'This more vigorous attitude [of the British Indian government]
towards public health was not expressed solely in increased expenditure on public
works, but also in greater attention to subjects like food adulteration. *Public Health
in British India*, p. 188.

62 Apparently, the Punjab act was the strongest of all the provincial laws that were
passed. Speaking against the strictness of the law in Punjab, Pandit Nanak Chand
noted in the Provincial Legislative Council that 'my part of the country... produced
the *Babbar Akalis*. If this Bill is passed, there will be many *Babbar Akalis*'. *Extract
from the Proceedings of the Meetings of the Punjab Legislative Council on 25th
November, 3rd, 5th, 6th, 9th and 14th December 1929*, in APAC, L/E/7/1540, p. 5.
Perhaps stricter rules were in place in Punjab as there was a widespread feeling that
ghee was much more central to the diet in Punjab than anywhere else. Expounding
upon this theme, Sayad Muhammad Husain noted that 'there is no denying the fact
that we, Punjabis, live upon ghi. Our life, our character, our physique and indeed
everything is dependent upon this article of food that we consume'. *Extract from the
Proceedings of the Meetings of the Punjab Legislative Council*, APAC, L/E/7/1540,
p. 59.

63 Marcus Daechsel notes that 'this Indian equivalent of margarine had made its
appearance in the late 1930s', but this is not entirely accurate. In *The Politics of
Self-Expression: The Urdu Middle-Class Milieu in mid-twentieth Century India
and Pakistan* (London: Routledge, 2006), p. 103. Mr Bhupat Sing, a landholder from
Bihar, noted at a Legislative Assembly debate in New Delhi in 1931 that 'it was
early in 1917 that this commodity first made its appearance in this country'. *Extract
from the Legislative Assembly Debates*, vol. I, no. 18 APAC, L/E/7/1450, n. p. The
'Lily Brand' of *banaspati* ghee, imported from Holland, was one of the most popular
during these initial years.

64 This was the approximate figure mentioned by V. Ramadas Pantulu during a debate
in the Council of State on 27 February 1929. APAC, L/E/7/1450, n. p.

65 The average annual quantity of condensed and preserved milk imported into India
during the quinquennium ending 1939–40 was valued at Rs. 3.47 million. *Report on
the Marketing of Ghee and Other Milk Products*, p. 22.

66 The Honourable Malik Firoz Khan noted in the Punjab Legislative Council that
'[banaspati] has ...this effect that it greatly reduces a man's vitality and the effect
of that article of food in the long run is, I think, as injurious as that of any poison'.
*Extract from the Official Report of the Punjab Legislative Council Debates, dated
23rd November 1927*, APAC, L/E/7/1450, n. p.

67 This was noted by Rai Bahadur Lala Ram Saran Das, *Extract from Debates in the
Council of State, dated 27th February 1929*, APAC, file no. L/E/7/1450, n. p.

68 *Extract from Official Report of the Council of State Debates, dated 8 February
1928*, APAC, L/E/7/1450, n. p.

69 In 1931 *The Times of India* reported that a new *banaspati ghee* factory was in the
process of being established at the cost of approximately Rs. 25,00,000. This was the
first among many other factories that were established in subsequent years. Report
titled 'Vegetable products: new factory being built in Bombay', dated 30 May 1931.

70 Michael Worboys, 'The Discovery of Colonial Malnutrition between the Wars',
in David Arnold (ed.), *Imperial Medicine and Indigenous Societies* (Manchester:
Manchester University Press, 1988), pp. 208–25.

71 David Arnold notes that vitamin C was, in fact, discovered as late as 1932. See 'The
"Discovery" of Malnutrition and Diet in Colonial India', *Indian Economic Social
History Review*, 31(1) (1994), 16.

72 There was a total of ten food inspectors working in 1922 in a city as large as Calcutta.
Ray, *Food for Thought*, p. 155.

73 Such strategies to circumvent laws have often been designated as acts of 'resistance' in recent historiography. However, in the present case they appear to have been survival strategies, or methods used for maintaining profit levels. The one explicit act of resistance against legislation by milkmen took place in Bombay in 1913 when, in opposition to a new law requiring compulsory licensing of milkmen within the city, a complete strike was declared for two days. This led to even greater hardship for the middle class as the price of milk rose in the subsequent days. Joshi, *Milk Problem of Indian Cities*, pp. 3–4.

74 Ray notes in the context of Calcutta that 'the work of Food Inspectors in checking adulteration was limited by the number of samples of food that could be analysed in laboratory by two analysts were not sufficient to cope with the work of so large a city as Calcutta'. Ray, *Food for Thought*, p. 40.

75 For more details on agricultural cooperatives, see I. J. Catanach, *Rural Credit in Western India: Rural Credit and the Co-operative Movement in the Bombay Presidency, 1875–1930* (Berkley, CA: University of California Press, 1970).

76 *Annual Report on the Working of Co-operative Societies in the United Province of Agra and Oudh for the year 1939–40* (Allahabad: Government Press, 1941), p. 11.

77 *Annual Report on the Working of Co-operative Societies in the United Province of Agra and Oudh for the Year 1938–39* (Allahabad: Government Press, 1940), p. 13.

78 'The quality of ghee sold by the societies is subjected to a double test before it is put on the market. The first test is with the *panches* (members of the *panchayats*) who apply a rule of thumb, but fairly effective test when the ghee is brought to *panchayats* ...Thereafter ghee is tested with a refractometer at the headquarters of the ghee union.' *Annual Report on the Working of Co-operative Societies in the United Province of Agra and Oudh for the Year 1937–38* (Allahabad: Government Press, 1939), p. 12.

79 For developments in other parts of the world, see Edward Geist, 'When Ice Cream Was Poisonous: Adulteration, Ptomaines, and Bacteriology in the United States, 1850–1910', *Bulletin of the History of Medicine*, 86(3) (Fall 2012), 333–60; Jim Phillips and Michael French, 'Adulteration and Food Law, 1899–1939', *Twentieth Century British History*, 9(3) (Jul. 1998), 350–69; Michael French and Jim Phillips, *Cheated Not Poisoned: Food Regulation in the United Kingdom, 1875–1938* (Manchester: Manchester University Press, 2000); P. J. Aitkins, 'Sophistication Detected: Or, the Adulteration of the Milk Supply, 1850–1914', *Social History*, 16(3) (Oct. 1991), 318–39; Marc T. Law, 'The Origins of State Pure Food Regulation', *Journal of Economic History*, 63(4) (Dec. 2003): 1103–30; Jeffrey M. Pilcher, *Sausage Rebellion: Public Health, Private Enterprise, and Meat in Mexico City, 1890–1917* (New Mexico: University of New Mexico Press, 2006).

80 This was partly because tuberculosis was not commonly seen in the country as spreading through milk. Even the spread of cholera, it was demonstrated by colonial scientists like D. D. Cunningham, was not due to infected or adulterated milk. *Scientific Memoirs by Medical Officers of the Army of India: On Milk as a Medium for Choleraic Comma-Bacilli* (Calcutta: Government Printing, 1890).

81 Quoted in Ray, *Food for Thought*, p. 170 (translation mine). It is difficult to hazard a guess regarding the exact date when this poem was written. Sukanta Bhattacharya, however, lived a very short life, lasting barely twenty years between 1926 and 1947, and many of his poems were published posthumously.

82 Interestingly, in many of these discussions, middle-class/elite representatives used the urban poor as a ruse to highlight their own concerns.

83 Swapna Banerjee notes that the Bengali *bhadralok*, during this period, was popularly known to be divided into two main groups: the *abhijat* (aristocratic) and the *madhya-bitto* (middling sort). In 'Down Memory Lane: Representations of Domestic Workers in Middle Class Personal Narratives of Colonial Bengal', *Journal of Social History*, 37(3) (spring, 2004), 681–708.

84 During the initial years the colonial state launched an exercise to compile 'traditional' Hindu and Muslim laws through consultation with those that were considered knowledgeable in the scriptures. See Bernard Cohn, *Colonialism and its Forms*

of Knowledge: The British in India (Princeton: Princeton University Press, 1996), pp. 57–75.

85 It seems that colonial officials were willing to reformulate their policies wherever they were felt to impinge on the question of female honour, especially the honour of womenfolk belonging to prosperous families. For example, medical inspection and vaccination measures were sometimes waived whenever they were felt to be unpalatable for such women and their families. Saurabh Mishra, *Pilgrimage, Politics and Pestilence: The Haj from the Indian Subcontinent, 1870–1920* (Delhi: Oxford University Press, 2011).

CHAPTER SIX

Cattle poisoning and the Chamar identity

The previous chapter briefly touched upon the process of the formation of stereotypes regarding certain caste groups, such as milkmen,
Ahir and Gujars. This chapter will carry that story forward, and will
look at the process of formation of stereotypes in detail. Admittedly,
though, it will focus much more on the activities, ideas, and notions
of colonial officials, and less on the indigenous responses to them. The
overall attempt of the chapter will be to highlight the process whereby
the identity of Chamars – popularly known as leather workers – was
crystallised.

Chamars have often been seen as one of the most underprivileged
caste groups in north India, and this is reflected in several literary
works that depict their sufferings. Perhaps the most well-known
among these is the sensitive and widely acclaimed short story *Sadgati*
(or 'The Deliverance'), written by Premchand, about the plight of
Dukhi Chamar and his wife Jhuria. Turned into a movie exactly
half a century later by the noted filmmaker Satyajit Ray,[1] the story
highlights the low-caste status of Dukhi, whose corpse was considered
so impure that it had to be dragged out of the village limits using a
rope. His impurity, and that of his caste members, was seen as a direct
consequence of an involvement in leather work. This was accepted
even by colonial ethnographers who quoted certain myths referring
to the 'original sin' of touching a carcass to explain the caste's low
status.[2] These ethnographers also made repeated mention of ancient
scriptures, starting from the institutes of Manu, to prove the ancient
and unquestionable link between Chamars and leather work.[3] Despite
all this, the association between occupation and caste status was, in
reality, not as obvious as it appears in these tracts. Census and other
figures show that the total population of Chamars touched the figure
of eleven million in 1916, and that it was the second largest caste
category after Brahmins all over India.[4] It is quite obvious that such

huge numbers could not possibly have been absorbed into the leather industry in India.[5] Even certain district-level surveys acknowledged this fact, noting that Chamars were 'good, hard working cultivators', or that they were mainly engaged in cultivation as labourers or tenants.[6] In fact, it is quite ironic that the period during which this occupational stereotype became widely accepted was also the period when the traditional role and position of the village tanner was being usurped by the rapidly growing leather industry in cities like Kanpur.[7] Why, then, did ideas about the low occupational and ritual status of the caste become so generally accepted? Was this a case of colonial ethnographers privileging certain ideas over others, thereby strengthening negative stereotypes about the group?

This takes us back to the debate over the historicity of modern castes: whether caste groups were, in effect, invented in their modern form through the codifying operations of the colonial state, or whether caste was a concrete pre-colonial reality that was reshaped through colonial intervention.[8] Susan Bayly has spoken strongly against the tendency to credit the state with great inventive powers. However, while noting that caste was not a 'mere exercise in the western "essentializing" of India',[9] she also simultaneously accepts the idea that significant new changes were introduced into caste configurations by the British. Perhaps this controversy arises out of the different degrees of emphasis laid upon colonial agency, and could be resolved through the use of more circumspect terminology. M. N. Srinivas appears to have done precisely this, even though his work on caste preceded these debates: he notes that, though caste was a social reality during pre-colonial times, census and other classificatory methods led to a 'livening up of the caste spirit'.[10] This 'livening up' was indeed quite evident in the numerous caste associations that were formed to lobby for official recognition as higher castes; it was also evident in the greater competition between various castes for jobs, government patronage, or political appointments.[11] Such developments however became discernible to a significant degree only in the late colonial period, and even the process of classification has been generally thought to have gathered pace in the 1880s, partly as a result of the influence of new fields of study such as anthropometry and ethnography.[12]

As a result of the accelerated pace of change during the 1880s and later, historians have tended to ignore similar caste-based developments that occurred during earlier decades. This chapter will provide a corrective to this general tendency while discussing colonial ideas about the Chamar caste; it will also look, in particular, at the process whereby the caste was both criminalised and unquestionably linked with leather work. Identification with both occupational and behavioural traits was

[124]

part of the larger trend towards fixing the caste with certain identifiable characteristics and we will show that, while Chamars began to be connected with crime as early as the 1850s, this was followed a few decades later by the tendency to see them as synonymous with tanning or leather work. These stereotypes of Chamars as criminals, poisoners, and leather workers were not disparate or unconnected, and could often dovetail into each other. This was especially true because leather work or tanning was often seen, within colonial discourse, as degraded or polluted work which had to be carried out by groups with questionable credentials.[13] That these stereotypes followed quickly on the heels of each other was not unusual either since, as Homi Bhabha has noted, each stereotype requires 'for its successful signification, a continuous and repetitive chain of other stereotypes', and this was certainly true of colonial ideas about the Chamar caste (see Figure 5).[14]

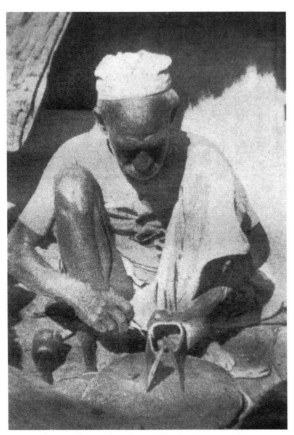

Figure 5 A 'typical Chamar leather worker'

This chapter will not only highlight these stereotypes but will also simultaneously look at the process whereby they were formed. For example, while looking at the notion of Chamars as poisoners or criminals, we will look at its links with ideas relating to 'oriental crime'; we will also look at the impact of emerging new areas of expertise such as medical jurisprudence or Toxicology. This study will also fill up the relatively neglected chronological space between the supposed elimination of Thuggee in the 1840s and the launch of the Criminal Tribes Act in 1871, both of which were important landmarks in the formation of colonial attitudes and stereotypes around criminal castes/tribes.[15] This interim period is important as it allows us to evaluate both the legacies of the anti-Thuggee operations as well as the background to the new campaign against 'criminal tribes'.

Cattle poisoning as an 'oriental' crime

Cattle poisoning as a crime made its first major appearance in 1854, when George Campbell claimed to have single-handedly unearthed an extensive network of Chamar poisoners who allegedly indulged in the crime for the sake of hides.[16] His campaign quickly turned into a witch-hunt against Chamars, and led to nearly 700 arrests within a very short period in the district of Azumgurh alone.[17] Most of these accused were also later convicted of their crime, which is not surprising at all, since Campbell was responsible for both arresting suspects and conducting trials against them. What is noteworthy, however, is the fact that his judgments and correspondences contained numerous references to Sleeman and Thuggee. This gives us a clue as to the conscious or subconscious inspiration behind his massive campaign: perhaps he, like many other ambitious young recruits working in India, yearned for the stature and influence of Sleeman, whose tracts on Thuggee had acquired a cult status in India and Britain.[18] These references were also to be expected as Thuggee was the most obvious and popular example of 'oriental crime', and cattle poisoning appeared to fall squarely within this bracket. Both offences, along with several others like Sati, female infanticide, and dacoity represented, for the colonial official, culturally distinct forms of crime that were peculiar to India.[19] Such an understanding resulted in major judicial innovations in the Indian context and, because many of these crimes were collective in nature, also led to a crystallisation of group identities at least in the official eye.[20] This was particularly true of crimes such as cattle poisoning which, unlike other crimes such as dacoity or Thuggee, were thought to have been perpetrated almost exclusively by a particular caste.

Before addressing these larger debates about the links between crime and caste identities, however, we must deal with certain fundamental questions regarding the incidence and spread of cattle poisoning. These questions are not as easy to address as they might appear at first sight, and authoritative data is hard to obtain even though provincial officers talked at length about the rampant nature of the crime. The magistrate of Jaunpur in the United Provinces, for example, went to the extent of blaming cattle poisoning for the dearth of cattle in his district, while another official saw it as being responsible for the extensive cattle mortality within his jurisdiction.[21] It is worth mentioning here though that, while such remarks were made principally within certain districts in Eastern United Provinces and Bihar, such as Jaunpur, Azumgurh, Gorakhpur, Benaras, and Saran,[22] the crime itself received great attention at the highest official levels; even the Cattle Plague Commission, which was formed in 1869 to investigate rinderpest in India, devoted a large chunk of its report to the question of cattle poisoning. Interestingly, though, the commission admitted rather freely that there was little concrete evidence to support claims about a high incidence of the crime. It noted that:

> The crime is mostly represented by isolated instances, or single cases with one or more defendants; but there is a general feeling evident in many of the judgements ... that one detected case is the evidence of many undetected cases.[23]

This 'general feeling' led to a surfeit of impressionistic and questionable evidence, most of which would not have been admissible even in the most lenient court. 'Oriental crimes' of a collective nature such as cattle poisoning or Thuggee were, however, treated very differently both by the police and the courts. As a result, all kinds of evidences and techniques of obtaining evidences became acceptable and appropriate, a topic that we will discuss in detail in the next section.

Keeping in mind the fact that even commissions of enquiry could not gather evidence to support the supposedly rampant nature of the crime, it is hardly surprising that 'natives' were mostly ignorant of the very existence of cattle poisoning. Campbell expressed his surprise at this ignorance in 1854 but, even two decades after he had first established the existence of the crime, his successors in the same district were equally amazed at the complete lack of 'native awareness'. It was noted in 1873, for example, that 'the ignorance of the people as to the real cause of mortality was perfectly wonderful', and that villagers suffered from 'an incapacity to detect crime by mere induction'.[24] In the same year, the Magistrate of Gorukhpur noted that petty Zamindars were 'ignorant and blindly unsuspicious' of the crime, while the Commissioner of the Benaras division referred to 'a population as unsuspecting [of the crime] as the beasts themselves',[25] which was inclined to fall back on superstitions about ghosts and spirits to explain unusual cattle mortality.[26] During times of exceptional mortality officials reported that money was being offered to village Chamars, but this was, apparently, not a bribe to stop them from poisoning cattle but a payment in lieu of various religious ceremonies that they performed to propitiate evil spirits.[27] These ceremonies appear to have been taken very seriously, and retribution could follow quickly on the heels of any perceived failure on the part of Chamars to dispel the curse of cattle mortality.[28] This was quite evident in a striking incident that occurred in the Gorukhpur district in 1872, when villagers raided a Chamar settlement, looted their crops, and swung the women up naked from the boughs of trees.[29] Such incidents reveal the fact that a connection was seen to exist between cattle and the Chamar caste;[30] however, they do not at all point towards any larger consensus about the caste group's responsibility for cattle poisoning.[31] The credit for 'discovering' the crime must therefore go to officials such as Campbell, who were keen to mould it within the larger framework of 'oriental crimes' provided by the Thuggee department.[32]

A wonderful narrative that was produced in 1882 by a government detective called H. Ramsay provides us with a remarkable instance of the influence of Thuggee operations on future investigations of collective crime in India. In his tract *Detective Footprints in India*, Ramsay describes in detail his method of gathering information on cattle poisoning, and there is an uncanny resemblance between his strategies and the ones that Sleeman has famously described in his tracts and reports.[33] The first step in his investigations was to find someone convicted of the crime who could become an authentic and believable colonial informant, and he soon decided upon one Sew Chamar as the approver.[34] No force or coercive tactics appear to have been used in obtaining testimony from him, but Sew Chamar was eager to please the White Sahib as the potential reward of a release from prison had been dangled before him.[35] Interestingly, Ramsay was less keen to obtain information about co-conspirators or gang members, and wanted to know about the specific method used to commit crime; perhaps he wanted to establish the modality of crime in the same way as strangulation had been established as the chief method adopted by thugs. Sew Chamar proved to be an exceptionally useful informant on this subject, and explained and demonstrated the 'sutari' method of cattle poisoning in great detail.[36] Testimonies and reports such as this not only established the crime on a solid footing, but also associated it strongly with the caste group and a peculiar and a suitably oriental method of committing it.

Ramsay's thesis about the 'sutari' method of poisoning cattle, though enticingly close to British notions of 'oriental crime', did not gain wide acceptance within official circles. In fact, the method that was commonly agreed upon was far coarser and required much less subterfuge: it involved quickly tossing arsenic balls into the fodder so as to minimise the possibility of being caught in the act.[37] Poisoning was therefore seen as less of an 'art' than Thuggee was. The two crimes were separated by another distinguishing feature – whereas Thuggee was seen as being extremely rampant during early nineteenth century, cattle poisoning made intermittent, though powerful appearances on the mental landscape of officials. After Campbell's initial campaign in 1854, which attracted a lot of attention, the issue of poisoning appears to have simply slipped out of the picture, only to make a reappearance nearly a decade and a half later in 1869, again in 1872–3, and finally in 1878. The subject received such great official attention in 1873 that cattle poisoning was turned into a cognisable offence under Act XI of 1874, but this was in turn followed by another dormant period.[38] This anomalous rise and fall in the crime graphs becomes strikingly apparent in the reports written by the Commissioner of Patna, who reported absolutely no incidents of poisoning for three consecutive years between 1867 and 1869,[39] but noted just three years later that 'if a search [were] to be made, we should find scarcely a Chamar's house without a certain amount of arsenic in it'.[40] What lay behind this periodic resurgence of the crime? Did Chamar poisoners consciously decide to forsake the practice after they became the subject of a campaign by the police, or does the answer to this lie somewhere else?

A clue to this mystery is provided by certain officials who did not subscribe to the hyperbole around poisoning. The personal assistant to the inspector-general of police for the North-Western province was, for example, quite sceptical of the existence of an organised network of poisoners and scoffed at the tendency to over-report or exaggerate the extent of crime. Adopting a very sarcastic tone, he noted that 'it is strange to notice how cases increase with the issue of the Inspector General's circular on the subject ... I have [had] several opportunities during the past cold weather of seeing the wonderful effect of the Police Circular.'[41] His theory was substantiated by a huge increase in cattle poisoning samples received by W. Walker, the Chemical Examiner for the North-Western Provinces, in the wake of the circular – he received one case for examination in 1867, two in 1868, but more than a hundred the very next year. Walker was convinced that this rise was due to the misplaced vigilance of police officials.[42] Other officials also raised significant doubts about the supposedly high prevalence rates. When Farrell, an officer placed on special duty to investigate the crime in 1869, submitted his remarks regarding the 'wholesale poisoning of cattle' in Bengal, his conclusions were strongly refuted by the Magistrate of Jessore. The magistrate placed a surprising amount of faith in the wisdom of 'villagers' and noted that:

> The majority of the people are not so ignorant as to make a rule of gener-
> ally mistaking poisoning by arsenic with death by disease. With one fact
> they are absolutely familiar, viz., that death by arsenic ensues much
> more rapidly and suddenly than death by disease.[43]

He also conducted a raid upon certain villages in order to test the truth of Farrell's conclusions, and reported that no arsenic was found in any of the households. Such evidences lead one to doubt the very existence of the crime or, at the very least, doubt inflated claims about the threat it presented. These doubts are further strengthened by traces in the records of the use of questionable tactics to obtain evidence. The following section will discuss these tactics and also the conduct of trials against those accused of poisoning.

Confessions, coercion, and trials

In 1854, during Campbell's anti-poisoning offensive, a strikingly gruesome incident occurred that revealed the coercive underpinnings of the campaign. Roshun Ally, a Thanedar and Campbell's reliable lieutenant, took it upon himself to conduct a raid on a Chamar settle-ment in order to discover incriminating evidence. Finding no arsenic or any other poisonous substance in any of the households, Ally decided to make an example out of one Ramdehul Chamar in order to encourage others to come forward with confessions. Ramdehul's fate has been recorded in graphic detail by an officer investigating the incident, who noted that his arms were tied behind his back with cruel violence, he was beaten with twigs of castor-oil plant while being suspended from a tree, and that he was released only intermittently for interrogation about the location of the alleged stockpile of poison. When he claimed ignorance the same treatment was repeated, and this cycle continued until the end of the day when he finally died due to the combined effects of torture, exhaustion, and hunger.[44]

Campbell received a lot of unwanted attention for this incident, especially for his tendency to rely completely on 'native subordinates' and his habit of bypassing higher authorities while investigating the crime. He, in turn, readily expressed regret for 'the view of the law [he had] taken', but contended that an opportunity to 'lay bare a vast criminal system' could not be allowed to pass due to the minor issues of legality or scruples.[45] In order to justify his own actions he represented the crime as a grave, pressing problem, noting that he had been forced to act 'as if the town was on fire'.[46] Though this argument was questioned by some, most officials agreed about the seriousness and severity of the crime, which is why Campbell was let off after being lightly chastised. Not only this, Roshun Ally – the man physically responsible for the exceptionally brutal murder of Ramdehul – was acquitted after merely being fined Rs. 5 and receiving a mention in the 'bad characters' book.[47] These light sentences were justified on grounds of practical exigencies: it was argued that a degree of gentle wheedling was indeed required to extract information out of the 'native'. Also, officials in colonial India could definitely expect to be the beneficiaries of a liberal interpretation of the law. This was stated clearly by the Officiating Magistrate dealing with the Roshun Ally case, who noted that: 'it might be murder in England, but I find that here the nature of the crime is determined by the intention, and there is no doubt that the defendants did not intend to kill the deceased'.[48] In any case, it was accepted wisdom that hereditary, professional, or collective crimes in India required a different approach to criminal investigations, and that exceptional measures were justified in such cases.[49]

Though the perpetrators might have got away lightly in this instance, this incident revealed the coercive tactics underpinning Campbell's campaign. Of far greater import in forging his reputation, however, was his evident success in establishing the crime, which was reflected in the massive numbers of confessions that he was able to obtain from Chamars in the Azumgurh district. In fact confessions became so common that Campbell called them a 'fashion' and noted that 'almost all the new men from day to day seized have frankly stated whatever share they had in the matter, and told their whole story'.[50] The large number of confessions led to the appointment of a special officer to handle and record them, and the entire police establishment in Azumgurh became, for at least a month, almost exclusively occupied with them. The extent to which these confessions were voluntary is, however, questionable. After all, the modus operandi that was used to obtain them included imprisonment without trials for those suspected of the crime. Prisoners were quite obviously alarmed by this, and it was not unusual for them to 'confess' to their crimes in the hope that such cooperation would reduce the possibility of a harsh sentence.[51] Campbell's report also provides certain clues and hints about other methods used to induce confessions. He notes, for example, that officers such as Roshun Ally were sent out to inspect places where the crime was suspected to have been common, and that subordinate officers were instructed to act 'at once and vigorously upon any information of the crime, whether a formal petition was received from a plaintiff or not'.[52] Such instructions and procedures were bound to lead to excesses and overzealous policing.

Campbell's campaign, it might be argued, was exceptionally harsh as he was trying to establish a crime that had little precedence in colonial penal history. However, similar coercive measures were employed by officials as late as two decades later. In the year 1874 Campbell's role as the leading investigator in the entire cattle-poisoning drama was assumed by H. D. Spedding, the Joint Magistrate of Gorukhpur. Spedding adopted a new approach towards solving the problem: having established Arsenic as the poisoning agent in most cases, he launched a drive to detect it within Chamar households. Arsenic had been recognised as the poisoning agent even earlier, but Spedding saw its discovery upon a person of the Chamar caste as the only proof required to establish his criminal intent or culpability. Using this strategy, he quickly concluded that Chamars in Gorukhpur were supported and encouraged in their criminal enterprise by an entire network of merchants and leather dealers.[53] What he had failed to consider was that arsenic was in fact used widely by leather workers in the tanning process, which was the reason behind its wide availability.[54]

Despite his new approach towards establishing crime, Spedding's methods of dealing with alleged criminals were just as extra-legal and arbitrary as Campbell's: he directed the police to take cognisance of the crime without waiting for orders; he directed them to make arrests without warrants; and he also authorised them to conduct raids whenever the presence of arsenic was suspected in any Chamar household. Waiting for the owners of poisoned cattle to make their complaints was, according to him, equivalent to 'facilitating the commission of crime'.[55] Not surprisingly, such orders led to a flood of arrests and 'confessions' on a daily basis. Spedding also claimed to have finally uncovered 'the vast network of cattle poisoning', and noted that all his investigations led to an individual named Bulaki, who was cast in the role of the villain of the piece. Bulaki was not only held responsible for supplying arsenic in large quantities but also for convincing 'gullible Chamars' to join his criminal system. A massive manhunt was launched for him and he was eventually apprehended in a wine shop in Calcutta with an 'accomplice' called Lekha, whom he named as his witness for defence. Interestingly, Lekha's reaction upon hearing this news was to abscond from the area – he was perhaps aware of the witch-hunt against poisoners and might have had an inkling that his association with Bulaki would turn him into a suspect in colonial eyes. His fears were, in fact, not at all unjustified as he was immediately branded as a 'chief worker in the entire matter'; his attempt at absconding was also seen as additional proof of guilt.[56]

In a remarkable case of déjà vu, a very similar drama unfolded again in 1878, only this time Lekha replaced Bulaki as the ringleader of the cattle-poisoning network. His own former position as the chief witness was taken over by Phulel Chamar and Bamlall Baniya, both of whom took a leaf out of Lekha's book and promptly absconded from the scene. They were, once again, suspected of being accomplices in the crime of 'secret trade of arsenic', even though there was very little concrete evidence against even the primary accused.[57] Lekha was eventually sentenced to fifteen months in prison, though Spedding himself noted that there was no likelihood of proving his guilt under section 109 of the Penal Code, which referred to aiding or abetting a criminal act. His witnesses were also tried and fined Rs. 100 each for the crime of knowing Lekha, though no charges had been originally levied against them.[58] In the colonial campaign against poisoning, where evidences were scarce and assumptions were treated as certainties, witnesses could fully expect to be prosecuted for the 'crime' of knowing the culprit.

Chamar as poisoner and leather worker: late colonial developments

Spedding's arsenic-based operations show clearly that officials were clutching at straws to authenticate the poisoning hypothesis, though, despite these efforts, police records continued to show negligible annual prevalence rates for the crime. The effort to establish arsenic as the poisoning agent was also a fallout of the new emphasis within the legal profession on scientific evidence. This was reflected in the advent of new 'sciences' such as toxicology and medical jurisprudence, both of which had made their first appearance in the early part of the nineteenth century and were well on the way towards establishing themselves professionally by the time Spedding launched his campaign.[59] The question of poisoning had a special place within these new specialisms, partly because the crime was less amenable to physical detection, and partly as cases of poisoning in upper class households created great sensation in Europe and therefore attracted greater medical and legal attention.

This is clearly illustrated by a landmark case of poisoning in France in 1840, which gained wide popularity all over Europe.[60] The Marie Lafarge affair is significant for us for more than one reason – it was one of the first cases where the accused was convicted largely on the basis of medical/toxicological evidence and, second, it was a case of arsenic poisoning that had significant implications for our own study of cattle poisoning. The case was reported in daily newspapers, and

Marie Lafarge was eventually convicted of poisoning her husband by arsenic, though public opinion was divided over her guilt. What was remarkable about this trial was the emphasis placed upon ascertaining the kind of poison used, so much so that the verdict depended almost entirely on the result of a new and relatively unknown procedure to detect arsenic called the 'Marsh method'.[61] The entire affair was also widely referred to within Anglo-Indian medical and non-medical circles, and the Marsh method to ascertain the presence of arsenic began to be used by chemical examiners in the subcontinent as well.[62] As a result of cases such as these, arsenic itself began to acquire reputation as a powerful murder weapon, which led to a legislative Act to control it in Britain (the Arsenic Act of 1851). It was, by the 1850s, easily the most well-known poison in Europe, which could partly be the reason for the quick association made by officers like Campbell and Spedding between cattle poisoning and arsenic.[63]

As a result of this association, people who suspected a case of cattle poisoning were asked to send samples from deceased animals to the chemical examiner in Calcutta. This advice was followed very rarely, primarily because, as mentioned before, cattle poisoning was hardly seen as a serious crime by the inhabitants themselves. In the few cases that samples were indeed sent out, the examiners failed to find evidences for arsenic poisoning as consistently as provincial officials might have expected him to. The examiner was, in fact, openly critical of officials who had created the cattle-poisoning controversy and, in this sense, he represented a viewpoint that contrasted strongly with the larger colonial consensus around the subject. Most other experts uncritically swallowed the hyperbole, including acknowledged authorities such as Norman Chevers, who wrote the first authoritative volume on medical jurisprudence in India in 1856.[64] Chevers referred vaguely to the 'ancient crime of cattle poisoning', though the earliest concrete evidence he could muster was from 1851 when four Chamars were convicted of the crime in the Saran district of present-day Bihar.[65] He also referred to Campbell's campaign in an approving fashion, and there appears to have been very little doubt in his mind about the collective guilt of the entire caste group.

This openness to the idea of criminal groups/tribes appears to have been the one major difference between Anglo-Indian and British experts on medical jurisprudence and becomes quite clear when we compare Chevers with British experts like A. S. Taylor, who wrote the first authoritative text on the subject in Britain.[66] The latter believed firmly in individual responsibility and guilt, while Chevers made it abundantly clear that medical experts appearing at trials needed to be fully abreast of both traces of crime and traits of character of various groups.[67] This point was heavily underlined by several authors who preceded and followed him, starting with C. A. Baynes, the Civil and Sessions Judge for Madura district, who published his tract in 1854. This tract presented a summary of A. S. Taylor's influential text, and also sought to Indianise this text for the benefit of Indian magistrates.[68] Others who wrote on the subject later reiterated the distinctiveness and peculiarity of Indian crime and criminals.[69] This was nowhere reflected as clearly as it was in case of poisoning, which acquired entirely different meanings and tones in the metropole and the colony. Whereas it was related strongly to upper-class household intrigues in Europe, it became strongly connected to lower-caste groups in India due to the strength of collective stereotypes.[70]

Such stereotypes became more entrenched by the last two decades of the century and were, in certain cases, further strengthened by an additional layer of occupational stereotypes about various groups. Chamars, for instance, began to be completely identified with leather work during this period as a result of ethnographic tracts by influential authors such as H. H. Risley, H. A. Rose, R. V. Russell, D. Ibbetson, M. A. Sherring, J. Wise, and others. Anthropometric judgements were also passed regarding the physical characteristics of the caste cluster.[71] Risley's first sentence about Chamars, for example, unequivocally branded the group as 'the tanner caste of Behar and Upper India'.[72] Similarly James Wise, whose tract published in 1883 was used as a model by Risley, noted that Chamars everywhere 'followed the same customs, and prosecuted the same trade [i.e. tanning]'.[73]

This trend was strengthened by the census of 1881, which used the categories of Chamars and leather workers interchangeably, and was used as a foundational text by many of these ethnographers. Influenced by its findings, even non-official British sources began to make this association – for example when G. A. Lefroy, a missionary working with 'Chamar Christians', wrote a tract in 1884 about his experiences, and called it *The Leather Workers of Daryaganj*.[74] Lefroy was also acutely and painfully aware of the low-caste nature of his congregation, and it is clear from his narrative that he was somewhat embarrassed about the nature of his flock.[75] His embarrassment should not cause us any surprise at all as, at the same time as gaining a strong and fixed occupational identity, Chamars had also begun to be increasingly identified with several undesirable habits, practices and traits of character. These perceptions, once they had gathered momentum, became even stronger in the twentieth century, so that the census of 1901 came up with a separate occupational category of 'cattle-poisoners' and lumped it together with prostitutes and others under main rubric of 'unproductive labour'.[76]

[135]

By this period even tracts on medical jurisprudence began to see the connection between Chamars and poisoning as unquestionable and automatic. While Chevers was partly trying to establish the severity of the crime, by the 1880s this had become an irrefutable fact known to everyone, and authors like Gribble and Lyons merely prescribed quick tips on identifying and dealing with the poison.[77] In fact, it appears to have broken free of its earlier geographical confines and was now depicted as being rampant all over India.[78] Reports about poisoning cases began to trickle in from the Madras and Bombay Presidencies, which had hitherto remained relatively untouched by the crime.[79] In the former it was the Madiga caste which took over the burden of crime from Chamars, whereas in Bombay Mahars were seen as the culprits.[80] Many officials even offered rational explanations for this supposedly irrational and oriental crime, noting, for example, that the spurt in crime had been caused by a massive boom in the leather export market, whose value had risen about forty times between 1860 and 1925.[81] Chamars, it was argued, had been turned into handmaidens of powerful leather dealers and merchants, who were keen to make a quick profit out of this exponential growth in demand. Officers noted that dealers had fanned out into the countryside and had offered huge loans to Chamars who, in turn, were forced to adopt criminal tactics in order to keep their benefactors happy.[82] Chamars were therefore simultaneously seen as gullible victims as well as agents of crime. This was reflected even in the sentences handed down to dealers, who were imprisoned for much longer periods than the poisoners themselves.[83] Notwithstanding all this, it is clear that, by the end of our period of study, the Chamar caste had become synonymous with both leather work and cattle poisoning, and this was the result of the process of ethnic and occupational stereotyping which had started as early as the 1850s in case of Chamars and gathered enormous pace during the 1880s. The new 'sciences' of toxicology, ethnography, and medical jurisprudence had a major part to play in this process, and together they led to a recasting of the Chamar caste in both occupational and caste terms.

Conclusion

This chapter has thrown light upon a wide range of issues, including the legal–judicial mechanism, the nature and meanings of what was known as 'oriental crime', the use of scientific rationale to establish crime, and the larger process of crystallisation of caste stereotypes. All these various strands acted together to lend a peculiar colour to the Chamar caste as a whole, and this did not remain confined to the level of colonial discourse, but also influenced more widespread notions about the caste group. By the early twentieth century, not only did gazetteers and other official tracts begin to see an automatic correlation between Chamars, leather work and poisoning, but a negative perception about their lifestyle and habits had also become much more pervasive and popular.[84] In fact even Gandhi, while talking about the 'psychologically repulsive' meat-eating habits of tanners in 1938, described a scene in a typical tanner household in the following words: 'children dance round the carcass, and as the animal is flayed, they take hold of bones or pieces of flesh and thrown them at one another. A tanner... tells me [that] the whole family is drunk with joy at the sight of a dead animal.'[85] Such negative perceptions are also reflected clearly in the widespread prevalence of pejorative phrases such as 'chor-Chamar' or 'Bhangi-Chamar' all over north India;[86] it can also been seen in the increasingly strong association between dirt, filth, and the caste group.[87] While it is certainly not being argued that such notions were being *invented* by the colonial state, there is strong evidence to suggest that they strengthened considerably due to colonial intervention. Srinivas's hypothesis about the 'livening up' of the caste spirit during colonial times therefore appears to hold true, to a certain extent, for the Chamar caste.

This chapter has also shown how various colonial ideas about the caste group dovetailed into each other: notions about 'oriental crime' and Thuggee merged with perceptions of cattle poisoning by Chamars; scientific developments in the fields such as toxicology reinforced colonial assumptions about crime; and stereotypes about Chamar criminality led to further stereotypes about their occupational status. The process of colonial discourse formation was therefore not simple or straightforward – it consisted of various strands and was created due to the force of several historical circumstances. To reduce it to the status of a monolith or to dissociate it from the processes that led to it would create false impressions about the power and prevalence of such ideas, and it is important to avoid such errors while studying colonialism and colonial rule.

Notes

1 This was a movie made in 1981 for a television audience and has been called Ray's 'cruellest film' due to its dark subject matter See Andrew Robinson, *Satyajit Ray: The Inner Eye* (Berkeley: University of California Press, 1989) p. 257. It was also one of Ray's two Hindi movies, the other one being *Shatranj ke Khiladi* (or 'The Chess Players').

2 According to one such myth, the 'original ancestor [of Chamars] was the youngest of four Brahman brethren who went to bathe in a river and found a cow struggling in a quicksand. They sent the youngest brother in to rescue the animal, but before

he could get to the spot it had been drowned. He was compelled, therefore, by his brothers to remove the carcase [*sic*], and after he had done this they turned him out of their caste and gave him the name of Chamar.' R. V. Russell, *The Tribes and Castes of the Central Provinces of India*, vol. II (London: Macmillan, 1916), p. 406.

3 See, for example, Geo. W. Briggs, *The Chamars* (Calcutta: Calcutta Association Press, 1920), p. 13.

4 Briggs, *Chamars*, p. 406.

5 The leather industry in India even today employs only 2.5 million people, and this number would have been considerably lower in 1916. *Towards Inclusive Growth* (Delhi: UN Publications, 2008), p. 3.

6 See for instance the District Gazetteers for Farrukhabad (1911), Bijnor (1908), Etawah (1911), or Pratabgarh (1920).

7 H. G. Walton, in his treatise on the leather industry in the United Provinces, noted that 'in Cawnpore small independent tanners are extremely rare. The same is the case elsewhere.' *A Monograph on Tanning and Working in Leather in the United Provinces* (Allahabad: Government Press, 1903), p. 27. This process had started much before Walton wrote his monograph.

8 A large number of authors have dealt with this subject in recent times, but key texts include: Nicholas B. Dirks, *Castes of Mind: Colonialism and the Making of Modern India* (Princeton: Princeton University Press, 2001); Susan Bayly, *Caste, Society and Politics in India* (Cambridge: Cambridge University Press, 1999); Ronald Inden, *Imagining India* (Oxford: Basil Blackwell, 1990); Lucy Carroll, 'Colonial Perceptions of Indian Society and the Emergence of Caste(s) Associations', *Journal of Asian Studies*, 37(2) (Feb. 1978), 233–50; Norbert Peabody, 'Cents, Sense, Census: Human Inventories in Late Precolonial and Early Colonial India', *Comparative Studies in Society and History*, 43(4) (2001), 819–50. Prachi Deshpande, 'Caste as Maratha: Social categories, Colonial Policy and Identity in Early Twentieth-Century Maharashtra', *Indian Economic and Social History Review*, 41 (Feb. 2004), 7–32; Brian P. Caton, 'Social Categories and Colonisation in Punjab, 1849–1920', *Indian Economic and Social History Review*, 41 (Feb. 2004), 33–50.

9 Susan Bayly, 'Caste and "Race" in the Colonial Ethnography of India', in Peter Robb (ed.), *The Concept of Race* (Delhi: Oxford University Press, 1995), p. 165.

10 M. N. Srinivas, *Social Change in Modern India* (Berkeley: University of California Press, 1966), p. 95.

11 See Carroll, 'Colonial Perceptions of Indian Society', 235.

12 Paul B. Rich notes that there was a growth in the 'scientific pretensions of anthropology' in the 1880s and 1890s. In *Race and Empire in British Politics* (Cambridge: Cambridge University Press, 1986), p. 101. For a detailed study of the impact of anthropometry on colonial policies in India, see Crispin Bates, *Race, Caste and Tribe in Central India* (Edinburgh: Edinburgh Papers in South Asian History, 1995). The impact of these 'sciences' was reflected in the huge expenses involved in launching the first comprehensive ethnographic survey of India in 1889.

13 This was, of course, due to a certain kind of interpretation of 'indigenous tradition', but also because connection with dead cattle and leather was considered unsavoury within European countries too. One of the popular negative stereotypes about gypsies, for example, was that they ate meat of dead cattle and sold the leather in markets.

14 Homi Bhabha, 'The Other Question ... Homi K. Bhabha Reconsiders the Stereotype and Colonial Discourse', *Screen*, 24(6) (1983), 29.

15 For more information on the suppression of Thuggee and Criminal Tribes, see Radhika Singha, '"Providential" Circumstances: The Thuggee Campaign of the 1830s and Legal Innovation', *Modern Asian Studies*, 23(1) (1993), 83–146; Radhika Singha, *A Despotism of Law: Crime and Justice in Early Colonial India* (Delhi: Oxford University Press, 1998); Meena Radhakrishna, 'Colonial Construction of a "Criminal" Tribe: Yerukulas of Madras Presidency', *Economic and Political Weekly*, 35(28/29) (15–21 Jul. 2000), 2553–63; Meena Radhakrishna, *Dishonoured by History: 'Criminal Tribes' and British Colonial Policy* (Hyderabad: Orient

Longman, 2001); Mukul Kumar, 'Relationship of Caste and Crime in Colonial India: A Discourse Analysis', *Economic and Political Weekly*, 39(10) (6 Mar. 2004), 1078–87; Basudeb Chattopadhyay, *Crime and Control in Early Colonial Bengal, 1770–1860* (Calcutta: Bagchi, 2000); Anand A. Yang, *Crime and Criminality in British India* (Tucson: University of Arizona Press, 1985); Sandria B. Freitag, 'Crime in the Social Order of Colonial North India', *Modern Asian Studies*, 25(2) (1991), 227–61; Sanjay Nigam, 'Disciplining and Policing the "Criminals by Birth", Part 1: The Making of a Colonial Stereotype – The Criminal Tribes and Castes of North', *Indian Economic and Social History Review*, 27(2) (1990), 131–65; Sanjay Nigam 'Disciplining and Policing the "Criminals by Birth", Part 2: The Development of a Disciplinary System 1871–1900', 27(3) (1990), 257–87.

16 The first case that was apparently discovered by Campbell involved a child who had been caught in the act of poisoning. The *Friend of India* reported this incident and the subsequent 'unravelling' of the whole network in the following words: 'A child was detected administering poison to a cow. Inquiries were made as to his motive, and his replies furnished a clue, which was vigilantly followed, and at last revealed the existence of a widely organised conspiracy. A few men, perhaps not more than two, had adroitly availed themselves of the village organization, and turned it into a source of vast pecuniary profit.' Quoted in Norman Chevers, *A Manual of Medical Jurisprudence for Bengal and the North Western Provinces* (Calcutta: Government of India Press, 1856), pp. 78–9.

17 From George Campbell, Officiating Magistrate of Azumgurh, to the Superintendent of Police, 5th Division (Benaras), dated 16 November 1854, in *Report of the Commissioners Appointed to Inquire into the Origin, Nature, etc of Indian Cattle Plagues* (Calcutta: Government of India Press, 1871), p. 687. [hereafter *Cattle Plague Commission Report*]

18 Sleeman's own tracts on Thuggee (such as *Ramaseeana* published in 1836) were read widely, but others also wrote widely read tracts about Thuggee, including Meadows Taylor's *Confessions of a Thug* (1839). Noting the importance of suppressing Thuggee, J. W. Kaye wrote in 1853 that 'the extirpation of Thuggee is an exploit worthy to be celebrated by every writer who seeks to chronicle the achievements of the English in the East'. Quoted in 'Sleeman, Sir William Henry', *Oxford Dictionary of National Biography* (Oxford: Oxford University Press, 2004).

19 Satadru Sen, 'The Savage Family: Colonialism and Female Infanticide in Nineteenth-Century India', *Journal of Women's History*, 14(3) (autumn 2002), 56.

20 Chattopadhyay, in his monograph on crime in Bengal, appears to argue that British ideas about crime were transplanted within India without much modification, and that Indian specificities were not recognised by colonial authorities. This does not appear to be the case if we focus on the category of 'oriental crimes'. *Crime and Control in Early Colonial Bengal*, p. 2.

21 Letter from the Magistrate of Jaunpur, dated 6 January 1869, *Cattle Plague Commission Report*, p. 715; see also letter from an official dated 20 March 1855, *Cattle Plague Commission Report*, p. 699.

22 Azumgurh and Jaunpur were in fact mentioned as 'the home of the cattle poisoner'. Eustace J. Kitts, *Serious Crime in an Indian Province, Being a Record of the Graver Crimes Committed in the North-Western Provinces and Oudh During Eleven Years, 1876 to 1886* (Bombay: Government Press, 1889), p. 60.

23 *Cattle Plague Commission Report*, p. 646

24 From R. D. Spedding, Joint Magistrate of Gorukhpur, to the Officiating Magistrate of Gorukhpur, dated 2 October 1873. *Selections from the Records of Government of India*, vol. 180, *Papers relating to the Crime of Cattle Poisoning* (Calcutta: Government of India Press, 1881), p. 45.

25 A few reasons were offered for the supposed underreporting of the crime by 'natives'. An official offered the explanation that 'from the standpoint of the villager it must sometimes appear wiser to bide one's time and take one's own measures of reprisal than to submit to a lengthy police investigation and a protracted hearing in a law court'. S. M. Edwards, *Crime in India: A Brief Review of the More Important*

Offences Included in the Annual Criminal Returns (Oxford: Oxford University Press, 1924), p. 69. Another reason often offered was that, since women from the Chamar caste usually acted as midwives in villages, people were afraid that reporting Chamars to the police authorities would lead to a boycott of their families by midwives.

26 From C. P. Carmichael, Officiating Commissioner of the Benaras Division to the Secretary to the Government of North Western Provinces, dated 4 November 1873, *Selections from the Records*, p. 31; see also letter from J. J. F Lumsden, Officiating Magistrate of Gorukhpur, to the Commissioner of the Benaras Division, dated 15 October 1873, *Selections from the Records*, p. 51.

27 C. P. Carmichael, letter dated 4 November 1873, *Selections from the Records*, p. 31.

28 Various others caste groups, such as Baniyas, were also seen as possessing cosmic powers that allowed them to communicate with gods and spirits. See for example David Hardiman, 'Usury, Dearth and Famine in Western India', *Past and Present*, 152 (Aug. 1996), 136–40.

29 C. P. Carmichael, letter dated 4 November 1873, *Selections from the Records*, p. 31.

30 This might, however, also refer to the fact that members of the caste were sometimes seen to possess magical powers in other contexts too. Russell noted that 'when children fall ill one of them [Chamars] is called in and he waves a branch of the *nim* tree over the child and taking ashes in his hand blows them at it; he is also consulted for hysterical women'. R. V. Russell, *The Tribes and Castes*, vol. II, p. 422.

31 It must also be clarified that, though a connection was seen to exist between Chamars and cattle, we do not get the impression that the caste was unquestionably linked with leather work. The credit for permanently and irrevocably linking Chamars with leather work must also go, at least partly, to colonial officials.

32 These officials also saw religious ceremonies to stop cattle mortality as another cunning device used by Chamars to earn some extra income. This fact was noted by Rudyard Kipling's father, who wrote in 1892 that 'Hindu villagers have been known to make "transactions" with their dangerous neighbours [or Chamars]. When the cattle were mysteriously dying...the leather-dressers gravely [note] that the village godlings, especially those of their own peculiar caste, had been neglected...So a feast [would be] made to the leather-dressers, and their godlings propitiated by offerings; both sides going through an elaborate semi-religious farce with perfect gravity.' John Lockwood Kiping, *Beast and Man in India: A Popular Sketch of Indian Animals in their Relation with the People* (London: Macmillan, 1891), pp. 120–1.

33 H. M. Ramsay, *Detective Footprints, Bengal, 1874–1881* (Charleston, 2009, first published in 1882).

34 *Detective Footprints*, p. 45.

35 For an interesting discussion on the dynamics involved in choosing an approver and obtaining an approver's testimony, see Shahid Amin, 'Approvers' Testimony, Judicial Discourse: The Case of Chauri Chaura', in Ranajit Guha (ed.), *Subaltern Studies*, vol. V (Delhi: Oxford University Press, 1987), pp. 166–202. Sew Chamar had to walk the tight rope between speaking the language the Sahib wanted to hear while at the same time appearing reliable and authentic. Ramsay notes that 'I took special care to impress upon the man that he would be required to let me fully behind the scenes, and that any reticence on his part, or withholding of full information, would at any stage in the proceedings cancel the agreement [regarding commutation of sentence] between us ... Sew Chamar promptly and unequivocally accepted my conditions, and in native fashion expressed his complete surrender by seizing my foot between his hands and placing his forehead on it.' *Detective Footprints*, p. 46.

36 Ramsay explains the process of making *sutaries* in the following words: 'the Chamar placed a convenient quantity of the softened seeds [of *Karjani*] on the flat stone, and proceeded to tap them out gently until they were flattened, and then rub them up, so as to produce a perfectly smooth paste. This achieved he scraped the paste together with the back of his thumb nail, and [made] it into a ball like a marble. Sew Chamar placed the paste on the flat stone and proceeded to roll it backwards and forwards

with the ball of his thumb, laying increased pressure on one end of the paste, so as to graduate it into a marvellously sharp point. A portion of this, about an inch or more in length, was then cut off. The detached portion presented the appearance of a sharp stout thorn. At the point of incision the remaining paste, though round and fairly slender, was of course blunt, and had to be further manipulated to form a second sharp point.' *Detective Footprints*, pp. 47–8.

37 In one of the first judgments passed by the Nizamat Adawlut on poisoning, the accused had apparently been caught throwing a bundle of arsenic-infused grass in front of a bullock 'upon eating which the bullock began to bellow'. Government and Nema Sahoo versus Girdharee, in *Reports of Cases Determined in the Nizamut Adawlut for 1856*, vol. VI, no. I, p. 313. Girdharee was sentenced to 'imprisonment with labour and irons' for seven years.

38 This piece of legislation, however, did not satisfy authorities and demands were made for special police measures. Extract from the Proceedings of the Government of India in the Home, Revenue and Agriculture Department, dated 25 April 1881, *Selections from the Records*, p. 3.

39 From A. C. Mangles, Officiating Magistrate of Patna to the President, Cattle Plague Commission, dated 18 July 1870, *Cattle Plague Commission Report*, p. 669.

40 Letter from A. Mackenzie, junior secretary to the government of Bengal, to the secretary to the government of India, dated Calcutta 5 December 1873, *Selection from the Records*, p. 13.

41 *Cattle Plague Commission Report*, p. 729.

42 Waller made the same assertion about the impact of the circular, noting that while he received only eight cases between 1 January and 1 April (the month when the circular was received), he received 109 during the rest of the year. *Cattle Plague Commission Report*, pp. 726–7.

43 E. J. Barton, Officiating Magistrate of Jessore to the Commissioner of the Presidency Division, dated 18 September 1869, *Cattle Plague Commission Report*, p. 657.

44 Memorandum by M. Smith, esq., on the proceedings on the trial of Roshun Ally and others, and Sheikh Mahomed Ally and others, sent for inspection. *Cattle Plague Commission Report*, pp. 694–5.

45 Letter from Campbell, dated 26 February 1855, *Cattle Plague Commission Report*, p. 697.

46 Letter from Campbell, dated 26 February 1855, *Cattle Plague Commission Report*, p. 698.

47 Memorandum by M. Smith, *Cattle Plague Commission Report*, p. 695.

48 Memorandum by M. Smith, *Cattle Plague Commission Report*, p. 694.

49 Harald Fischer-Tine and Michael Mann (eds.), *Colonialism as a Civilizing Mission: Cultural Ideology in British India* (London: Anthem Press, 2004), p. 34; Singha, *Despotism of Law*.

50 From Campbell to the Superintendent of Police, the 5th or Benaras Division, dated 21 October 1854, *Selections from the Records*, p. 26.

51 Many British authors themselves have written about the doubtful validity of confessions in the colonial context. One author, for example, noted that 'the idea is seized that narrating a long series of crimes will lead to escape from penalties ... sometimes false confessions are extorted by the police to forward their own interests, and are so skilfully made as to baffle detection'. A. H. Giles, 'Poisoners and Their Craft', *Calcutta Review*, 81(161) (Jul. 1885), 108.

52 *Selections from the Records*, p. 26.

53 From R. D. Spedding to the Officiating Magistrate of Gorukhpur, dated 2 October 1873, *Selections from the Records*, pp. 37–8.

54 Arsenic was used for several purposes, including as a medicine and as a preservative for wood and timber. The chemical had also begun to be widely used to paint the bottom of ships. In Copy of a letter from the apothecary to the Honourable East Indian company, to the officiating secretary, Medical Board, no. 145, dated 31October 1855, APAC, V/23/119, p. 283).

55 R. D. Spedding, dated 2 October 1873, *Selections from the Records*, p. 41.

56 These remarks were made by one Mr Daniell, who was presiding over Bulaki's case. *Selection from the Records*, p. 66.

57 *Selections from the Records*, p. 67.

58 Both of them were able to pay the fine levied upon them and this, for Spedding, was additional proof that they had made huge profits out of the 'business' of cattle poisoning.

59 The first classes in Britain on the subject of medical jurisprudence were started by Andrew Duncan Sr. at Edinburgh University in 1781. In 1807 the government in London authorised the creation of a formal chair in medical jurisprudence at Edinburgh. This chair was subsequently taken up by Andrew Duncan Jr. By 1833 medical jurisprudence became a required course at Edinburgh and some other universities. See James C. Mohr, *Doctors and the Law: Medical Jurisprudence in Nineteenth Century America* (New York: Oxford University Press, 1993), pp. 4–6.

60 The incident left such an impact on popular memory that a movie was made on the subject in 1937, entitled *L'Affaire Lafarge*.

61 The method had been discovered by a Scottish scientist called James Marsh in 1836 but became famous only due to the Lafarge affair.

62 See for example *Report on the Investigations of Cases of Real or Supposed Poisoning* (Calcutta: Government of India Press, 1841), p. 4.

63 The use of the poison also became popular in literary tracts. For example, in *Madam Bovary* (1856), which absolutely gripped public attention, Emma Bovary commits suicide by ingesting arsenic.

64 Chevers's volume became so authoritative that it was quoted as the final word on jurisprudence as late as early twentieth century. It was also quoted extensively by the Cattle Plague Commission in its discussion on the subject of cattle poisoning.

65 Chevers, *Manual of Medical Jurisprudence*, p. 77.

66 *Manual of Medical Jurisprudence* (Philadelphia: Henry C. Lea, 1848). Taylor justified his book with the argument that it was necessary for doctors or scientific experts to be aware of legal requirements in order to protect themselves from the tactics employed by wily lawyers. He also provided a list of elaborate instructions for the medical practitioner and noted that: 'the hour, the day of the week, and the month, should be invariably mentioned. The words yesterday, next day, &c., should never be used. The facts which it will be necessary to enter in the report [should be] specially stated under the heads of investigation...In drawing up a report of symptoms and appearances after death, the facts should be plainly and concisely stated *seriatim*, in language easily intelligible to non-professional men' (pp. 13–17).

67 Quoting sources such as Macaulay, he noted that Bengalis were a feeble, sedentary, and delicate race that lacked courage and independence, while Rajputs were superstitious but loyal and austere. Chevers, *Manual of Medical Jurisprudence*, pp. 6–7.

68 C. A. Baynes, *Hints on Medical Jurisprudence Adapted and Intended for the Use of Those Engaged in Judicial and Magisterial Duties in British India* (Madras: Pharaoh and co., 1854). Baynes also noted that 'he is thrown upon the study of lengthy treatises, not one-tenth of which can, at present at all events, have practical application in this country' (p. iii). Clarifying his position further, Baynes noted how, while a corpse abandoned at an isolated spot would be investigated on the basis of available evidence in Europe, a similar circumstance would automatically point towards Thuggee in India.

69 Several historians have also, in line with the argument presented in this article, noted that the peculiarity of the Indian situation lay not in cultural differences, but in the colonial nature of legal authority in India, so that laws and sentences were passed on the basis of stereotypes about social groups. See for example Elizabeth Kolsky, 'Crime and Punishment on the Tea Plantations of Colonial India', in Markus D. Dubber and Lindsay Farmer (eds.), *Modern Histories of Crime and Punishment* (Stanford, CA: Stanford University Press, 2007), pp. 272–98.

70 This was true in case of both Thugs and cattle poisoners. Authors such as Chevers, William Crooke, and others in fact argued that many former Thugs had turned to the use of poison in order to kill their victims. William Crooke, *Things Indian:*

Being Discursive Notes on Various Subjects Connected with India (New York: Scribner's, 1906), p. 378.

71 They were often described as dark, strong, well made with dull expressions and high cheek bones.

72 H. H. Risley, *The Tribes and Castes of Bengal, Ethnographic Glossary*, vol. I (Calcutta: Government of India Press, 1891), p. 175. Highly influenced by the science of anthropometry, Risley also adduced several physical features to the caste group and even quoted the following proverb in Bhojpuri which bolstered his hypothesis: *Karia Brahman gor Chamar, Inke Sath na utariye paar* [do not cross a river in the same boat with a black Brahmin or a fair Chamar] (p. 175). The fact that Risley's tract was required reading for civil services is an indicator of the kind of influence it must have exerted in terms of determining official policies.

73 James Wise, *Notes on the Races, Castes and Tribes of Eastern Bengal* (London: Harrison & Sons, 1883), p. 251.

74 The term 'Chamar Christians' was used frequently by Lefroy to refer to converts into Christianity. *The Leather Workers of Daryaganj* (Delhi: Cambridge Mission, 1884).

75 He narrated the events in a congregation in the following words: 'a real crisis in the life of our little congregation had come, the calling out commenced. Designedly or otherwise it happened that the first five names called were those of men of very weak character, low esteem, and poor position among both their old and their new caste-fellows, and it was with less surprise than sorrow that I (who knew them best) saw them one after the other step forward in obedience to the summons and raise the water to their heads' (p. 18). For more details on Lefroy and his work in India, see Jeffrey Cox, 'G. A. Laffroy (1854–1919): A Bishop in Search of a Church', in Susan Pedersen and Peter Mendler (eds.), *After the Victorian: Private Conscience and Public Duty in Modern Britain* (London: Routledge, 1994), pp. 55–78.

76 Cited in Edwards, *Crime in India*, p. 68.

77 J. D. B. Gribble, *Outlines of Medical Jurisprudence for India* (3rd edn, London: Higginbotham, 1892); L. A. Waddell, *Lyon's Medical Jurisprudence in India* (Calcutta: Thacker, Spink & co., 1888). This was also true for various other authors who came much later: see for example R. C. Ray, *Medical Jurisprudence and Treatment of Poisoning* (Calcutta: Hare Pharmacy, 1910); Rai Bahadur Jaising P. Modi, *A Textbook for Medical Jurisprudence and Toxicology* (Calcutta: Kothari Book Depot, 1920).

78 See for example Robert Wallace, *India in 1887* (Edinburgh: Oliver and Boyd, 1888), pp. 114–15.

79 Though a Poisons Act had been passed in Bombay as early as 1866, this measure was not targeted at cattle poisoners.

80 Gribbles for example noted that 293 cases of poisoning had been reported from the Madras presidency in the five year period between 1885 and 1889. *Outlines of Medical Jurisprudence*, p. 421. The Report on the Administration of the Madras Presidency for 1886–7 also noted that during the year 114 samples of cattle poisoning were sent to the Chemical Examiner, and 68 of them were confirmed as poisoning cases. Report in *Calcutta Review*, 86(172) (1887), 409.

81 Walton, *Monograph on Tanning and Working in Leather*, pp. 4–5; Sir John Watt, *The Commercial Products of India Being an Abridgement of the 'Dictionary of Commercial Products of India'* (John Murray, London, 1908), p. 633; J. R. Martin, *Tanning and Working in Leather in the Bombay Presidency* (Bombay: Government Central Press, 1903), pp. 4–5; Nilanda Chatterjee, *The Condition of Cattle in India: Being an Enquiry into the Causes of the Present Deterioration of the Cattle with Suggestions for Their Remedy* (Calcutta: All India Cow Conference Association, 1926), p. 34.

82 See for instance L. S. S. O'Malley, *Bengal District Gazetteers: Saran*, p. 14; *Bengal District Gazetteers: Palamau*, p. 140.

83 It was noted that 'the instigators of the offence deservedly received much more severe punishment than the actual poisoners'. The majority of actually poisoners

received two years' rigorous imprisonment, whereas dealers received six years or more. *Selections from the Records*, p. 36.

84 Their wives were, for example, often seen as cohabiting with several males while drunkenness was supposed to be 'a common caste failing'. Biggs, *The Chamars*, p. 45.

85 Gandhi, M. K., *Cent Per Cent Swadeshi or the Economics of Village Industries* (Ahmedabad: Navjivan, 1938), p. 40.

86 *Chor* could be literally translated as 'thief', while Bhangi was another low caste that was seen as engaging in menial and unclean work. Ibbetson notes that 'the Chuhra or Bhangi of Hindustan is the sweeper and scavenger *par excellence*'. *Punjab Castes* (Lahore: Government Printing, 1916), p. 293. In his gazetteer on Saran district, written in 1908, O'Malley noted that 'such is their reputation for stealing that the word *"Chamari"* is equivalent to *"chori"*'. *Bengal District Gazetteers*, p. 44.

87 A monograph published in 1991, supposedly carrying out rigorous sociological research, noted rather unapologetically that 'his [Chamar's] quarters abound in all kinds of abominable filth. His foul mode of living is proverbial. Except when it is absolutely necessary, a clean living Hindu will not visit his part of the village' R. R. Prasad and G. Rajanikanth, *Development of Scheduled Caste Leather Artisans* (Delhi: Discovery Publishing House, 1991), p. 48.

CONCLUSION

Like many other objects and things from India, cows have become unquestionably linked with the question of religion in the western imagination. Historians of South Asia, too, appear to focus on religious themes connected with cattle, such as the Cow Protection Movement, which has been the subject of a number of historical works till now.[1] This monograph has consciously moved beyond the realm of religion to touch upon several other themes of great importance. Owing to the lack of much previous work on the subject, it has also, of necessity, adopted an exploratory stance, pointing towards a number of key developments in various interrelated fields that need to be studied in much greater detail in future. If, as a result, there appears to be a certain lack of unity, perhaps this has been compensated for by a survey of a number of exciting new themes.

The wide-ranging nature of this work is, however, extremely useful in several ways. It allows us, for instance, to reach interesting conclusions regarding the nature of the colonial state. One of the conclusions that emerges clearly from this work is that, for the colonial state, the question of military welfare was of central importance throughout the period of our study. This might appear to be a somewhat obvious point, but this study has highlighted the fact that the preoccupation with military interests continued to guide policies for much longer than has generally been assumed to be the case by historians of public health. In fact, down to the very end of the nineteenth century, veterinary officials appear to have been preoccupied with carrying out military tasks such as horse breeding, and military officials appear to have had a disproportionate influence in determining functioning of the Civil Veterinary Department. The question of funds, too, appears to have had a much greater influence in the case of policies framed around the question of welfare of 'public cattle': the meagre relief organised during times of famine, and the rigorous process for screening out poorer cattle owners is a case in point. Further, the question of military dominance and the issue of funds often fed into each other, as the preoccupation with military issues led to a lack of funds for areas that were of great concern to the larger public.

This book has also argued that it was these military and financial compulsions that drove the colonial state away from the concerns of the rural population, especially the concerns of the poorer class of peasants. In fact, in several cases one also notices a clear failure to understand the peasants' concerns and actions. Officials were taken aback, for example, when even the poorest peasants chose not to avail themselves of liberal *taccavi* loans at the time of famines, and instead sought help from the notoriously dishonest moneylenders. This appeared, to them, to justify longstanding assumptions regarding the inherent irrationality of the Indian peasant. However, we have shown that this was really a 'crisis of comprehension', which was caused partly due to a lack of official empathy with these sections. In fact, once one digs a little below the surface, the reasons for the peasants' lukewarm response to official policies become abundantly clear. While not wishing to get here into the debate about whether the peasantry was 'rational' or otherwise, one would still like to emphasise that responses were framed within a certain context, and it is important to understand these larger contexts that were at work. These assumptions regarding the peasants' inability to look after their own interests continue to be extremely powerful in post-colonial India, both amongst policy makers and the middle classes. It is perhaps time to rid oneself of such insular notions.

Though such colonial notions have been highlighted and critiqued, we have also underlined the fact that there was no single uniform or coherent colonial policy that was applicable across all regions, groups, and periods. Colonial response to middle-class anxieties could, for instance, be noticeably different compared to its stand vis-à-vis the peasantry. This was partly because of the greater colonial dependence on the 'enlightened' middle class by the end of the nineteenth century. As the state's dependence on this class grew, so did its eagerness to allay its anxieties, which is clearly apparent in the spate of regulations that were passed on the subject of milk/ghee adulteration. Many of these regulations, it is true, were not implemented fully; however, purely in terms of the number of laws that were passed, it seems that subjects that concerned the urban middle class received much more attention than much larger calamities that regularly affected the rural population. We are not, of course, suggesting a *quid pro quo* between the colonial state and the urban middle class, but the concerns of this class do appear to have received greater attention from colonial officials.

Besides looking at the relationship between the colonial state and various classes or castes, one of the major preoccupations of this book has also been to integrate the larger social history of cattle in India with medical or veterinary issues. Far too often there has been a tendency to look at medical issues in an isolated manner, as if they were divorced from larger social realities. This book challenges such approaches and seeks to bring together medical and social history in a common narrative. This is reflected also in the choice of themes that it chooses to examine: for instance it studies famines together with epizootics; it also looks simultaneously at bacteriological developments and the new middle-class obsessions with the question of germs and purity. All these issues are intimately connected with each other and an attempt to artificially separate them would only lead to a partial or lopsided picture of historical developments. In line with this 'integrative approach' adopted by the book, we have engaged throughout with not just the historiography on medical history in South Asia, but also with the much larger literature on modern South Asian history.

While dealing with these themes, this book has chosen to examine a rather long period of Indian history. This has allowed us to look closely at a number of changes that occurred over nearly a century and a half. Overall, the early colonial period has been covered less extensively than the late colonial one, but we have nevertheless been able to highlight the salient features of early colonial policies regarding cattle, namely the links with land settlements, the reliance upon middlemen and landlords, and the desperate efforts to kick-start horse-breeding operations. While some of these questions remained relevant throughout the long nineteenth century, the colonial state was also forced to contend with some larger developments such as urbanisation, new medical innovations such as bacteriology, the use of new methods of enumeration like the censuses, and the impact of famines (which began to occur with much greater frequency in the second half of the nineteenth century). The state's response to these stimuli/developments has been studied in detail, as has been the response of various indigenous sections to them.

What we would have liked to examine, but have not been able to due to limitations of space, is the question of continuities and changes between colonial and post-colonial times. In the South Asian context the question of the well-being of cattle affects nearly all classes to varying extents, and this is therefore the ideal subject for studying the nature of state and its interactions with various sections. Perhaps this would require a separate project in itself, but an initial survey points towards more continuities rather than changes or breaks with the colonial context.

Note

1 See, for instance, Peter Robb, 'The Challenge of Gau Mata: British Policy and Religious Change in India, 1880–1916', *Modern Asian Studies*, 20(2) (Mar. 1986), 285–319; Anand A. Yang, 'Sacred Symbol and Sacred Space in Rural India: Community Mobilization in the "Anti-Cow Killing" Riot of 1893', *Comparative Studies in Society & History*, 22(4) (Oct. 1980), 576–96; Anthony Parel, 'The Political Symbol-

ism of the Cow in India', *Journal of Commonwealth Political Studies*, 7(3) (1969), 179–203; Sandria B. Freitag, 'Sacred Symbol as Mobilizing Ideology: The North Indian Search for a "Hindu" Community', *Comparative Studies in Society & History*, 2(4) (Oct. 1980), 597–625; Gyanendra Pandey, The Construction of Communalism in Colonial North India (Delhi: Oxford University Press, 1991); Gyanendra Pandey, 'Rallying Round the Cow: Sectarian Strife in the Bhojpur Region *c.*1888–1917', in Ranajit Guha (ed.), *Subaltern Studies II* (Delhi: Oxford University Press, 1983).

BIBLIOGRAPHY

Unpublished primary sources

National Archives of India

Home Department – Medical Branch
Home Department – Sanitary Branch
Home Department – Public Branch

Asia, Pacific and Africa Collections, British Library, London

Board's Collections
Crown Representative's Records
Economic Department Records
Education, Health and Land
Famine Department
Home Miscellaneous
Military Department Records
Parliamentary Papers
Public and Judicial Department Records

Journals and periodicals

British Medical Journal
The Graphic
The Lancet
Pall Mall Gazette
Punch, or the London Charivari
The Times
The Times of India

Published primary sources (vernacular and English)

Anand, Roshan Lal, *The Milk Supply of Lahore* (Lahore: Civil and Military Gazette Press, 1933).

Annual Administration Reports of the Civil Veterinary Department in India.

Annual Administration Reports of the Civil Veterinary Department in the Presidency of Bombay.

Annual Reports of the Bombay Veterinary College.

Annual Reports of the Imperial Bacteriologist.

Annual Reports on the working of co-operative Societies in the United Province of Agra and Oudh.

'The Bengal Veterinary Department', *British Medical Journal*, 1 (2625) (22 Apr. 1911), 964–5.

'Presentation of the Mary Kingsley Medal to Dr. Griffith Evans', *Annals of Tropical Medicine and Parasitology*, 12 (1918), 1–16.

'Veterinary Work in India', *Journal for the Royal Society of Arts*, 63(3280) (1 Oct. 1915).

Baynes, C. A., *Hints On Medical Jurisprudence Adapted and Intended for the Use of Those Engaged in Judicial and Magisterial Duties in British India* (Madras: Pharaoh & Co., 1854)

Bose, Chunilal, *The Milk Supply of Calcutta* (Calcutta: Central Press, 1918).

Briggs, Geo W., *The Chamars* (Calcutta: Association Press, 1920).

Burton, I., *Prevention of Cruelty, and Antivivisection, etc, [extracted from Arabia, Egypt and India]* (London and Belfast: William Mullan, 1879).

Chatterjee, Nilanda, *The Condition of Cattle in India: Being an Enquiry into the Causes of the Present Deterioration of the Cattle with Suggestions for their Remedy* (Calcutta, 1926).

Chevers, Norman, *A Manual of Medical Jurisprudence for Bengal and the North Western Provinces* (Calcutta: Government of India Press, 1856).

Christophers, S. R., *Souvenir: The Indian Empire* (Calcutta: Thacker's Directories, 1927).

Copy of Correspondence between the Secretary of State for India and the Government of India on the Subject of Famine in Western and Southern India (London: George Edward Eyre and William Spottiswoode, 1877).

Crooke, William, *The Popular Folklore and Religion and Folklore of North India* (first published in 1896, repr. Kessinger Publishing, Montana, 2004).

Cunningham, D. D., *Scientific Memoirs by Medical Officers of the Army of India: On Milk as a Medium for Choleraic Comma-Bacilli* (Calcutta: Government Printing, 1890).

Doshi, Tarachandra, *Dugdhopchar aur Dugdh ka Khana* (publisher not mentioned, Sirohi, 1918).

Duthie, J. F., *The Fodder Grass of Northern India* (Roorkee: Thomason Civil Engineering College Press, 1888).

Dutt, R. C., *Famines and Land Assessment in India* (London: Kegan Paul, 1900).

— *The Economic History of India in the Victorian Age* (London: Kegan Paul, 1904).

Dutta, S., 'Indian Veterinary Research Institute, 1890–1950', in *Indian Veterinary Research Institute, Diamond Jubilee, 1890–1950, Indian Farming: Special Number* (Delhi: Government Press, 1950).

Edwards, S. M., *Crime in India: A Brief Review of the More Important Offences Included in the Annual Criminal Returns* (Oxford: Oxford University Press, 1924).

Famine Code of the North Western Provinces and Oudh, rev. edn (Lucknow: Government Press, 1895).

Famine in the Bombay Presidency, 1899–1902 (Bombay: Government Central Press, 1903).

Further Papers Regarding the Famine and the Relief Operations in India during the Years 1896–97: Correspondence Regarding the Appointment of a Famine Commission (London: Darling & Son, 1897).

Further Papers Regarding the Famine and the Relief Operations in India during the Years 1896–97, no. V, Resolution on the Administration of Famine Relief in the North Western Provinces and Oudh (London: Darling & Son, 1898).

Gandhi, M. K., *Cent per Cent Swadeshi or the Economics of Village Industries* (Ahmedabad: Navjivan Press, 1938).

Geddes, J. C., *Administrative Experience Recorded in Former Famines: Extracts from Official Papers Containing Instructions for Dealing with Famine, Compiled Under Orders of the Government of Bengal* (Calcutta: Bengal Secretariat Press, 1874).

Goyal, Babu Hanumandas, *Doodh Hi Amrit Hai* (Prayag: Nagri Press, 1937).

Gribble, J. D. B., *Outlines of Medical Jurisprudence for India* (3rd edn, Calcutta, 1892).

Hailey, H. R. C., *The Improvement of the Milk Supply in the Towns of the United Provinces of Agra and Oudh* (Allahabad: Government Press, 1913).

Hare, William Loftus, *Famine in India: Its Causes and Effects* (London: King & son, 1902).

Harnamdas, Kaviraj, *Keval Bhojan Dwara Swasthya-Prapti* (Lahore: Madan Mohan Printing Press, 1944).

Hartley, Percival, 'The Imperial Bacteriological Laboratory, Muktesar, India', *Nature* (9 Apr. 1914), 137–8

Holmes, Major J. D. E., *A Description of the Imperial Bacteriological Laboratory* (Superintendent Calcutta: Government Printing, 1918).

Imperial Gazetteer of India, The Indian empire, vol. III (Clarendon press, Oxford, 1907).

Jensen, Rev. Herman, *A Classified Collection of Tamil Proverbs* (London: Trubner & co, 1897).

Kipling, John Lockwood, *Beast and Man in India: A Popular Sketch of Indian Animals in Their Relation with the People* (London: Macmillan, 1891).

Kitts, Eustace J., *Serious Crime in an Indian Province, Being a Record of the Graver Crimes Committed in the North-Western Provinces and Oudh During Eleven Years, 1876 to 1886* (Bombay: Government Press, 1889).

Lefroy, Rev. G. A., *The Leather Workers of Daryaganj* (Delhi: Cambridge Mission, 1884).

BIBLIOGRAPHY

Lemuel Lucas Joshi, *Milk Supply of Indian Cities – with Reference to Bombay* (Bombay: Tarporewala & Sons, 1916).

Lethbridge, Sir Roper, *The Golden Book of India: A Genealogical and Biographical Dictionary of the Ruling Princes, Chiefs, Nobles, and other Personages, Titled or Decorated of the Indian Empire* (Delhi: Aakar Books, 2005; originally published in 1893).

Manson, Patrick, *Tropical Diseases: A Manual of the Diseases of Warm Climates* (London: Cassell, 1900).

Martin, J. R., *Tanning and Working in Leather in the Bombay Presidency* (Bombay: Secretariat Press, 1903).

Merewether, F. H. S., *A Tour through Famine Districts in India* (London: Innes, 1898).

Modi, Rai Bahadur Jaising P., *A Textbook for Medical Jurisprudence and Toxicology* (Calcutta: Kothari Book Depot, 1920).

Moorcroft, William, *Directions for using the Contents of the Portable Horse Medicine Chest, Adapted for India and Prepared by W. Moorcroft* (London, 1795).

Muktesar: Its Works and Products (Superintendent Calcutta: Government Printing, 1913).

Olver, Arthur, 'Animal Husbandry in India', *Journal of the Royal Society of Arts* (29 May 1942), 433–9.

Palmer, Dr. D. C., *Report on the Calcutta Epizootic or Cattle Disease of 1864 in Calcutta and Its Neighbourhood* (Calcutta: Government of India Press, 1865).

Papers and Correspondence relative to the Famine in Bengal and Orissa, Including the Report of the Famine Commission and the Minutes of the Lieutenant Governor of Bengal and the Governor General in India (London: Eyre and Spottiswoode, 1867).

Papers Regarding the Famine and the Relief Operations in India during 1899–1900, vol. I – British States (London: Darling & Son, 1900).

Papers Regarding the Famine and the Relief Operations in India during 1899–1900, vol. II – Native States (Darling & Son, London, 1900).

Papers Relating to Cattle Disease, from the Records of the Government of Bengal, XLIII (Calcutta: Central Press Company, 1869).

Piggott, J. P., *Treatise on the Horses in India* (Calcutta: Government of India Press, 1794).

Proceedings of the Cattle Conference held at Bangalore on 22nd and 23rd January, 1924 (Calcutta: Government of India Press, 1924).

Proceedings of the First Meeting of Veterinary Officers in India (Superintendent Calcutta: Government Printing, 1919).

Proceedings of the Third All-India Sanitary Conference held at Lucknow in January 1914 (Calcutta: Government of India Press, 1914).

Provincial Reports of the Civil Veterinary Department of Punjab.

The Punjab Famine of 1899–1900 (Government Press, Lahore, 1901).

Ramsay, H. M., *Detective Footprints, Bengal, 1874–1881* (Charleston, 2009, first published in 1882).

Ray, R. C., *Medical Jurisprudence and Treatment of Poisoning* (published by the author, Calcutta, 1910).

Records of the Government of India, Papers Relating to Cattle Diseases, LXIX (Calcutta: Government of India Press, 1868).

Report by Zal R. Kothawala, in *Proceedings of the Cattle Conference* (Calcutta: Government of India Press, 1924).

Report of Colonel Baird Smith to the Indian government, dated 8 May 1861, on the Commercial Condition of the North West Province of India; and Report of the Same Officer to the Indian Government on the Recent Famine in the Same Province (London: Eyre and Spottiswoode, 1862).

Report of the Central Executive Committee, Indian Famine Charitable Relief Fund, 1900 (Calcutta: Government Press, 1901).

Report of the Commissioners Appointed to Inquire into the Origin, Nature, etc of Indian Cattle Plagues (Calcutta: Government Press, 1871).

Report of the Committee Appointed by the Central Advisory Board of Health to Investigate the question of Food Adulteration in India with Particular Reference to Legislation now in Force in Difference Provinces and to the Varying Standards which are in Force (Government Press, Simla, 1940).

Report of the Indian Famine Commission, 1901, and Papers Relating Thereto (London: Darling & son, 1901).

Report on a Village Enquiry regarding Cattle and the Production and Consumption of Milk in Seven Breeding Tracts of India (Simla: Government of India Press, 1939).

Report on a Village Enquiry regarding Cattle and the Production and Consumption of Milk in Seven Breeding Tracts of India (Government of India Press, Delhi, 1939).

Report on the Famine in the Central Provinces in 1899–1900.

Report on the Investigations of Cases of Real or Supposed Poisoning (Calcutta: Government of India Press, 1841).

Report on the Marketing of Ghee and Other Milk Products in India (Delhi: Government of India Press, 1947).

Reports of Cases Determined in the Nizamut Adawlut for 1856 (Calcutta: Government of India Press, 1857).

Risely, H. H., *The Tribes and Castes of Bengal, Ethnographic Glossary* (Calcutta: Government of India Press, 1891).

Royal Commission on Agriculture in India (Government of India Publications, Calcutta, 1927).

Russell, R. V., *The Tribes and Castes of the Central Provinces of India* (London: Macmillan, 1916).

Selections from the Records of Government of India, CLXXX, *Papers relating to the Crime of Cattle Poisoning* (Calcutta: Government of India Press, 1881).

Selections from the Records of the Government of the Punjab and its Dependencies: Treatment of Cattle Disease in the Punjab, new series(XX (Lahore: Punjab Government Secretariat Press, 1883).

Shastri, Acharya Shri Chatursen, *Arogya Shashtra* (Sanjeevni Institute, Delhi, 1932).

Shastri, Chandreshekhar, *Sharir Vigyan* (Delhi, publisher not mentioned, 1937).

[153]

Singh, Ganpati Verma, *Dugdh Gun Vidhan* (publisher not mentioned, Bikaner, 1934).

Taylor, Meadows, *Confessions of a Thug* (London: Richard Bentley, 1839).

Taylor, A. S., *A Manual of Medical Jurisprudence* (Philadelphia: Henry C. Lea, 1848).

Waddell, L. A., *Lyon's Medical Jurisprudence in India* (Calcutta: Thacker, Spink & Co., 1888).

Wallace, Robert, *India in 1887* (Edinburgh: Oliver and Boyd, 1888).

Walton, H. G., *A Monograph on Tanning and Working in Leather in the United Provinces* (Allahabad: Government Press, 1903).

Watt, Sir John, *The Commercial Products of India Being an Abridgement of the 'Dictionary of Commercial Products of India'* (London: J. Murray, 1908).

Weston, S. T., *Cattle and Dairying in the Punjab* (Lahore: Civil and Military Gazette Press, 1910).

Wise, James, *Notes on the Races, Castes and Tribes of Eastern Bengal* (London: Harrison and Sons, 1883).

Wright, Norman C., *Report on the development of the Cattle and Dairy Industries of* India (Simla: Government of India Press, 1937).

Wroughton, R. C., *Famine in the Bombay presidency, 1899–1902* (Bombay: Government Central Press, 1902).

Secondary sources

Aitkins, P. J., 'Sophistication detected: or, the Adulteration of the Milk Supply, 1850–1914', *Social History*, 16(3) (Oct. 1991), 318–39.

Alder, G. J., 'The Asian years of William Moorcroft, 1808–25', *Asian Affairs*, 18(1) (1987), 3–10.

Alter, Joseph, *The Wrestler's Body: Identity and Ideology in North India* (Berkeley: University of California Press, 1992).

Ambirajan, S., 'Malthusian Population Theory and Indian Famine Policy in the Nineteenth Century', *Population Studies*, 30(1) (Mar. 1976), 5–14

Amin, Shahid, 'Small Peasant Commodity Production and Rural Indebtedness: The Culture of Sugarcane in Eastern U.P., c.1880–1920', in Ranajit Guha (ed.), *Subaltern Studies, vol. I* (Delhi: Oxford University Press, repr. 2010).

Anderson, Warwick, 'Climates of Opinion: Acclimatization in Nineteenth-Century France and England', *Victorian Studies*, 35(2) (1992), 135–57.

Appleby, Andrew B., 'Famine, Mortality, and Epidemic Disease: A Comment', *Economic History Review*, 30(3) (Aug. 1977), 508–12.

Arnold, David, 'Medical Priorities and Practice in Nineteenth Century British India', *South Asia Research*, 5(2) (1985), 167–83.

— (ed.), *Imperial Medicine and Indigenous Societies* (Manchester: Manchester University Press, 1988).

— *Colonizing the Body: State Medicine and Epidemic Disease in Nineteenth-Century India* (Berkeley: University of California Press, 1989).

— 'Social Crisis and Epidemic Disease in the Famines of Nineteenth-century India', *Social History of Medicine*, 6(3) (1993), 385–404.

— 'Crisis and Contradictions in India's Public Health', in Dorothy Porter (ed.), *The History of Public Health and the Modern State* (Rodopi, Amsterdam, 1994), 335–55.

— 'The "Discovery" of Malnutrition and Diet in Colonial India', *Indian Economic Social History Review* 31(1) (1994), 1–26.

— 'The Place of the "Tropics" in Western Medical Ideas since 1750', *Tropical Medicine and International Health*, 24 (1997), 303–13.

— *Science, Technology and Medicine in Colonial India* (Cambridge: Cambridge University Press, 2000).

— *Tropics and the Travelling Gaze: India, Landscape and Science, 1800–1856* (Washington, DC: University of Washington Press, 2006).

Bagchi, Amiya Kumar, 'Land Tax, Property Rights and Peasant Insecurity in Colonial India', *Journal of Peasant Studies*, 20(1) (1992), 1–49.

Bahre, Conrad J. and Shelton, Marlyn L., 'Southwest Rangeland Destruction: Cattle and Drought in Southeastern Arizona at the Turn of the Century', *Journal of the Southwest*, 38(1) (spring 1996), 1–22.

Bala, Poonam, *Imperialism and Medicine in Bengal* (New Delhi: Sage, 1991).

Balland, Daniel, 'Nomadism and Politics: The Case of Afghan Nomads in the Indian Subcontinent', *Studies in History*, 7 (1991), 205–29.

Banerjee, Himadri *et al.* (eds.), *Calcutta Mosaic: Essays and Interviews on the Minority Communities of Calcutta* (Delhi: Anthem Press, 2009).

Banerjee, Swapna M., 'Down Memory Lane: Representations of Domestic Workers in Middle Class Personal Narratives of Colonial Bengal', *Journal of Social History*, 37(3) (spring 2004), 681–708.

Banerjee-Dube, Ishita (ed.), *Caste in History* (Delhi: Oxford University Press, 2008).

Barendse, R. J., 'The Feudal Mutation: Military and Economic Transformations of the Ethnosphere in the Tenth to Thirteenth Centuries', *Journal of World History*, 14(4) (Dec. 2003), 503–29.

Barua, Pradeep P., *Gentlemen of the Raj: The Indian Army Officer Corps, 1817–1949* (Westport: Praeger, 2003).

Basalla, George, 'The Spread of Western Science', *Science*, 156(3775) (5 May 1967), 611–22.

Bates, Crispin, *Race, Caste and Tribe in Central India* (Edinburgh: Edinburgh Papers in South Asian History, 1995).

Bayly, C. A., 'Knowing the Country: Empire and Information in India', *Modern Asian Studies*, 27(1) (Feb. 1993), 3–43.

— *Empire and Information: Intelligence Gathering and Social Communication in India, 1780–1870* (Cambridge: Cambridge University Press, 1996).

Bayly, Susan, *Caste, Society and Politics in India: From the Eighteenth Century to the Modern Age* (Cambridge: Cambridge University Press, 1999).

Bearce, G. D., 'Lord William Bentinck: The Application of Liberalism to India', *Journal of Modern History*, 28 (1956), 234–46.

Beinart, William, *The Rise of Conservation in South Africa: Settlers, Livestock, and the Environment 1770–1950* (New York: Oxford University Press, 2003).

Bhabha, Homi, 'The Other Question ... Homi K. Bhabha Reconsiders the Stereotype and Colonial Discourse', *Screen*, 24(6) (1983), 18–36.

Bhalla, Lt. Col. J. S., *History of the Remount and Veterinary Corps* (New Delhi: Additional Directorate General Remount and Veterinary Press, 1988).

Bhatia, B. M., *Famines in India: A Study in Some Aspects of the Economic History of India, 1860–1965* (London: Asia Publishing House, 1967).

Bhattacharya, Nandini, *Contagion and Enclaves: Tropical Medicine in Colonial India* (Liverpool: Liverpool University Press, 2012).

Bittel, Carla, *Mary Putnam Jacobi and the Politics of medicine in Nineteenth-century America* (North Carolina: University of North Carolina Press, 2009).

Blaisdell, John D., 'With Certain Reservations: The American Veterinary Community's Reception of Pasteur's Work on Rabies', *Agricultural History*, 70(3) (summer 1996), 503–24.

Bose, Pradip Kumar (ed.), *Health and Society in Bengal: A Selection from Late 19th-Century Bengali Periodicals* (Delhi: Sage, 2006).

Bose, Sugata (ed.), *Credits, Markets and the Agrarian Economy of Colonial India* (Delhi: Oxford University Press, 2004), pp. 197–247.

Brahme, Sulabha, 'Drought in Maharashtra', *Social Scientist*, 1(12) (Jul. 1973), 47–54.

Brewis, Georgina, 'Fill Full the Mouth of Famine: Voluntary Action in Famine Relief in India 1896–1901', *Modern Asian Studies*, 44(4) (2010), 887–918.

Brown, Karen, 'Tropical Medicine and Animal Diseases: Onderspoort and the Development of Veterinary Science in South Africa, 1908–1950', *Journal of South African Studies*, 31(3) (2005), 513–29.

Brown, Karen and Gilfoyle, Daniel (eds.), *Healing the Herds: Disease, Livestock Economies, and the Globalization of Veterinary Medicine* (Ohio: Ohio University Press, 2010).

Butalia, Romesh C., *The Evolution of the Artillery in India: From the Battle of Plassey to the Revolt of 1857* (Delhi: Allied Publishers, 1999).

Callahan, Raymond, *The East India Company and Army Reform, 1783–1798* (Cambridge, MA: Harvard University Press, 1972).

Carroll, Lucy, 'Colonial Perceptions of Indian Society and the Emergence of Caste(s) Associations', *Journal of Asian Studies*, 37(2) (Feb. 1978), 233–50.

Caton, Brian P., 'Social Categories and Colonisation in Punjab, 1849–1920', *Indian Economic and Social History Review*, 41 (Feb. 2004), 33–50.

Chakrabarti, Pratik, 'Beasts of Burden: Animals and Laboratory Research in Colonial India', *History of Science*, 48, 2(160) (Jun. 2010), 125–52.

— *Bacteriology in British India: Laboratory Medicine and the Tropics* (Rochester: University of Rochester Press, 2012).

Chakravarti, Ranabir, 'Early Medieval Bengal and the Trade in Horses: A Note', *Journal of the Economic and Social History of the Orient*, 42(2) (1999), 194–211.

Chandravarkar, Rajnarayan, *Imperial Power and Popular Politics: Class, Resistance and the State in India, c.1850–1950* (Cambridge: University Press, 1988).

Chatterjee, Partha, *Our Modernity* (Rotterdam: SEPHIS, 1997).

Chattopadhyay, Basudeb, *Crime and Control in Early Colonial Bengal, 1770–1860* (Calcutta: Bagchi, 2000).

Chaudhuri, Binay Bhushan, 'The Land Market in Eastern India, 1793–1940. Part 1: The Movement of Land Prices', *Indian Economic and Social History Review*, 12(1) (1976), 1–42.

Chaudhuri, K. N., *Asia before Europe: Economy and Civilisation of the Indian Ocean from the Rise of Islam to 1750* (Cambridge: Cambridge University Press, 1990).

Cohn, Bernard, *Colonialism and its Forms of Knowledge: The British in India* (Princeton: Princeton University Press, 1996).

Collingham, E. M., *Imperial Bodies: The Physical Experience of the Raj* (Cambridge: Polity, 2001).

Cranefield, Paul, *Science and Empire: East Coast Fever in Rhodesia and the Transvaal* (Cambridge: Cambridge University Press, 1991).

Cunningham, A. and Williams, P. (eds.), *The Laboratory Revolution in Medicine* (Cambridge: Cambridge University Press, 1992).

Currie, Bob, 'Public Action and Its Limits: Re-Examining the Politics of Hunger Alleviation in Eastern India', *Third World Quarterly*, 19(5) (Dec., 1998), 873–92.

Curth, Louise Hill, 'The Care of the Brute Beast: Animals and the Seventeenth-Century Medical Market-Place', *Social History of Medicine*, 15(3) (2002), 375–92.

Damodaran, Vinita, 'Famine in Bengal: A Comparison of the 1770 Famine in Bengal and the 1897 Famine in Chotanagpur', *Medieval History Journal*, 10(1–2) (2007), 143–81.

Dangwal, Dhirendra Datt, 'State, Forests and Graziers in the Hills of Uttar Pradesh: Impact of Colonial Forestry on Peasants, Gujars and Bhotiyas', *Indian Economic Social History Review*, 34(4) (1997), 405–35.

Davis, Diana K., 'Prescribing Progress: French Veterinary Medicine in the Service of Empire', *Veterinary Heritage*, 29(1) (May 2006), 1–7.

— 'Brutes, Beasts and Empire: Veterinary Medicine and Environmental Policy in French North Africa and British India', *Journal of Historical Geography*, 34(2) (2008), 242–67.

Davis, Mike, *Late Victorian Holocausts: El Nino Famines and the Making of the Third World* (London: Verso, 2001).

Deshpande, Prachi, 'Caste as Maratha: Social Categories Colonial Policy and Identity in Early Twentieth-Century Maharashtra', *Indian Economic and Social History Review*, 41 (Feb. 2004), 7–32.

Dictionary of National Biography (Oxford: Oxford University Press, 2004).

Dirks, Nicholas B., *Castes of Mind: Colonialism and the Making of Modern India* (Princeton: Princeton University Press, 2001).

— *The Scandal of Empire: India and the Creation of Imperial Britain* (Cambridge, MA: Harvard University Press, 2006).

Drayton, R., 'Science and the European Empires', *Journal of Imperial and Commonwealth History*, 23 (1995), 503–10.

Dubber, Markus D. and Farmer, Lindsay (eds.), *Modern Histories of Crime and Punishment* (Stanford: Stanford University Press, 2007).

Dyson, Tim (ed.), *India's Historic Demography: Studies in Famine, Disease and Society* (London: Curzon, 1989).

— 'On the Demography of South Asian Famines: Part I', *Population Studies*, 45(1) (Mar. 1991), 5–25.

Edwards, Peter, *Horses of Tudor and Stuart England* (Cambridge: Cambridge University Press, 1988).

Ernst, Waltraud and Pati, Biswamoy (ed.), *India's Princely States: People, Princes and Colonialism* (London: Routledge, 2007).

Fallis, Murray A., 'Griffith Evans 1835–1935: Discoverer of the First Pathogenic Trypanosome', *Canadian Veterinary Journal*, 27 (1986), 336–8.

Firth, R. (ed.), *Themes in Economic Anthropology* (London: Tavistock, 1967), pp. 229–52.

Fischer-Tine, Harald and Mann, Michael (eds.), *Colonialism as a Civilizing Mission: Cultural Ideology in British India* (London: Anthem Press, 2004).

Fisher, John R., 'Cattle Plagues Past and Present: The Mystery of Mad Cow Disease', *Journal of Contemporary History*, 33(2) (1998), 215–28.

Fox-Genovese, Elizabeth, *Origins of Physiocracy: Economic Revolution and Social Order in Eighteenth Century France* (New York: Cornell University Press, 1976).

Freitag, Sandria B., 'Sacred Symbol as Mobilizing Ideology: The North Indian Search for a "Hindu" Community', *Comparative Studies in Society & History*, 22(4) (Oct. 1980), 597–625.

— 'Crime in the Social Order of Colonial North India', *Modern Asian Studies*, 25(2) (1991), 227–61.

French, Michael and Phillips, Jim, *Cheated Not Poisoned: Food Regulation in the United Kingdom, 1875–1938* (Manchester: Manchester University Press, 2000).

Frykenberg, R. E. *Guntur District, 1788–1848: A History of Local Influences and Central Authority in South Asia* (Oxford: Clarendon Press, 1965).

— (ed.), *Land Control and Social Structure in Indian History* (Wisconsin: University of Wisconsin Press, 1969).

Geist, Edward, 'When Ice Cream Was Poisonous: Adulteration, Ptomaines, and Bacteriology in the United States, 1850–1910', *Bulletin of the History of Medicine*, 86(3) (Fall, 2012), 333–60.

Ghose, Ajit Kumar, 'Food Supply and Starvation: A Study of Famines with Reference to the Indian Subcontinent', *Oxford Economic Papers*, 34(2) (1982).

Ghosh, Suniti Kumar, 'Marx on India', *Monthly Review*, 35(8) (Jan. 1984), 41–2.

Ghotge, Nitya S., *Livestocks and Livelihoods: The Indian Context* (Delhi: Foundation Books, 2004).

Gilfoyle, Daniel, 'Veterinary Research and the African Rinderpest Epizootic: the Cape Colony, 1896–1898', *Journal of Southern African Studies*, 29(1) (2003), 133–54.

— 'Veterinary Immunology as Colonial Science: Method and Quantification in the Investigation of Horse Sickness in South Africa, c.1905–1945', *Journal of the History of Medicine and Allied Sciences*, 61(1) (2005), 26–65.

Gilmartin, David, 'Cattle, Crime and Colonialism: Property as Negotiation in North India', *Indian Economic and Social History Review*, 40(1) (2003), 33–56.

Gommans, Jas, 'The Horse Trade in Eighteenth Century South Asia', *Journal of the Economic and Social History of the Orient*, 37(3) (1994), 228–50.

— *The Rise of the Indo-Afghan Empire, c.1710–1780* (Leiden: Brill, 1997).

Greenough, Paul R., 'Comments from a South Asian Perspective: Food, Famine, and the Chinese State', *Journal of Asian Studies*, 41(4) (Aug. 1982), 789–97.

— *Prosperity and Misery in Bengal: The Famine of 1943–44* (New York: Oxford University Press, 1982).

Guha, Ramchandra, *The Unquiet Woods: Ecological Change and Peasant Resistance in the Himalayas* (Delhi: Oxford University Press, 1989).

Guha, Ranajit, *A Rule of Property for Bengal: An Essay on the Idea of the Permanent Settlement* (Paris: Mouton, 1963).

— *Elementary Aspects of Peasant Insurgency in Colonial India* (Durham: Duke University Press, 1999).

Hall-Matthews, David, *Peasants, Famines and the State in Colonial Western India* (Basingstoke: Palgrave, 2005).

Hannaway, Caroline C., 'Veterinary Medicine and Rural Health Care in Pre-Revolutionary France', *Bulletin of the Institute of Science*, 51(3) (1977), 431.

Hardiman, David, 'Usury, Dearth and Famine in Western India', *Past and Present*, (152) (Aug. 1996), 113–56.

— *Feeding the Baniya: Peasants and Usurers in Western India* (Delhi: Oxford University Press, 1997).

Hardy, Anne, 'Pioneers in the Victorian Provinces: Veterinarians, Public Health and the Urban Animal Economy', *Urban History* 29(3) (2003), 372–87.

— 'Professional Advantage and Public Health: British Veterinarians and State Veterinary Services, 1865–1939', *Twentieth Century British History*, 14(1) (2003), 1–23.

Harris, Marvin, 'The Cultural Ecology of India's Sacred Cattle', *Cultural Anthropology*, 33(1) (Feb. 1992), 261–76.

Harrison, Mark , 'Towards a Sanitary Utopia? Professional Visions and Public Health in India, 1880–1914', *South Asia Research*, 10(1) (1990), 19–40.

— *Public Health in British India: Anglo-Indian Preventive Medicine, 1859–1914* (Cambridge: Cambridge University Press, 1994).

— '"The Tender Frame of Man": Disease, Climate and Racial Difference in India and the West Indies, 1760–1860', *Bulletin of the History of Medicine*, 70(1) (spring 1996), 68–93.

— *Climates and Constitutions: Health, Race, Environment and British Imperialism in India 1600–1850* (Delhi: Oxford University Press, 2000).

— *Disease and the Modern World, 1500 to the Present Day* (Cambridge: Polity, 2004).

— 'Science and the British Empire', *Isis*, 96 (2005), 56–63.

Harrison, Mark and Pati, Biswamoy (eds.), *Health, Medicine and Empire: Perspectives on Colonial India* (Delhi: Orient Longman, 2001).

Hill, Christopher, 'Philosophy and Reality in Riparian South Asia: British Famine Policy and Migration in Colonial North India', *Modern Asian Studies*, 25(2) (1991), 263–79.

Hobsbawm, E. J., 'Peasants and Politics', *Journal of Peasant Studies*, 1(1) (1973), 3–22.

Illiah, Kancha, *Buffalo Nationalism: A Critique of Spiritual Fascism* (Kolkata: Samya, 2004).

Inden, Ronald, *Imagining India* (Oxford: Basil Blackwell, 1990).

Jeffrey, Roger, *The Politics of Health India* (Berkeley: University of California Press, 1988).

Jordan, William Chester, *The Great Famine: Northern Europe in the Early Fourteenth Century* (New Jersey: Princeton University Press, 1996).

Kanwar, Pamela, 'The Changing Profile of the Summer Capital of British India: Simla 1864–1947', *Modern Asian Studies*, 18(2) (1984), 215–36.

— *Imperial Simla: The Political Culture of the Raj* (Delhi: Oxford University Press, 1990).

Kennedy, Dane, 'Imperial History and Post-colonial Theory', *Journal of Imperial and Commonwealth History*, 24(3) (1996), 345–63.

— *The Magic Mountains: Hill Stations and the British Raj* (Berkeley: University of California Press, 1996).

Kenny, Judith T., 'Climate, Race, and Imperial Authority: The Symbolic Landscape of the British Hill Station in India', *Annals of the Association of American Geographers*, 85(4) (Dec. 1995), 694–714.

Klein, Ira, 'Death in India, 1871–1921', *Journal of Asian Studies*, 32(4) (Aug. 1973), 639–65.

— 'When the Rains Failed: Famine, Relief, and Mortality in British India', *Indian Economic Social History Review* 21(2) (1984), 185–214

Kraft, Alison, 'Breaking with Tradition: The Reform of British Veterinary Education 1900–20', *History of Education*, 33(3) (2004), 317–36.

Krishnan, S. (ed.), *A Town Called Malgudi* (Delhi: Penguin, 2002).

Kumar, Anil, *Medicine and the Raj: British Medical Policy in India, 1835–1911* (Delhi: Sage, 1998).

Kumar, Deepak (ed.), *Disease and Medicine in India: A Historical Overview* (Calcutta: Indian Historical Congress, 2001).

— 'Health and Medicine in British India and Dutch Indies: A Comparative Study', in Joseph Alter (ed.), *Asian Medicine and Globalization* (Pennsylvania: University of Pennsylvania Press, 2005).

Kumar, Dharam, *Land and Caste in South India: Agricultural Labour in Madras Presidency in the Nineteenth Century* (Cambridge: Cambridge University Press, 1965).

— 'Famine Deaths in China', *Economic and Political Weekly*, 18(5) (29 Jan. 1983), 132.

Kumar, Dharma and Raychaudhuri, Tapan (eds.), *Cambridge Economic History of India*, vol. II, c.1757–c.1970 (Cambridge: Cambridge University Press, 1983).

Kumar, Mukul, 'Relationship of Caste and Crime in Colonial India: A Discourse Analysis', *Economic and Political Weekly*, 39(10) (6 Mar. 2004), 1078–87.

Kumar, Ravinder, *Western India in the Nineteenth Century: A study in the Social History of Maharashtra* (Toronto: University of Toronto Press, 1968).

Kupperman, Karen Ordahl, 'Fear of Hot Climates in the Anglo-American Colonial Experience', *William and Mary Quarterly*, 41 (1984), 213–40.

Lardinois, Roland, 'Famine, Epidemics and Mortality in South India: A

Reappraisal of the Demographic Crisis of 1876–1878', *Economic and Political Weekly*, 20(11) (16 Mar. 1985), 454–65.

Law, Marc T., 'The Origins of State Pure Food Regulation', *Journal of Economic History*, 63(4) (Dec. 2003), 1103–30.

Lowy, Ilana, 'From Guinea Pigs to Man: The Development of Haffkine's Anticholera Vaccine', *Journal of the History of Medicine and Allied Sciences*, 47 (1992), 270–306.

McAlpin, Michelle Burge, *Subject to Famine: Food Crises and Economic Change in Western India, 1860–1920* (Princeton: Princeton University Press, 1983).

Macleod, Roy and Lewis, Milton (eds.), *Disease, Medicine and Empire: Perspectives on Western Medicine and the Experience of European Expansion* (London and New York: Routledge, 1988).

Maharatna, Arup, 'Infant and Child Mortality during Famines in Late 19th and Early 20th Century', *Economic and Political Weekly*, 31(27) (6 Jul. 1996), 1774–783.

Marks, Shula, 'What Is Colonial about Colonial Medicine? And What Has Happened to Imperialism and Health?', *Social History of Medicine* 10(2) (1997), 205–19.

Marriott, McKim, 'Caste Ranking and Food Transactions: A Matrix Analysis', in Bernard S. Cohn and Milton Singer (eds.), *Structure and Change in Indian Society* (Chicago: Aldine, 1968).

Mishra, Arima, 'Local Perceptions of Famine: Study of a Village in Orissa', *Economic and Political Weekly*, 40(6) (5–11 Feb. 2005), 572–8.

Mishra, Saurabh, *Pilgrimage, Politics and Pestilence: The Haj from the Indian Subcontinent, 1870–1920* (Delhi: Oxford University Press, 2011).

Mitchell, A. R. (ed.), *History of Healing Professions*, III (Cambridge: Cambridge University Press, 1993), pp. 119–30.

Mohanty, Bidyut, 'Orissa Famine of 1866: Demographic and Economic Consequences', *Economic and Political Weekly*, 28(1/2) (2–9 Jan. 1993), 55–66.

Mohr, James C., *Doctors and the Law: Medical Jurisprudence in Nineteenth Century America* (New York: Oxford University Press, 1993).

Nag, Sajal, 'Tribals, Rats, Famine, State and the Nation', *Economic and Political Weekly*, 36(12) (24–30 Mar. 2001), 1029–33.

Nigam, Sanjay, 'Disciplining and Policing the "Criminals by Birth" Part 1: The Making of a Colonial Stereotype – The Criminal Tribes and Castes of North', *Indian Economic and Social History Review*, 27(2) (1990), 131–65.

— 'Disciplining and Policing the "Criminals by Birth"', Part 2: The Development of a Disciplinary System 1871–1900', 27(3) (1990), 257–87.

Otter, Sandra Den, 'Rewriting the Utilitarian Market: Colonial Law and Custom in Mid Nineteenth-Century British India', *European Legacy*, 6(2) (2001), 177–88.

Pandey, Gyanendra, 'Rallying Round the Cow: Sectarian Strife in the Bhojpur Region c.1888–1917', in Ranajit Guha (ed.), *Subaltern Studies II* (Delhi: Oxford University Press, 1983).

— *The Construction of Communalism in Colonial North India* (Delhi: Oxford University Press, 1991).

Pankhurst, Alula, *Resettlement and Famine in Ethiopia: The Villagers' Experi-ence* (Manchester: Manchester University Press, 1992).

Parel, Anthony, 'The Political Symbolism of the Cow in India', *Journal of Commonwealth Political Studies*, 7(3) (1969), 179–203.

Parry, Benita, 'The Postcolonial: Conceptual Category or Chimera?', *Yearbook of English Studies*, 27 (1997), 3–21

— *Postcolonial Studies: A Materialist Critique* (London: Routledge, 2004).

Parthasarthi, Prasannan, *The Transition to a Colonial Economy: Weavers, Merchants and Kings in South India, 1720–1800* (Cambridge: Cambridge University Press, 2001).

— 'The State of Indian History', *Journal of Social History*, 37(1) (2003), 47–54.

Pathak, Akhileshwar, *Laws, Strategies, Ideologies: Legislating Forests in Colonial India* (Delhi: Oxford University Press, 2002).

Pati, Biswamoy, *Situating Social History: Orissa, 1800–1997* (London: Sangam Books, 2001).

Patterson, K. David, 'The Veterinary Department and the Animal Industry in the Gold Coast, 1909–1955', *International Journal of African Historical Studies*, 13(3) (1980), 457–91.

Peabody, Norbert, 'Cents, Sense, Census: Human Inventories in Late Pre-colonial and Early Colonial India', *Comparative Studies in Society and History*, 43(4) (2001), 819–50.

Pedersen, Susan and Mendler, Peter (eds.), *After the Victorians: Private Conscience and Public Duty in Modern Britain* (London: Routledge, 1994).

Peers, Douglas M., *India under Colonial Rule, 1700–1885* (London: Longman, 2006).

Phillips, Jim and French, Michael, 'Adulteration and Food Law, 1899–1939', *Twentieth Century British History*, 9(3) (Jul. 1998), 350–69.

Phoofolo, Pule, 'Epidemics and Revolutions: The Rinderpest Epidemic in Late Nineteenth-Century Southern Africa', *Past and Present*, 138 (Feb. 1993), 112–43.

Pilcher, Jeffrey M., *Sausage Rebellion: Public Health, Private Enterprise, and Meat in Mexico City, 1890–1917* (New Mexico: University of New Mexico Press, 2006).

Post, John D., 'Famine, Mortality, and Epidemic Disease in the Process of Modernization', *Economic History Review*, 29(1) (Feb. 1976), 14–37.

Pouchepadass, J., Markovits, C., and Subramanyam, S. (eds.), *Society and Circulation: Mobile People and Itinerant Cultures in South Asia* (Delhi: Permanent Black, 2003).

Prakash, Gyan (ed.), *The World of the Rural Labourer in Colonial India* (Delhi: Oxford University Press, 1992).

Prasad, R. R. and G. Rajanikanth, *Development of Scheduled Caste Leather Artisans: Profile, Problems and Prospects* (New Delhi: Discovery Publishing House, 1991).

Prasad, Srirupa, 'Crisis, Identity, and Social Distinction: Cultural Politics of Food, Taste, and Consumption in Late Colonial Bengal' *Journal of Histor-ical Sociology*, 19(3) (Sept. 2006), 245–65.

BIBLIOGRAPHY

Prindle, Peter H., 'Peasant Society and Famine: A Nepalese Example', *Ethnology*, 18(1) (Jan. 1979), 49–60.

Radhakrishna, Meena, 'Colonial Construction of a "Criminal" Tribe: Yerukulas of Madras Presidency', *Economic and Political Weekly*, 35(28/29) (15–21 Jul. 2000), 2553–63.

— *Dishonoured by History: 'Criminal Tribes' and British Colonial Policy* (Hyderbad: Orient Longman, 2001).

Ramanna, Mridula, *Western Medicine and Public Health in Colonial Bombay, 1845–1895* (Hyderabad: Orient Blackswan, 2002).

Ramasubban, Radhika, *Public Health and Medical Research in India: Their Origins under the Impact of British Colonial Policy* (Stockholm: SAREC, 1982).

Rangarajan, Mahesh, *Fencing the Forest: Conservation and Ecological Change in India's Central Provinces, 1860–1914* (Delhi: Oxford University Press, 1999).

Ranger, Terence and Slack, Paul (eds.), *Epidemics and Ideas: Essays on the Historical Perception of Pestilence* (Cambridge: Cambridge University Press, 1992).

Ratan, Jai and Lal, P. (tr.), *Godan: A Novel of Peasant India* (Mumbai: Jaico, 2002).

Ray, Kabita, *Food for Thought: Food Adulteration in Bengal, 1836–1947* (Calcutta: Papyrus, 2003).

Raychaudhuri, Tapan and Habib, Irfan (eds.), *Cambridge Economic History of India, vol. I, c.1200–c.1750* (Cambridge: Cambridge University Press, 1982).

Reed, Robert R., 'The Colonial Genesis of Hill Stations: The Genting Exception', *Geographical Review*, 69(4) (1979), 463–8.

Rich, Paul B., *Race and Empire in British Politics* (Cambridge: Cambridge University Press, 1986).

Robb, Peter, 'The Challenge of Gau Mata: British Policy and Religious Change in India, 1880–1916', *Modern Asian Studies*, 20(2) (Mar. 1986), 285–319.

— 'Peasants' Choices? Indian Agriculture and the Limits of Commercialization in Nineteenth – Century Bihar', *Economic History Review*, 45(1) (Feb. 1992), 97–119.

— (ed.), *The Concept of Race* (Delhi: Oxford University Press, 1995).

Robinson, Andrew, *Satyajit Ray: The Inner Eye* (Berkeley: University of California Press, 1989).

Rogers, J. D., 'Introduction: Caste, Power and Region in Colonial South Asia', *Indian Economic & Social History Review*, 41(1) (Feb. 2004), 1–6.

Roy, Kaushik (ed.), *War and Society in Colonial India* (Delhi: Oxford University Press, 2006).

Roy, Tirthankar, 'Questioning the Basics', *Economic and Political Weekly*, 37(23) (8–14 Jun. 2002), 2223–8.

Sarkar, Sumit, 'Popular Culture, Community and Power: Three Studies of Modern Indian Social History', *Studies in History*, 8(2) (Aug. 1992), 309–23.

— *Writing Social History* (Delhi: Oxford University Press, 1997).

Satya, Laxman, *Ecology, Colonialism and Cattle: Central India in the Nineteenth Century* (Delhi: Oxford University Press, 2004).

BIBLIOGRAPHY

Sengupta, Jayanta, 'Nation on a Platter: the Culture and Politics of Food and Cuisine in Colonial Bengal', *Modern Asian Studies*, 44(1) (Jan. 2010), 81–96.

Sharma, Sanjay, 'The 1837–38 Famine in U.P.: Some Dimensions of Popular Action', *Indian Economic Social History Review*, 30(3) (1993), 337–72.

— *Famine, Philanthropy, and the Colonial State: North India in the Early Nineteenth Century* (Delhi: Oxford University Press, 2001).

Sharma, V. P., Morton, J. and Kohler-Rollefson, I., *Pastoralism in India: A Scoping Study* (Delhi: DFID, 2003).

Shears, P., 'Epidemiology and Infection in Famine and Disasters', *Epidemiology and Infection*, 107(2) (Oct. 1991), 241–51.

Siddiqui, Asiya (ed.), *Trade and Finance in Colonial India, 1750–1860* (Delhi: Oxford University Press, 1995).

Simoons, F. J., *Eat Not this Flesh* (Madison: University of Wisconsin Press, 1961).

Singer, M. and Cohn, B. S. (eds.), *Structure and Change in Indian Society* (Chicago: Aldine, 1978).

Singha, Radhika, '"Providential" Circumstances: The Thuggee Campaign of the 1830s and Legal Innovation', *Modern Asian Studies*, 27(1) (1993), 83–146.

— *A Despotism of Law: Crime and Justice in Early Colonial India* (Delhi: Oxford University Press, 1998).

Sinha, Mrinalini, *Colonial Masculinity: The 'Many Englishman' and the 'Effeminate Bengali' in Late Nineteenth Century* (Manchester: Manchester University Press, 1995).

— (ed.), *Selections from the Controversial 1927 Text Mother India* (Michigan: University of Michigan Press, 2000).

Sinha, Sasadhar, *The Drought and Other Stories* (Delhi: Sahitya Akademi Press, 2004).

Spinage, Clive A., *Cattle Plague: A History* (New York: Kluwer, 2003).

Spivak, Gayatri Chakravorty, 'The Rani of Sirmur: An Essay in Reading the Archives', *History and Theory*, 24 (1985), 247–70.

Srinivas, M. N., *Religion and Society amongst the Coorgs of South India* (Oxford: Clarendon Press, 1952).

— *Social Change in Modern India* (Berkeley: University of California Press, 1966).

Stalheim, Ole H. V., 'The Hog Cholera Battle and Veterinary Professionalism', *Agricultural History*, 62(2) (1988), 116–21.

Stein, Burton (ed.), *The Making of Agrarian Policy in British India, 1770–1900* (Delhi: Oxford University Press, 1992).

Stern, Rebecca F., '"Adulterations Detected": Food and Fraud in Christina Rossetti's "Goblin Market"', *Nineteenth-Century Literature*, 57(4) (Mar. 2003), 477–511.

Stokes, Eric, *The Peasant and the Raj: Studies in Agrarian and Peasant Rebellion in Colonial India* (Cambridge: Cambridge University Press, 1978).

— *English Utilitarians and India* (Delhi: Oxford University Press, 1989).

Strasser, Susan (ed.), *Commodifying Everything: Relationships of the Market* (New York: Routledge, 2003).

[164]

Thompson, E. P., *The Making of the English Working Class* (2nd edn, London: Penguin, 1968).

— 'The Moral Economy of the English Crowd in the Eighteenth Century', *Past and Present*, 50(1) (1971), 76–136.

Tomes, Nancy K., 'American Attitudes towards the Germ Theory of Disease: Phyllis Allen Richmond Revisited', *Journal of the History of Medicine*, 52 (Jan. 1997), 17–50.

Vaughan, Megan, *The Story of an African Famine: Gender and Famine in Twentieth-Century Malawi* (Cambridge: Cambridge University Press, 1987).

Venkataratnam, R., 'A History of Western Medicine in India, 1664–1945', *Indian Journal of History of Medicine*, 19 (1974), 5–14.

Vinten-Johansen, P. (*et al.*), *Cholera, Chloroform and the Science of Medicine: A Life of John Snow* (Oxford: Oxford University Press, 2003).

Waddington, Keir, *The Bovine Scourge: Meat, Tuberculosis and Public Health, 1850–1914* (Woodbridge: Boydell Press, 2006).

Waller, Richard, '"Clean" and "Dirty": Cattle Disease and Control Policy in Colonial Kenya, 1900–40', *Journal of African History*, 45 (2004), 45–80.

Washbrook, David, 'The Commercialization of Agriculture in Colonial India: Production, Subsistence and Reproduction in the "Dry South", *c.*1870–1930', *Modern Asian Studies*, 28(1) (Feb. 1994), 129–64.

Watts, Sheldonm, *Epidemics and History: Disease, Power and Imperialism* (New Haven: Yale University Press, 1997).

— 'British Development Policies and Malaria in India, 1897–1929', *Past and Present*, (165) (Nov. 1999), 141–81.

Weiss, Holger, '"Dying Cattle": Some Remarks on the Impact of Cattle Epizootics in the Central Sudan during the Nineteenth Century', *African Economic History*, (26) (1998), 173–99.

Whetham, E. H., 'The London Milk Trade, 1860–1900', *Economic History Review*, 17(2) (1964), 369–80.

Wilkinson, L., 'Medicine and Veterinary Medicine in Common Pursuit of a Contagious Disease', *Medical History*, 25(4) (Oct. 1981), 363–84.

— *Animals and Disease: An Introduction to the History of Comparative Medicine* (Cambridge: Cambridge University Press, 1992).

Wilson, Jon E., 'A Thousand Countries to Go to: Peasants and Rulers in Late Eighteenth-Century Bengal', *Past and Present*, 189 (Nov. 2005), 81–109.

Wiser, Charlotte Viall, 'The Foods of an Indian Village on North India', *Annals of the Missouri Botanical Garden*, 42(4) (Nov. 1955), 303–412.

Worboys, Michael, 'Germ Theories of Disease and British Veterinary Medicine, 1860–1890', *Medical History*, 35(3) (Jul. 1991), 308–27.

— 'Was There a Bacteriological Revolution in late Nineteenth-century Medicine?', *Studies in the History and Philosophy of Biology and Biomedical Science*, 38 (2007), 20–42.

Worboys, Michael and Condrau, Flurin, 'Second Opinions: Epidemics and Infections in Nineteenth-Century Britain', *Social History of Medicine*, 20(1) (2007), 147–58.

Yang, Anand A. 'Sacred Symbol and Sacred Space in Rural India: Community

Mobilization in the "Anti-Cow Killing" Riot of 1893', *Comparative Studies in Society & History*, 22(4) (Oct. 1980), 576–96.

— (ed.), *Crime and Criminality in British India* (Tucson: University of Arizona Press, 1985).

— *The Limited Raj: Agrarian Relations in Colonial India, Saran District, 1793–1920* (New Delhi: Oxford University Press, 1989).

— *Bazaar India: Markets, Society, and the Colonial State in Gangetic Bihar* (Berkeley: University of California Press, 1998).

INDEX

adulteration laws and the scandalous trade in milk and ghee 107–12
Afghan war, Second (1880) 50, 69
Afghanistan, Amir
  horses 15
agrarian processes, importance of cattle 1–3
agricultural cycles in South Asia 12
agricultural productivity, impact of famine 93
Agriculturists Loans Act (1884) 86
Ahirs and Gujars 109, 123
All-India Sanitary Conference (1921) 108
Anglo-Indian horse breeder 21
Anglo-Indian veterinary practice 25
animal and human disease, linkages 3
animal experimentation 61
anthrax 3, 63, 69
anti-serum 66
anti-vivisectionist lobby 62–3
Arabian horse breed 21
Arcot
  training of local ferries 24, 25
Army Veterinary School, Pune/ Poona 40, 47
Arnold, David 51, 62
Arsenic Act (1851) 134
Asiatic mode of production 15
autonomy or integration with native economy 12
Ayurveda 105
Azumgarh, United Provinces (Uttar Pradesh)
  cattle poisoning by Chamars 126, 127, 131

Bacteriological Department 68
bacteriological research 43, 59–70
bacteriology 5, 36, 49, 59–64, 69–70, 147
  as a colonial science, incredible scientific destitution 65–9
Ballygunge, Calcutta, training of local ferries 24, 25, 26
banaspati ghee 112–13
  See also food adulteration
Banerjee, Sudeshna 107
Baniya, Bamlall 133
banjara traders 1, 18–19
Bardi, Dr 107
Basalla, George 65
Basu, Rajnarayan 106
Bayly, Susan 124
Baynes, C. A. 135
beef-eating 90
Bengal cavalry 14
Bengal famine (1874) 81–2
Berar
  cattle mortality 38
Bhabha, Homi 125
bhadralok 107
Bhalla, Lieutenant Colonel J. S. 11
Bharatpur cavalry, horses 15
Bhattacharya, Sukanta 114
Bihar
  famine migration and resettlement 89
Board for the Superintendence of Horse Breeding Operations 21, 26
Bombay system (abolition of remount agency and contract system) 40
Bombay Veterinary College 49, 50
bovine tuberculosis and anthrax 3
Brahmins 123
British Medical Journal 68
British notion of quality 15
British quota system 49
Buchenwald concentration camp 84

budgetary deficits 44
Bulaki 132
Burton, Isabel 92

Calcutta Corporation 108
Calcutta Veterinary College 50
Campbell, George 126–9, 130–2,
    134
caste identities 4, 5, 90, 104
    and crime, link 127
    impurity 123
    menial 80
    stereotypes 109–11, 123, 136–7
cattle
    and cultivation 1–2, 38
    famine relief and the raj 81–7
    famines, and the colonial state
        77–94
    migration 88–9, 91
    and milk and ghee trade 103–7
    ownership, economic significance
        90
    power in rural India 1
    for preparing vaccines 60, 66
    preservation and agrarian produc-
        tion 47
    theft 4
cattle camps 82–3, 92
cattle diseases and bacteriological
        research 66, 69, 70
    and civil veterinary departments
        43–8
    colonial neglect 38–41, 43, 44–6
    epizootics 2, 3, 4, 5, 25, 36, 37–8,
        46, 47, 48, 51, 52, 70, 77, 115,
        147
    glanders 42, 43
    lack of investment 66
cattle mortality 2, 3, 4, 5, 25, 37–8,
        42, 43, 115
    cattle poisoning 127, 128
    during famines 77, 78–81
    and famine relief 81–7, 88–9
cattle plague 36, 37, 39–42, 47, 51,
        81
    See also rinderpest; veterinary
        health

Cattle Plague Commission 39, 40,
        43, 44, 48, 127
cattle poisoning
    arsenic poisoning 129, 130, 132,
        133–4
    and Chamar identity 123–37
    as an oriental crime 126–30
    confessions, coercion, and trials
        130–3
    sutari method 128–9
Central Asian horses, overland trade
        12
Chamar, Phulel 133
Chamar, Ramdehul 130–1
Chamars 4, 80
    associated with criminality
        124–37
    identity 123–37
    as poisoner and leather worker,
        late colonial developments
        133–6
charitable grants and tacavi loans 88
charity and public welfare notions 3
charwahas (cow herders) 22–3
Chatterjee, Partha 106
Chatterjee, Sarat Chandra 90
Chevers, Norman 134, 136
child mortality, and adulterated
        milk, link 107, 113
cholera 38, 39, 63, 69
    anti-cholera vaccination 69
Choloroform Commission (1889) 62
Civil Veterinary Department 37,
        43–7, 49, 51, 52, 145
civilising mission, notion of 70
climatic conditions and bacterio-
        logical research 59–60
Coleman, Mr 24
colonial
    bureaucracy 107
    cavalry 39, 46, 68
    laboratories
        autonomy 59
        financial support from wealthy
            Indians 61–3
        metropolitan influences 61–5
    medicine in India 3, 50

policies, indigenous reactions 77

policy on veterinary health 36–52

suspicion, mistrust and disparagement 18, 19, 24–5, 27

Contagious Diseases (Animals) Act (1869) 41

contract system 40

Coonoor 52, 60

Cornwallis, Lord 13, 27

corruption 20–1

cottage industry 103

cow-protection 104

Criminal Tribes Act (1871) 126

cropping patterns 81

cultural difference 11

Cunningham, D. D. 59

Datta, J. N. 108

Davis, Mike 84

Deshmukhs 17

Deshpandeys 17

Dinapore cattle fair 19

diphtheria 63, 114

Dirks, Nicholas B. 20

diseased livestock, segregating and slaughtering 41, 47

displacement 11

drugs and vaccines 61

Dutch colonial settlements in India 44

East India Company, horse breeding network 12–13, 14, 15, 16, 28

military needs 13

native market 19–22

ecology and natural resources 22

economy, economic factors/ measures famines and 77, 80, 81, 84, 88, 90, 93

in horse breeding 12, 15, 23, 26, 27

reductionism 11

role of milk 103, 105

veterinary health and 36, 37, 49, 51

employment opportunities for native

farriers 49–50

ensilage 84

epizootics 36, 48, 51, 52, 77, 147

See also veterinary

and cattle mortality 2, 3, 4, 5, 25, 37–8, 115

colonial neglect 37, 38, 47, 70

prevention 46

Epstein, Scarlett 91

Essex farm 21

Europeans fears regarding tropics 60

Evans, Griffith 69

experimental pathology 41

famine(s) 3, 4, 5, 38, 77–94

(1896–7) 78, 83, 85

(1899–1900) 79, 83, 85, 88, 92

Bengal (1874) 81, 84

food prices 84

human cost 93

impact on livestock economy of rural India 77, 78–81

insurance 15

leather and meat trade due to livestock deaths 80

Madras (1876–7) 84

migration for food and employment 91

Orissa (1866) 78, 85

Famine Charitable Relief Committee 80–1, 87

Famine Commission (1880) 91

Famine Commission (1901) 90

famine relief

colonial policies 5, 82–7, 93–4

expenditure 81, 83, 84, 85

indigenous reactions 4, 77, 83, 87

and the irrational peasant , 85, 87–93

meagreness and ineffectiveness 3, 81–7

reluctance to provide for weaker cattle 82–3, 92

farming and breeding 15–16

Farrell 129–30

female infanticide 126

Ferozepur, Punjab
  epizootics and cattle mortality 37
finance question, influence on policy
  making 65
Fisher, John R. 42
Fleming, George 44
fodder
  crisis/scarcity during famine 4,
    22, 77, 78, 79, 91
  distribution, 84–5, 88–9
  ensilage technique to preserve
    green fodder 84
  government measure inadequate
    to tackle 3, 81–7
  wasted 85, 87, 88, 89
food adulteration, public health,
  and middle-class anxieties
  102–15
  in 1920s and 1930s 112–15
food inspectors 113
foot-and-mouth disease 48
forest-grazing 22, 82, 83, 87, 88, 89
Francis, Philip 27
fraudulence and nepotism 20
Frazer, Major 16, 17, 20, 22–3, 25, 27
free market and free enterprise 15, 18
free trade, Malthusianism, and
  financial prudence 77, 82, 83,
  84, 85, 93

Gandhi, M. K. 137
Ganjam stud 14, 20
germ theory of disease 51
ghee scandal 110–11
  See also food adulteration
Gilmartin, David 4
glanders 42, 43
Glanders and Farcy Act (1879) 42
  Amendment Act of 1899 42
Gorukhpur, United Provinces (Uttar
  Pradesh)
  cattle poisoning by Chamars 127,
    128, 132
Gribble, J. D. B. 136
growth and development 15

Haffkine, Waldemar Modecai 69

Hallen, J. H. B. 40, 44, 45, 50, 52, 64
Hall-Matthews, David 88
Hankin, E. H. 60
Hapur stud 22
hariali grass 91
Harrison, Mark 111
Harsajh system of sharing cattle 1
Hart, Ernest 68
Hartogs 112
Hill, Christopher 89
Hindu beliefs 47
  and bacteriology 61
Hissar, famines, impact on livestock
  82
Hodgson, 22, 24, 25, 26
horse breeding in colonial studs
  autonomy and efficiency
    compromised 21, 27
  colonial preoccupation with 3, 5,
    6, 37, 44–5, 47, 51, 145
  disengagement from local setting
    18–23
  expenditure 17, 19–20, 21, 27, 44
  failed 16–17, 20–1
  functions handed over to Horse
    Breeding Commission 52
  indecisiveness on questions 12
  markets as the measure of success
    13–18
  network under East India
    Company 12–13, 14, 15, 16
  network of native breeders 14
  unprofitability 20, 27
Horse Breeding Commission, 52
horses, no use from agrarian
  perspective 43
Hughes, Mr 24
human diseases 43, 44
human medicine 39, 46
humanitarian hysterics 84
Hyderabad Nawab 62
hydrophobia 63

Ibbetson, D. 135
immunity for animals 48
Imperial Bacteriological Laboratory,
  Muktesar 3, 51, 59–70

obstacles 60
Inchcape Committee 66
Indian Charitable Relief Fund 85–6
Indian Medical Service 67
indigenous knowledge systems 24–5, 48
infant mortality, and adulterated milk, link 108, 113
inoculation programmes 52
insubordination 22
jajmani system 91
Journal of Tropical Veterinary Science 68
Jurgens 112

Kattra 14
Koch, Robert 63, 64, 68, 69, 70
    bile theory of treating rinderpest 64
    demonstrations of tubercle bacillus 64
Kulkarnis 17
Kunbis 17

Lafarge, Marie affair 133–4
Lahore Veterinary College 50, 64
Land Improvement Act (1883) 86
land resources, use for horse breeding 46
land revenue settlement 11–12, 15, 16
    See also Ryotwari
Lawrence, John 39
Lefroy, G. A. 135
Lekha 132–3
Lingard, Dr Alfred 52, 60, 63, 64, 66, 68–9
Linlithgow, Lord 108
Lyons 136
Lytton, Lord 84

Madiga caste 136
mahajans, and famine relief measures 91–2
Malthusianism 77, 82, 83, 93
Mamlatdar 17
Manbhum, Bengal

epizootics and cattle mortality 37–8
Mansfield, Sir W. 40
Manson, Patrick 60
Manu 123
Marathas 27
maritime trade in horses 12
market forces in scarcity conditions 11, 80, 84, 85
market-driven rationality 94
Marsh method 134
Marwari Association 110
Mayo, Catherine 92
McKenzie, Captain 22
medical bureaucracy 39
medical jurisprudence 5, 126, 133–4, 136
Merewether, F. H. S. 78
middle-class in India 61, 62
    notions of health, hygiene and food 4, 102–15
middlemen, fear and distrust of 18–19
military
    authority and halting march of veterinary medicine 38–43
    and economic compulsions 51
    horses 36, 41
    preoccupation with livestock 3, 42
    and the veterinarians 23–6, 27
Military Board 22, 26
milk and ghee, adulteration laws and the scandalous trade 107–12
milk suburbs 103
modernisation and efficiency 11
modernity 61, 102, 106
Molineux, Mr 24
moneylenders 88
Moorcroft, William 17, 25–6, 52
More, Thomas 27
Municipal Health Offices 39
Murray, Sir John 21
Mussolini, Benito 104–5

Narayan, R. K. 102

native
  bookkeepers and *babus* 21–2
  distrust and suspicion 18–19,
    24–5, 27, 28
  ignorance and apathy 48
  market and the horse breeding in
    colonial studs 18–23
  press 61
  uncooperative 22
Naulbunds (native horse breeders)
  16, 17, 21, 25
new germ theory 70

occupational stereotypes 123–4, 135,
  137
Onderstepoort Veterinary Institute,
  South Africa 59
Orissa famine (1866) 78, 85
Otherness and assimilation 11

Pasteur Institutes 52, 59, 62, 65–6
Pasteur, Louis 63, 64–5, 69
pastoralist groups, cattle
  ownership 1
Patils 17
peasant(s)
  and the colonial state 102
  economy 2
  indebtedness 1, 2, 81
  reluctance to take advantage of
    famine relief measures 81–2,
    87–93
  silent capitulation 4
  victims of colonial policies 47
pinjrapoles 92
plague (human) 43, 63, 69
plague inspector 42
Porter, Roy 50
Powindah caravans 12
preferential treatment to respectable
  classes 87
Premchand, Munshi 123
  Godan 2
private donations for bacteriological
  research 61–3
private property, notion of 15, 27
property rights 4, 11

prophylactic 66
provincial legislative councils on
  adulteration 112
public consciousness 42
public good, question 67
Pusa stud 14, 16, 20, 21, 22, 25

rabies 63
  treatment for European patients
    65–6
Ramruttun Sain 22
Ramsay, H. 128–9
Rangpur *dhing* (insurgency, 1783),
  Bengal 1–2
Ray, Satyajit 123
Registration of Births and Deaths,
  Bombay Presidency 39
religious sentiments, prejudices 61,
  90
Remount Committee 26
revenue deficits 2
rinderpest (*puschima*) 38, 41, 47, 48,
  63, 66, 127
  bile theory of treatment 64
rinderpest sera, serum 61, 66, 68
Risley, H. H. 135
Rose, H. A. 135
Roshun Ally 130–1
Royal Commission on Agriculture
  (1927) 69
rural development and colonial
  policies 102–3
rural landscape and livelihood,
  dependence on livestock 1–2,
  5–6
  impact of cattle mortality due to
    famines 77, 78–81
Russell, R. V. 135
Ryotwari land settlement 19

Sadgati 123
sanitary commissions 39
Sanitary Department 43
Sanskritization 90
Sarkar, Sumit 107
Sati 126
Satya, Laxman 4, 38

scandal of empire 20
Schultz, Theodore 93
scientific policies in India, colonial
    roots 68
Scott, James C. 93
Seager, Lieutenant Colonel E. 40
sera, manufacture and sale 66
Seringapatam, Lord Cornwallis's
    advance on (1791) 13
Shashtri, Acharya Chatursen 105–6
Sherring, M. A. 135
Simoons 90
Sleeman, 126, 128
Smith, Baird 15
social evils 126
Society for Prevention of Cruelty
    against Animals (SPCA) 61, 92
Spedding, H. D. 132, 133, 134
Spinage, Clive A. 38
Srinivas, M. N. 124, 137
Steel, J. H. 49
superstitions 128
surra 43, 69

tacavi loans 82
    underutilised 86–7, 88
Taylor, A. S. 134–5
Temple, Richard 84
Thompson, E. P. 93, 103
Thuggee 14, 126, 128–9, 137
tijara system of sharing cattle 1
toxicology 5, 126, 133, 136
Tropical Veterinary Bulletin 68
tubercle bacillus 64
tuberculosis 63, 114
typhoid 63, 114

unemployment 107
United Provinces Prevention of
    Adulteration Act (1912)
    111–12

urban middle-class in India. See
    middle-class
urbanisation 102–3, 107, 147

Van den Berghs 112
vegetarianism 104
Venkatarungapilly 19
Verschure Creameries 112
veterinarians
    between the treasury and the
        military 23–6
    economic utility 23
veterinary administration 3, 5, 6, 36,
    43, 51, 52, 59
veterinary health
    colonial policies 39, 67–9
    colonial foundations 42
    epizootics and cattle mortality 2,
        3, 4, 5, 25, 36, 37–8, 46, 47, 48,
        51, 52, 70, 77, 115, 147
    glanders 42, 43
veterinary medicine in India 3, 23,
    46, 53
veterinary reforms 41, 43
veterinary training (farriers) 25, 36,
    48–50
villages, lost, and magical milk
    103–7

Walker, W. 129
Warboys, Michael 113
Williams, Raymond 106
Wise, James 135
World War I 11, 52
World War II 11
Wyatt, Captain 14

Zamindari system of horse breeding
    16, 17, 27
Zamindars 15, 25, 91
    ignorant of cattle poisoning 127